DOCUMENTS
ON THE MEXICAN REVOLUTION

Volume IX

OTHER VOLUMES IN THIS SERIES

Volume I — The Origins of the Revolution in Texas, Arizona, New Mexico and California, 1910-1911.

Volume II — The Madero Revolution as Reported in the Confidential Dispatches of U.S. Ambassador Henry Lane Wilson & the Embassy in Mexico City, June 1910 to June 1911.

Volume III — The Election of Madero, the Rise of Emiliano Zapata and the Reyes Plot in Texas.

Volume IV — The Murder of Madero and the Role Played by U.S. Ambassador Henry Lane Wilson.

Volume V — Blood Below the Border. American Eye-witness Accounts of the Mexican Revolution.

Volume VI — ¡Abajo el Gringo! Anti-American Sentiment During the Mexican Revolution.

Volume VII — Counter Revolution Along The Border.

Volume VIII — The Rebellion of Felix Diaz.

Volume IX — The Bad Yankee — El Peligro Yankee. American Entrepreneurs and Financiers in Mexico. In 2 volumes.

THE BAD YANKEE

EL PELIGRO YANKEE

THE BAD YANKEE

EL PELIGRO YANKEE

AMERICAN ENTREPRENEURS AND FINANCIERS IN MEXICO

by
Gene Z. Hanrahan

VOLUME II

DOCUMENTARY PUBLICATIONS

Table of Contents

VOLUME ONE

INTRODUCTION i

Chapter One   DOHENY EL CRUEL 1

Chapter Two   MORDELO VINCENT: KING OF THE
                   TAMPICO WILDCATTERS 17

Chapter Three   LOST LEGENDS OF THE GOLDEN
                   LANE 25

Chapter Four   FROM BROTHERS BUCKLEY TO
                   BIG OIL 41

Chapter Five   EL PATRON GRANDE 59

Chapter Six   THE MULATOS MINE AND
                   YANKEE DOLLARS 75

Chapter Seven   "AMERICAN SMELTING,
                   SON-OF-A-BITCH!" 93

Chapter Eight   STEEL RAILS AND YANKEE
                   GOLD 109

Chapter Nine   THE BROTHERS BRANIFF, CITIZEN
                   HEARST, AND OTHER MATTERS 127

Chapter Ten   FINAL THOUGHTS AND NOTABLE
                   QUOTES 147

DOCUMENTS

Document I   AMERICAN INVESTMENTS, INVESTORS,
                   AND ENTREPRENEURS IN MEXICO, 1902 . . . D-1

Document II   AMERICAN INVESTMENTS & ECONOMIC
                   CONDITIONS, 1909-1910 . . . . D73

VOLUME TWO

Document III   AMERICAN INVESTMENTS AND ENTRE-
                  PRENEURS IN MEXICO, 1907-1926 ...... D135

Document IV   U.S. & FOREIGN INVESTMENTS, 1927 .... D-151

Document V   A UNITED STATES GOVERNMENT
                  OFFICIAL TESTIFIES ON INVESTMENTS
                  (FRANKLIN K. LANE) D-179

Document VI   A RAILROAD ENTREPRENEUR
                  TESTIFIES (EDWARD N. BROWN) D-195

Document VII   A MINING ENTREPRENEUR TESTIFIES
                  (MICHAEL J. SLATTERY) D-223

Document VIII   A UNITED STATES SENATOR
                  TESTIFIES (ALBERT B. FALL) D-235

Document IX   AN OIL ENTREPRENEUR TESTIFIES
                  (WILLIAM FRANK BUCKLEY) D-241

Document X   A UNITED STATES AMBASSADOR
                  TESTIFIES (HENRY LANE WILSON) D-251

Document XI   A MINING ENGINEER TESTIFIES
                  (NILS OLAF BAGGE) D-263

Document XII   AN OIL PIONEER TESTIFIES
                  (EDWARD L. DOHENY) D-273

Document XIII   THE WEALTH OF MEXICO IN 1911, AND
                  AMERICAN LOSSES DURING THE
                  REVOLUTION D-381

                  STATISTICAL TABLES D-389

                  1. Mexican Foreign Trade (1910) D-390
                  2. Mexican Exports (1910-1911) D-392
                  3. American Investments in Mexico
                     (Estimate—1911) D-393

4. Most Profitable U.S. Companies
   Operating in Mexico (1900-1911) D394
5. Losses Claimed by Americans in
   Mexico. First 10 Years of Revolution
   (1910-1920) D-395
6. U.S. Oil Companies & Entrepreneurs
   with Operations in Mexico Prior to
   May 1917 . . . . D-396
7. Effect of 1917 Constitution on
   U.S. Oil Companies D-397
8. World Petroleum Production and
   Mexican Output (1927) D-398
9. American Investments in Mexico by
   Industry (Estimates—1929) D-399

CHAPTER SOURCES 401

INDEX 413

AMERICAN INVESTMENTS AND
ENTREPRENEURS IN MEXICO, 1907 - 1926

Some notion of the amount of our total investment in Mexico and its growth over a period of years may be gained by considering the following estimates gleaned from a variety of sources and authorities, official and unofficial.

These total figures are but rough approximations. Their accuracy depends much upon the skill of the "authority" in determining what proportion of the authorized and issued capital of the enterprises represents actual investment. However, they may be taken in relation to each other and considered as fairly reliable guesses. The wide variation is due to the fact that some figures represent capitalization, others value and still others the actual money invested.

In 1902 a careful estimate by the United States consul in Mexico, Andrew D. Barlow, read: "Five hundred million dollars gold is in round figures the American capital invested in Mexico."[1]

In 1907, it was estimated by the United States Bureau of Manufactures that "American investments in Mexico aggregate probably more than $750,000,000." In the same report: "Of the total investments in Mexican railways eighty per cent belongs to Americans."[2]

Wilfred H. Schoff,[3] in 1911, placed the figure at a round billion dollars.

[1]*Mexican Year Book,* 1920-21, p. 167.
[2]Idem.
[3]*Annals,* v. 37, p. 643.

A year later, Marion Letcher, the United States consul at Chihuahua, put the total American investment at $1,057,770,000 and the
British investment at $321,301,800.[4]   As the figure for the total
wealth of Mexico at that time was $2,434,241,422 it would appear
that United States investors owned nearly half of it. John Barrett,
former Director of the Pan-American Union, gave the same figure
for the American investment.   However, certain bankers familiar
with Mexico pointed out that a large part of the American share invested in the Mexican National Railways was placed there by British
citizens through American banks, which would make it appear that
the bonds were registered in the name of United States citizens.
For this reason they estimated that probably $700 million covered,
at that time, the amount of American investment in Mexico.[5]

Since 1913 many estimates have been made, based on little more
than partisan speculation. For example Albert B. Fall, when Chairman of the Senate Sub-Committee on Mexican Relations, put the
American investment at a billion and a half, while figures by Cabrera and Salinas of the Carranza government indicated an even
higher figure for American holdings.[6]

The latest estimate from a government source comes from the
Finance Division of the Bureau of Foreign and Domestic Commerce
in a statement issued to the press June, 1924, which puts the total
of our industrial and commercial investment in Mexico at roughly a
billion dollars, adding the estimated amounts known to be tied up
in Mexican Government obligations.

In view of the tremendous development in oil and the growing
interest in mines, lands and public utilities, we are inclined to base
our present estimate on a still more recent set of figures issued semi-
officially by the Department of Commerce. Though only the rough-
est approximations, and in the case of government bonds underestimated, they show at least the present relative importance of our
various interests in Mexico:

Government bonds	$ 22	million
Railroads	160	
Mining and smelting	300	
Oil lands and refineries	478	
Manufacturing	60	
Wholesale and retail stores	50	
Plantations and timber	200	
Banks, telephone and telegraph companies, light and power companies and tramways	10	
Total	$1,280	million

*Not including provincial and municipal bonds held here.

[4]*Mexican Year Book,* p. 168.
[5]*Annalist,* v. 1, p. 166.
[6]Beals, *Mexico,* p. 233.

Considering only the bonded debt of the country, several authorities have estimated that American citizens hold one-fifth of the total debt, distributed as follows: 17 per cent of the railway bonds, 28 per cent of the direct government obligations, 22 per cent of the municipal bonds and 19 per cent of the internal government bonds (see page 40).

1. *Oil.*

Oil, as the table indicates, leads the field.

Pierre L'Espagnol de la Tramerye estimates that 70 per cent of the capital invested in the Mexican oil fields is American in origin, while the Anglo-Dutch share is only 27 per cent.[7] Other figures for the relative British and American investment in Mexican oil have shown approximately the same ratio, the American interest usually running at least twice that of the British. The greatest number of leases and concessions are, of course, held by United States citizens, and in 1919 "American companies produced about 70 per cent of the Mexican crude oil production," according to William S. Culbertson.[8]

Moody's opinion on oil is as follows: "The petroleum industry in Mexico is valued at more than $1,000,000,000, according to official figures. The exact figures as of March 10, 1923 are $1,050,532,434, of which American oil magnates own $606,043,239, or 57.7 per cent. British capital has $354,776,199 invested, or 33.8 per cent of the total."[9] This figure, which is more than a hundred million higher than that given in the table above, includes wells, tanks, pipe lines and equipment as well as land owned by American companies.

At least 300 oil companies organized in the United States, Britain or Mexico are at work in the Mexican fields. Most of them are incorporated in the United States. Below are mentioned a few of those believed to be owned or controlled by American capital. In view of the lack of uniformity in the information it has been impossible to make any satisfactory table that would show at a glance the relative size of the different companies and their complete and exact relationships. However, a statement from the Mexican Secretary of the Treasury, January, 1923, gives the names of companies, both American and European, in their order of importance on the basis of export tax paid and production in barrels for the year 1922.

[7] L'Espagnol, *World Struggle for Oil*, p. 125.
[8] *Annals*, v. 112, p. 106.
[9] Moody's *Governments and Municipals*, p. 518.

The companies as mentioned in their order of importance are: Huasteca, Mexican Gulf Oil, Transcontinental, Corona, Mexican Eagle, International Petroleum, Texas Company of Mexico, Atlantic Gulf Oil, Freeport and Mexican Fuel Oil, Island Oil and Transport, Cortez Oil, Penn-Mex Fuel, East Coast Oil, New England Fuel Oil, Atlantic Lobos, Continental Mexican Petroleum, Empire Transport and Oil, National Oil, U.S. Mexican Oil, Surfsure Oil, Pierce Oil, Panuco-Boston Oil, Tal Vez and Terminal Union.

In the following list, the companies, at least the larger ones, are also arranged in the order of their importance:

Mexican Petroleum Co., Ltd. (Del.) is the largest and most important American company; it operates through Mexican Petroleum Co. (Cal.) and other subsidiaries. In the spring of 1925 the properties of the Mexican Petroleum Co., controlled by the Pan-American Petroleum and Transport Co., were sold by the Doheny interests to a new company, the Pan-American Eastern Petroleum Corporation. A syndicate headed by Blair & Co., and dominated by the Standard Oil Co. of Indiana, holds control in this new company which also acquires the stock of the British Mexican Petroleum Co., a Doheny company which has a controlling interest in the British Equatorial Oil Co., and Lago Petroleum Co. Concerning this oil deal, then under negotiation, the *New York Times* reported: "Acquisition of the Mexican oil properties will give the Standard Oil Co., of Indiana second rank among the larger oil companies of the world, exceeded only by the Standard Oil Co. of New Jersey."[10] The Mexican properties represented in this transaction were estimated conservatively to be worth over $125 million and to cover between 1.5 million and 2 million acres of producing or prospective oil lands. Daily production is estimated at 150,000 barrels.

Mexican Petroleum Co. (Cal.) was the first company to secure the commercial production of oil in Mexico. It owns storage facilities for a million barrels, 80 tank cars, pipe lines and refineries and a tanker fleet second in size only to that of the Standard Oil of New Jersey.[11] The Mexican Petroleum Co., Ltd. (Del.) controls among other companies the important Huasteca Petroleum Co., with an authorized capital of $15 million and approximately 1,050,000 acres with tanks, wharves and steamers.[12] It produced in 1922 over 15 million barrels. Other Mexican Petroleum subsidiaries are the Tamiahua Petroleum Co. and the Tuxpan Petroleum Co.

[10]*New York Times,* Mar. 11, 1925.
[11]*New York Times,* May 12, 1925. Moody's *Industrials,* p. 2278.
[12]Moody's *Industrials,* p. 2278.

The more important Standard Oil companies operating in Mexico directly or through subsidiaries are Transcontinental Petroleum Co., one of the heaviest producers, Atlantic Lobos Oil Co. (controlling Cortez Oil Corporation), Port Lobos Petroleum Corporation, New England Fuel Oil Co., Atlantic Refining Co., Atlantic Oil Producing Co., Panuco-Boston Oil Co., and the recently acquired Doheny companies referred to above.

The Atlantic Refining Co. has a subsidiary, Atlantic Oil Shipping Co., interested in the large Producers Terminal Corporation at Tampico;[13] the Atlantic Lobos Oil Co., controlled by Atlantic Refining Co., owns some 140,374 acres in the Mexican light oil fields. It has $20 million preferred stock outstanding.[14] The New England Fuel Oil Co. has transferred some of its extensive leases to Magnolia Petroleum Co., also a Standard Oil subsidiary. A New England Fuel Oil subsidiary has a lease on 1500 acres, about half of which it has sub-leased to Corona Oil Co., a Royal Dutch company.[15] The Panuco-Boston Oil Co., has a proven area of 500 acres and an unproven one of 15,000 and a capital of $1 million.[16]

The extent of the various interests in Mexico of the Standard Oil of New Jersey is suggested by a statement in *The Lamp*: "We have a pipeline system handling about 100,000 barrels a day of heavy crude, some two-thirds of which we produce ourselves."[17]

Sinclair Consolidated Oil Corporation owns concessions on more than 1 million acres, some 150,000 of which are now producing.[18] Sinclair concerns operating in Mexico are Freeport and Mexican Fuel Oil Corporation and International Petroleum Co., both among the largest producers in the country. The Mexican Seaboard Oil Co. holds most of the shares of International, which directly and through several subsidiaries owns over 6 million acres of fee and leasehold land with 12 producing wells, 12 drilling and 11 locations. It also controls a Mexican company with pipe lines, tanks and storing stations.[19] Freeport and Tampico Fuel Oil Transportation Co. is the Sinclair subsidiary, operating tankers and pipe lines, through which the Freeport and Mexican Fuel Oil Corporation is controlled.[20]

[13]Ibid., p. 1764.
[14]*Petroleum Register*, 1923, p. 394.
[15]Moody's *Industrials*, p. 1451.
[16]*Petroleum Register*, 1923, p. 397.
[17]*The Lamp*, v. 7, Feb. 1925, p. 7.
[18]*Oil Trade Blue Book*, 1923, p. 234. *Petroleum Register*, 1923, p. 110.
[19]Moody's *Industrials*, p. 2197.
[20]*Petroleum Register*, 1923, p. 396.

In addition to the fast-growing Standard and Sinclair interests the following important American companies may be mentioned:

Texas Co. of Mexico has 17,000 acres leased in the Panuco and Tuxpam fields, 5,000 in fee, and 231,000 acres leased in unproven regions. The total investment of the company is over 5 million pesos.[21] It is one of the heaviest producers among the independents.

Marland Oil Co. (Md.): Morgan interests own the majority of stock in this company with concessions on 15 million acres. It operates through several subsidiaries.[22]

Gulf Oil Corporation (Mellon interest) operates, through subsidiaries, wells and pipe lines in Mexico and holds all the capital stock of several companies including Mexican Gulf Oil Co., one of the largest producers, South American Gulf Oil Co., and Panama Gulf Oil Co.[23]

Atlantic Gulf Oil Corporation, common stock $20 million, is controlled by Atlantic, Gulf and West Indies Steamship Lines and owns 11 wells with a daily average of 18,000 barrels, and leases on 35,000 acres in producing areas. It also owns a refinery, pipe lines, docks, tanker fleets, etc.[24]

New National Oil Co. is controlled by the Penrose interests of Philadelphia. It owns over 30,000 acres of leases together with cars, pipe lines, storage tanks, railroads, river transport and several Mexican subsidiaries.[25]

Cities Service Co. (Henry Doherty interests) controls the following companies:—

(a) Cities Fuel and Power Co., controlling Empire Pipe Co. of Mexico.[26]

(b) Cia. de Gas y Combustible "Imperio."

(c) Cia. Emmex de Petroleo de Gas.

(d) Cia. Terminal de "Imperio."

(e) Cia. de Terrenos Petroliferos "Imperio" — leases on 20,000 acres.[27]

(f) Empire Pipe Line Co.

(g) Gulf Coast Corporation.

(h) Holden Evans Steamship Co.

(i) Lagunita Oil Co. (Tampascas Oil Co.)

[21]U.S. Congress, 66: 2; *Sen. Doc.*, v. 9, p. 536.
[22]Moody's *Industrials*, p. 2183.
[23]Ibid., p. 2048.
[24]Ibid., p. 1762. *Petroleum Register*, 1923, p. 180.
[25]Moody's *Industrials*, p. 1454.
[26]Poor and Moody, *Public Utilities*, p. 1653.
[27]Ibid., p. 1661.

(j) National Petroleum Co.
(k) Southern Fuel and Refining Co.
(l) Sentinel Oil and Gas Co.

South Penn Oil Co., a Standard Oil unit which should have been mentioned among the other Standard companies above, owns the majority of the stock in Penn-Mex Fuel Co., the latter controlling 160,000 acres, terminals, pipe lines and railroads.[28]

Mexican-Panuco Oil Co. with a capital of $3 million, produced 143,976 barrels in 1923; it has storage and pipe-line facilities and subsidiaries.[29]

Pierce Oil Corporation has lands and a plant in Mexico. One of its subsidiaries is Mexican Fuel Co.[30]

Mexico Oil Corporation, capital stock $15 million, owns entire stock of Cia. Nueva de Petroleo Mexicana with leases on 25,000 acres, and Nuenhoffer & Co. with leases on 5,000.[31]

Island Oil and Transport Co., controlled by A. B. Leach & Co., has several Mexican subsidiaries and a capital of $30 million covering also properties in Cuba and Colombia. Capuchinas Oil Co., one of its subsidiaries, has rights on 7,925 acres.[32]

Port Lobos Oil Co., with subsidiaries and $2 million capital, owns some 6,636 acres.

Other American companies of apparently lesser importance, but all controlled by American capital, are the following:

Gulf Consolidated Oil Corporation — capital issued, $2.9 million, and 30,000 acres.[33]

East Coast Oil Co., controlled by Southern Pacific R. R.[34]

Mexican Investment Co., controlling Otontepec Petroleum Co., with terminal at Tampico and leases in south fields of Mexico.[35]

Union Oil Co. of Cal. controls the Union Oil Co. of Mexico.[36]

Gulf States Oil and Refining Co., controlled by Middle States Oil Corporation, has refineries and subsidiaries.[37]

Caltex Oil Co. (Nev.), stock $2.5 million; lease, option and royalty on 471,761 acres.[38]

---

[28]Moody's *Industrials*, p. 2386.
[29]Ibid., p. 674.
[30]*Petroleum Register*, 1923, p. 104.
[31]Moody's *Industrials*, p. 674.
[32]*Petroleum Register*, 1923, p. 394.
[33]Ibid., p. 396.
[34]Ibid., p. 395.
[35]Ibid., p. 397.
[36]Moody's *Industrials*, p. 2455.
[37]Ibid., p. 2202.
[38]*Petroleum Register*, 1923, p. 394.

Mexican Producing and Refining Co. (Del.), owning some 32,000 acres, with wells, terminals, railways, and the entire stock of two other Mexican oil companies.[39]

General Petroleum Co., controlling Continental Mexican Petroleum Co.[40]

Hidalgo Petroleum Co., over $1 million capital.[40]

Noco-Mexican Oil Co., controlled by North American Oil Co. through the Noco Petroleum Co.[41]

Interocean Oil Co., with a plant at Tampico.[42]

Curyon Oil Co., $1 million capital, 472 acres.[40]

Tex-Mex Fuel Oil Co. with subsidiary.[40]

Eastern Oil Corporation with subsidiary.[40]

Boston Mexican Petroleum Trust.[43]

Boston-Mexican Leasing Co.[40]

Ventura Consolidated Oil Fields.[44]

Lewis Oil Corporation — 28,000 acres.[45]

New York-Mexican Oil Co.[40]

National Oil Co.[40]

Kumfort Oil and Gas Co.[40]

Mexican Oil Co.[40]

Federal Oil Co. — 8,000 acres.[40]

Equity Petroleum Corporation.[40]

Casiana Petroleum Co.[40]

Sun Oil Co., S. A., a subsidiary of the Mexican Sun Oil Co.[40]

Tuxpan Oil Co., controlled by Producers Oil Corporation of Mexico.[46]

2. Mining and Smelting.

Our second largest interest in Mexico is in mining and smelting, the chief investments being owned by the Guggenheim, Green and Ryan interests and the Phelps Dodge Corporation. Out of a total of approximately $460 to $500 million invested in mines and smelters in Mexico, various authorities agree that the American share must be at least $275 to $300 million. We have used the higher figure in the table on page 91. Our interests are from five to six times as

[39]Moody's *Industrials*, p. 1424.
[40]*Petroleum Register*, 1923, pp. 394-8.
[41]Moody's *Industrials*, p. 1458.
[42]Ibid., p. 627.
[43]Moody's *Industrials*, p. 1121.
[44]Ibid., p. 2508.
[45]Ibid., p. 652.
[46]Ibid., p. 1509.

large as the British, which come second in this field. The four chief American companies are the following:

(a) American Smelting and Refining Co. (Guggenheim controlled) represents one of the largest capital investments in Mexico, very conservatively estimated at $30 million, and operating over 30 mines directly and through subsidiaries. According to the latest statement this company through American Smelters Securities Co. owns 2 silver mines, 1 silver and lead mine, 1 silver and copper mine, 1 lead and zinc, 1 silver, lead and zinc, 2 silver, lead and copper, 1 gold, silver, lead and zinc, 1 copper, silver, lead and zinc. In addition it has the following mines leased or owned in part: 2 silver, 1 silver and gold, 1 silver, lead and copper and 1 silver, lead and zinc. It has the following smelters in Mexico: lead, 4 (19 furnaces with daily capacity of 3,300 tons); copper, 3 (15 furnaces with daily capacity of 3,200 tons).[47]

Some of the producing units controlled by the American Smelting and Refining Co. are:

1. National Metallurgical Co.

2. Rosita Coal and Coke Co.

3. Mexican Northern Mining and Railroad Co., organized in 1923 to take over the properties of Alvarado Mining and Milling Co., with 4 mines in Mexico, mill sites and 700 acres.[48]

4. Towne Mines, Inc., which owns or controls the various mines and mineral, railways, land and lead companies formerly under Cia. Metallurgica Mexicana of which George Foster Peabody is President and Treasurer. It represents an investment of some $12 million. One of the best paying subsidiaries of Guggenheim Bros. is the Great National Mexican Smelting Co.

(b) Phelps Dodge Corporation, the second mining interest in importance, operates through a Mexican subsidiary, the Moctezuma Copper Co., owning 2,500 acres in Sonora, 38 mining claims, and a concentrator with a daily capacity of 2,000 tons. In 1919 it produced 27,943,000 pounds of copper, 432,000 ounces of silver and 2,211 ounces of gold.[49]

(c) Next comes the Green Cananea Copper Co., capital $50 million, a holding corporation for a number of companies operating in Mexico. It is controlled by the Cole-Ryan Syndicate.[50] Its production in 1919 amounted to 41,404,810 pounds of copper, 1,759,790

[47]Moody's *Industrials*, pp. 841-2.
[48]Ibid., p. 841.
[49] U.S. Geological Survey, *Mineral Resources*, 1919, pt. 1, pp. 537-614.
[50]U.S. Congress, 66: 2; *Sen. Doc.*, v. 9, p. 62.

ounces of silver, 9,168 ounces of gold. The Department of Commerce has estimated its Mexican investment very conservatively at $10 million.

(d) American Metal Co. owns the entire stock of one important Mexican company, Cia. Minera de Penoles, with an investment estimated at $15 million and 90 per cent of the stock of another; and it operates also on a lease the properties of the San Toy Mining Co.[51] The American Metal Co. is the largest coke producer in Mexico and stands second in the production of lead. It produces also silver, gold and coal. It leases and operates also the Mexican Northern Railway.[52]

In addition to the four major mining companies, just mentioned, dozens of other American companies are represented among those exploiting the 32,000 patented mining claims in Mexico. A few of them follow:

United States Smelting, Refining and Mining Co. controls three copper, lead, gold, silver and zinc mines, and has a substantial interest in three others.[53]

Bethlehem Steel Co. has a subsidiary in the Cia. de Minas de Fierro "Las Truchas," S. A.[54]

General Development Co. (a Lewisohn company) holds stock in the South American Gold and Platinum Co. and other mining properties in Mexico.[55]

The Consolidated Copper Mines Corporation owns 99 per cent of the stock of Giroux Consolidated Mines Co. with claims in Sonora.[56]

United Eastern Mining Co. (Ariz.) in 1922 acquired a controlling interest in an El Tigre group of gold claims in Mexico.[57]

Howe-Sound Co., a holding company with 53,000 shares in the El Potosi Mining Co., with silver mines, also owns nearly all the stock of the Chihuahua Mining Co. The Howe-Sound Co. owns also the entire stock of the Calera Mining Co., with 3 mining claims in Mexico.[58]

Guanajuato Reduction and Mines Co. owns 2 mills and a cyanide plant.[59] (Protective committee in charge.)

[51]Moody's *Industrials,* p. 836.
[52]Powell, *Railways of Mexico,* p. 36.
[53]Moody's *Industrials,* p. 2491.
[54]Ibid., p. 1794.
[55]Ibid., p. 1277.
[56]Ibid., p. 1188.
[57]Ibid., p. 798.
[58]Ibid., p. 1332.
[59]Ibid., p. 1300.

Lucky Tiger-Combination Gold Mining Co. owns all the capital stock of Tigre Mining Co. operating a gold and silver mine at El Tigre, 936 acres of mineral rights, 55,718 acres of surface rights, and a 20-stamp mill with a capacity of 200 tons daily.[60]

Canario Copper Co. controls two copper companies working in Mexico.[61]

Batopilas Mining Co. owns over 2,200 acres in mineral land, and 130,000 acres of ranch and timber land, and has a capital of $9 million.[62]

Amparo Mining Co. operates 5 mines and a mill with a daily capacity of 400 tons.[63]

The Fresnilloa Co.,[64] gold and silver.

The Barnsdall Corporation owns silver, copper, gold and lead properties in Mexico.[65]

Ahumada Lead Co. (Del.) operates chiefly through Cia. Minera Erupcion y Anexas, S. A., and Cia. Minera de Ploma, S. A. Through a third subsidiary it has built 47 miles of railroad. It also has a minority interest in two other properties.[66]

Real del Monte Mining Co. holds an option on a large property in the States of Mexico and Guerrero.[67]

A Department of Commerce report estimates an American investment of $3 million in Mexican coal mines.

3. Railroads.

We have estimated the American holdings in Mexican railroads at approximately $160 million, this amount, of course, including the lines owned exclusively by American interests, the roads in which interest is shared with native and foreign capitalists, and the National Railways of Mexico, the government controlled line, which may return to private management in 1926.

The principal independent American-owned roads in Mexico, according to the "Mexican Year Book,"[68] are the following:

Southern Pacific Railroad Co. of Mexico. The First National Bank of New York has recently acquired a large interest in this road

[60]Ibid., p. 2170.
[61]Ibid., p. 1148.
[62]Ibid., p. 1099.
[63]Ibid., p. 1070.
[64]Ibid., p. 584.
[65]Ibid., p. 1778.
[66]*Magazine of Wall Street,* v. 36, p. 149.
[67]*New York Times,* June 19, 1925.
[68]*Mexican Year Book,* 1920-21, p. 169.

which up to December 31, 1922, had spent nearly $43 million in providing railroad facilities for Northwestern Mexico, and in 1924 was reported to be spending another $15 million for new construction.[69] Its total construction up to date is well over 1300 miles.

Kansas City, Mexico and Orient Railroad, covering at least 35 miles. In 1924, it was reported that this road had been sold for $3 million to exclusive American interests in order to eliminate the (at the time) small remaining British interest in the road.

The other independents are:

Mexican Northern Railroad	75 miles
Nacozari Railroad	75
Line of American Smelting and Refining Co.	43
Potosi and Rio Verde Railroad	40
Parral and Durango Railroad	60

The total mileage of these independent roads, including 160 miles of 7 shorter lines, is at present approximately 2,103 miles.

American capital to the amount of $50 million is invested in the National Railways of Mexico, formed in 1910 and consolidating, in addition to five narrow gauge lines, the following standard gauge lines which previously had been completely controlled by American interests:

1. The Mexican International Railroad;
2. The Pan-American Railroad;

and the following lines in which United States investors had put a moderate amount of capital, British interests controlling the first two:

3. The Mexican Central Railway;
4. The National Railroad of Mexico;
5. The Vera Cruz and Isthmus Railroad.[70]

Several of the directors of the National Railways of Mexico are New York bankers representing Kuhn, Loeb & Co., Speyer & Co., Hallgarten & Co., Ladenburg, Thalmann & Co., Metropolitan Life Insurance Co., and the Mercantile Bank of the Americas.

The National Railways of Mexico recently granted a 99-year lease to a group financed by the Colorado River Land Co., of Calexico to build a railroad between Mexicali and San Felipe.[71]

The comparative mileage under United States, British and other

[69]*Annalist,* v. 1, p. 166. *New York Commercial,* July 17, 1924.
[70]*Mexican Year Book,* 1920-21, p. 169.
[71]*Annalist,* v. 24, p. 286.

foreign control, including the investment in all Mexican railroads as above indicated, was in 1921:[72]

British	2,723 miles
United States	2,101
German	16
French	113
Mexican	172
Mexican Government	252
	5,377
National Railways (partly)	
American investment	7,000
Total	12,377 miles

4. *Public Utilities.*

Although the total United States investment in this field is comparatively unimportant the following units are worth mentioning:

The Mexican Telegraph Co., controlled by All America Cables, Inc., has an investment of $250,000.[73]

The Mexican Telephone and Telegraph Co., with an authorized capital of approximately $1 million, serves a population of $1,110,000 and has over 5,800 stations. (Protective Committee now in charge.)[74]

The Mexican Cable Co. has an investment of $5 million in the country.

Central Power and Light Co., Nueva Laredo, Mexico. Electric light and traction service.[75]

Guanajuato Power and Electric Co. transmits power from Mexico to the city of Guanajuato. Owns the entire $1 million stock of the Michoacan Power Co. and controls by stock ownership the Central Mexico Light and Power Co. with approximately $3 million capital.[76]

5. *Manufacturing Industries, including Construction Companies.*

Only a few of the American firms interested in this form of enterprise have been listed, as the number and amounts of capital invested are constantly changing. However, a number are mentioned to show the range of industry in which American capital is working.

Mexican Crude Rubber Co. operates two factories.

[72]*Journal of Commerce,* June 2, 1922.
[73]Moody's *Industrials,* p. 1045.
[74]Poor and Moody, *Public Utilities,* p. 255.
[75]Ibid., p. 77.
[76]Ibid., p. 1807.

Intercontinental Rubber Products Corporation (controlled by Intercontinental Rubber Co.) owns approximately two million acres of rubber property together with a plant for extracting guayule.[77] The Firestone company has leased 35,000 acres.

Motzorongo Co., producing sugar and alcohol and engaging also in cattle raising with properties in Vera Cruz.[78]

Consolidated Rolling Mills Co. — iron goods, with approximately $1 million.

Roessler and Hasslacher Chemical Co. of New York.

Mexican National Construction Co. (Kuhn, Loeb & Co. is interested in this company).

National Iron and Steel Co. with a $500,000 investment.

Mexican International Corporation.

Astoria Mahogany Co.

Honey Iron and Steel Co.

Richardson Construction Co. owns land and dams.

Ford Motor Co. — plant.

Hidalgo Cement Co.

Air Reduction Co., developing patents.

Cia. Industrial Jabonera, cotton seed oil and soap, capital $5 million.

Buen Tono, a $15 million tobacco concern, is owned by an American syndicate.

Besides these there are flour mills, foundries and machine shops, glass and bottle works, shoe factories, textile, printing and other industries in which American capital is invested.[79]

6. *Lands.*

Under this heading come all lands used for timber, agricultural and cattle raising purposes — the sort referred to in a dispatch over the Universal wires September 4, 1923:

"A syndicate of Texas capitalists have acquired 300,000 acres in Mexico,"

and reporting the capital investment to have been $15 million and the use of the land as desired for the cultivation of rice and other cereals, and the exploitation of timber. The wire closed with the statement:

[77]Moody's *Industrials,* p. 2088.
[78]Ibid., p. 684.
[79]*Journal of Commerce,* June 7, 1922. Gives a detailed list of plants in Mexico, their nationality and amount of investment.

"This is the first, big investment coming as a result of the renewal of diplomatic relations between Mexico and the United States."

American citizens have many investments in sisal, chicle, tobacco, coffee, and sugar lands, fruit haciendas, vegetable oil production, vine culture, cereal growing, guayule rubber and hardwood production and other land enterprises in Mexico.

Investments of this kind ranging from $200,000 to $10 million were reported in 1921 by an American business man residing in Mexico. Some of the American companies mentioned were the American Chicle Co., the Di Giorgio Fruit Co., with 20,000 acres, the United Sugar Co., the West Coast Cattle Co., Palomas Land and Cattle Co., Corralitos Cattle Co., Mormon Colonies investment, San Jose Babicora (Hearst investment), estimated at that time at $2 million, Cia. Maderera Hartment, Richardson Construction Co. with 400,000 hectares, Atascador Land Co., Rascon Sugar Plan, Choco Colony, Valley of Paradise Development Association, Mexican American Land Co., and dozens of other private and company owners of haciendas and other real estate. The list included approximately 75 names of relatively equal importance with those here mentioned.[80]

The American investment in this form of holding in the various states of Mexico is estimated at $200 million.

7. Banks and other interests.

The National City Bank and several Morgan banks, some of which are mentioned above, are extensively interested in Mexican enterprises, and private citizens of the United States have holdings, and in some instances complete control, in native Mexican banks.[81] *The Annalist*[82] states that Speyer & Co., Kuhn, Loeb & Co., Ladenburg, Thalmann & Co., Hallgarten & Co., H.B. Hollins & Co., Brown Bros. & Co., William Salomon & Co., are the chief American banking houses interested in Mexican securities. In addition to the first four of these seven firms, representatives of the following banking houses are included on the American Section of the International Committee of Bankers on Mexico: J.P. Morgan & Co., Central Union Trust Co., Illinois Merchants Trust Co., National City Bank, Guaranty Trust Co., Chase National Bank, Kidder, Peabody & Co.

The Association of Oil Producers in Mexico is made up of companies already mentioned in this study led by the Doheny and Standard

[80]Ibid., June 12, 1922.
[81]*Boston Transcript,* Oct. 15, 1923.
[82]*Annalist,* v. 1, p. 166.

interests. Mr. Doheny's oil interests have made substantial loans to the Mexican Government, one during 1924 for 10 million pesos. "The Doheny interests, it was stated last week, had almost completed arrangements for a loan of 10,000,000 pesos to the Mexican Government. The advance will be made on the oil tax, similar to the one last year."[83]

The National Association for the Protection of American Rights in Mexico (17 Battery Place, New York City) includes in addition to the larger banking units above mentioned a long list of American industrial corporations engaged in the exploitation of Mexican properties.

[83]Ibid., v. 24, p. 644.

U.S. & FOREIGN INVESTMENTS, 1927

A population of 14,234,799 people is living in a vast territory of 760,290 square miles. To compare Mexico with the United States, its area equals that of the states of Wisconsin, Nebraska, Ohio, Indiana, Illinois, Minnesota, Missouri, Michigan, Kansas, Iowa, Vermont, Connecticut, North and South Dakota together. No wonder that there is a great difference in temperature and different kinds of agricultural occupations. The density of population is about 20 per square mile.

The 28 federal states are self-governing and have the right to contract loans and to regulate their own budgets.

About four-fifths of the soil of Mexico is adaptable for agriculture of cattle raising.

The chief staple product is corn, but coffee, sugar, beans and cotton are also raised.

Mexico is extremely rich in mineral resources. During the colonial days, Mexico was an important silver producing country, and silver is still the leading product of the mining business. Coal is found in the State of Coahuila, with an annual output of about 800,000 tons.

However, it is the petroleum wealth of the country which more than any other product has contributed to the influx of foreign capital into the republic.[1] Of the total exports of petroleum, the

[1]On the controversy over petroleum properties, see Charles W. Hackett, *The Mexican Revolution,* World Peace Foundation Pamphlets, Vol. IV, No. 5.

United States imports 90%, only 10% going to Europe. Petroleum production has declined steadily since 1921, and this has entailed serious loss in Government revenues with accompanying difficulties, but its effects upon the life of the people as a whole are less than might be thought from a purely statistical study. From 64,121,142 barrels in 1927 production dropped to 50,150,610 barrels in 1928.[2]

Domestic consumption in a country of some 15,000,000 population is considerable, and with the exception of the mineral products, which are 90% foreign owned, is of far more importance to the country at large than the export demand.

After the election of Obregon in July, 1928, there was a general feeling of increased optimism, which received a setback following his assassination in the same month, but was revived by the peaceful election of Señor Portes Gil in November. There was no tangible improvement during 1928 in Mexican economic conditions which reached their nadir toward the close of 1927, but there has been a decided feeling of optimism since that time owing to political rather than to economic causes.

Of Mexico's foreign commerce, 70% of the imports come from the United States, while of the exports about 75% go to the United States. Leaving petroleum out of consideration, United States imports from Mexico showed a 12% drop in 1927 and a further decline in our total imports from Mexico of 18% in 1927 and 13% in 1928.

United States exports to Mexico were 7% less in 1926 than in the previous year, and dropped a further 19% in 1927, increasing some 6% during 1928. Mexico dropped from its position as our leading customer in Latin America in 1921 to second place in 1924, and to third place since that date.

Public Finance. The public debt of Mexico is extensively held abroad and was in default from July, 1914, until an arrangement was effected with an international committee of bankers in 1925. Since that date, some irregularity has occurred in taking up cash warrants issued in connection with the settlement. The total included in the agreement as of December 31, 1925, amounted to 1,561,438,348 gold pesos, or $778,337,000. Of this amount 671,236,456 pesos was the railway debt, which is especially secured on the revenues of the National Railways, the accounts of which were gone over by auditors in a report due in 1929. The "direct debt" included in the agreement amount to 890,201,892 gold pesos.

[2]*Bulletin of Pan American Union,* LXIII, p. 610.

In addition, there was a banking debt and a floating debt. The minister of finance in a statement submitted to Congress on November 29, 1928, gave the debt as follows:

MEXICAN DEBT, 1928

Bonded debt	$18,820,976
Classified floating debt	139,870,350
Unclassified floating debt, estimated	614,421,124
Total	$773,112,450

This total was apparently independent of the settlement of 1925. Business respecting the external debt is being handled by the International Committee of Bankers of Mexico.[3]

The Mexican unit of currency is the gold peso of $0.4985. On exchange it maintains a position slightly below par.

Foreign Investments. Total United States investments in the republic, at the close of 1928, may conservatively be placed at $1,550,096,000, distributed as follows:

FOREIGN INVESTMENTS

Government bonds (external)	$140,000,000
Government bonds (internal)	15,800,000
State bonds	3,500,000
Municipal bonds	2,500,000
Railroads	300,000,000
Mining and smelting	391,000,000
Oil	408,000,000
Manufacturing	60,000,000
Wholesale and retail	50,000,000
Public utilities	37,500,000
Banks	3,500,000
Plantation and timber	138,296,000
Total	$1,550,096,000

According to the Mexican Department of Industry and Commerce, foreign capital invested in the Mexican oil industry was distributed as follows:

	Amount (Peso)
American	606,043,000
British	354,776,000
Dutch	71,191,000
Mexican	11,582,000
Miscellaneous	6,933,000
Total	$1,050,535,000

[3]For the present status see *55th Annual Report . . . Corporation of Foreign Bondholders,* p. 243.

This value of roughly $525,000,000 compares with a total investment of $583,159,000 in 1926, when the land costs represented $193,000,000, or one-third of the total. Of the $390,000,000 invested in petroleum enterprises in addition to the land — well construction, tanks, pipe lines, etc. — $224,000,000, or 57.46%, was American.

In connection with the large investments in Mexican oil enterprises, it is of interest to call attention to the completion of a task undertaken by the Mexican Ministry of Industry and Commerce, involving the listing of companies and persons legitimately engaged in petroleum exploitation, for the purpose of avoiding frauds which have so often occurred by the sale of shares in so-called oil companies which in reality do not exist.

The capital invested in industrial establishments is reported to be as follows:[4]

CAPITAL IN INDUSTRIAL ESTABLISHMENTS

NATIONALITY	Amount (Pesos)	Percentage of Total
Mexican.	98,180,155	23.78
Canadian	85,566,657	20.72
United States	71,610,092	17.34
English	27,701,906	6.71
French	23,408,947	5.67
Spanish	16,010,012	3.88
German	1,949,921	0.47
Other nationalities and unspecified	88,539,752	21.43
Total	412,967,450	100.00

At $0.48 per peso, $202,364,000.

Oil Interests. Some of the larger American controlled or owned petroleum companies operating in Mexico are:

The Mexican Petroleum Company of California was the first to secure the commercial production of oil in Mexico. It owns storage facilities for about 1,000,000 barrels, tank cars, pipe-lines, refineries and tanker fleet;

The Standard Oil Company of New Jersey operates through various subsidiaries, particularly the Compañía Transcontinental de Petroleo.

The Atlantic Gulf Oil Corporation, organized under the laws of

[4]*Bulletin of the Pan American Union*, LXIII, p. 609.

Virginia in 1919, with a capitalization of 200,000 shares of $1 par value, is a subsidiary of the Atlantic Gulf and West Indies Steamship Lines. The company's properties have been sold to the Warner Quinlan Company of New York.

The Atlantic Lobos Oil Company was organized in Delaware in 1919, and has a capitalization of 500,000 shares of no par value, of which 499,433 have been issued, and 200,000 shares of preferred stock of $50 par value. The company owns extensive oil bearing lands in Mexico, and is interested in the Cortex-Aguada Petroleum Corporation, the Adrian Petroleum Company, Inc. and the "La Atlantica", Compañía Mexicana Productora y Refinadora de Petroleo, S. A.

The California Investment Company of New York is a subsidiary of the Venezuela Mexicana Oil Corporation, and owns a terminal at Tampico, Mexico.

The California Standard Oil Company de Mexico, a subsidiary of the Standard Oil Company of California, was organized in Delaware in 1925. Capital consists of 1,000 shares of common stock of no par value.

Compañía de Gas y Combustible "Imperio" is a subsidiary of the Cities Service Company, and was organized in Mexico in 1919 with a capitalization of 2,000 shares of $50 par value.

Compañía de Terrenos Petroliferos "Imperio", also a Cities Service subsidiary, was organized in Mexico in 1921 with a capitalization of $50,000. The company owns acreage in Tamaulipas and Vera Cruz, Mexico.

Compañía Emmex de Petroleo y Gas, a subsidiary of Cities Service, was organized in Mexico in 1918 and owns acreage in northern Mexico.

The Compañía Petrolera del Agwi, S. A., was organized in Mexico in 1921 with a capitalization of 6,250 shares of common stock of $100 par value. The company owns pipe lines with a capacity of 100,000 barrels per day.

Compañía Transcontinental de Petroleo was organized in Mexico in 1912 with a capitalization of 400,000 shares of common stock of 10 pesos par value. It owns extensive holdings of producing and undeveloped fields in various parts of Mexico.

The Consolidated Oil Companies of Mexico, a subsidiary of Marland Oil Company of Mexico, was organized in 1920 under the laws of Mexico with a capitalization of 10,000,000 shares of one peso par value. The company also has an interest in the Compañía Pet. Franco Espanola, S. A. It owns acreage in Lemon, Vera Cruz, with an output of 1,300 barrels per day.

The Continental Mexican Petroleum Company was organized in 1911 with a capitalization of 5,000 shares of $100 par value, all owned by the General Petroleum Corporation. The company owns a terminal site opposite Tampico; part of 597 acres of unproven land in the Panuco district; 3,563 acres in the Tantoyuca district; and a joint ownership of leases with the Texas Corporation on 83,165 acres of unproven land in Nuevo Leon.

The Continental Oil Company, incorporated in Delaware in 1929 for the purpose of merging the Marland Oil Company, the Continental Oil Company of Maine and the Prudential Oil Company of Delaware, controls through the Marland Oil Company the Marland Oil Company of Mexico, S. A., with a capitalization of 2,000,000 shares of two pesos par value. This company owns 7,308,135 shares of stock of the Consolidated Oil Companies of Mexico, S. A., leaving 1,018,937 shares in the hands of the public. Shares have a par value of one peso.

The Cortez-Aguada Petroleum Corporation was organized in New York in 1913 with a capitalization of 1,500 shares of $100 par value, as the Mexican subsidiary of the Atlantic Lobos Oil Company.

The Empire Pipe Line Company of Mexico, S. A., a subsidiary of Cities Fuel & Power Company, has a capitalization of 500 shares of $50 par value. It holds acreage under lease in the Cacalilao and Maguabes districts, with an average daily production of 2,450 barrels.

The English Oil Company, S. A., a subsidiary of the Intercontinental Petroleum Corporation, is capitalized at 1,000 shares of one peso (gold) par value. It owns 241 acres in the Panuco district and 1,600 acres in the Tampico district. Daily production averages 2,000 barrels.

The Globe Petroleum Corporation was organized in Virginia in 1922, with 500,000 shares of $10 par value, of which 311,253 shares are outstanding. The company's Mexican properties comprise 4,172 acres in the Tampico district, and 15,692 acres in northern Mexico. It also is interested in the Globe Oil Company, S. A.

The Gulf Coast Corporation, a subsidiary of Cities Fuel & Power Company, was organized in 1910 under the laws of Virginia, with 200,000 shares of $5 par value, of which 170,000 shares are outstanding.

The Hidalgo Petroleum Company was organized in Delaware in 1921, with 3,000,000 shares of $1 par value, of which 1,205,000 shares are outstanding. Properties consist of 640 acres of unproven land in Port Lobos, Mexico.

The Huasteca Petroleum Company was organized in Delaware in

1907 with an authorized capital of $15,000,000, of which $14,680,000 is outstanding, all owned by the Mexican Petroleum Company, Ltd., of Delaware. It owns or controls about 1,050,000 acres in Mexico, together with pipe lines, railroad, wharfage and terminal facilities.

The International Petroleum Company, a subsidiary of the Mexican Seaboard Oil Company, was organized in Maine in 1910 with 60,000 shares of $10 par value. It owns the entire capital stock of the Compañía Internacional de Petroleo y Oleductos, S. A., and Compañía Mexicana de Terrenos y Petroleo. Properties comprise about 1,377,540 acres, of which 1,000,000 acres are in the state of Tamaulipas.

The Kern Mexican Oil fields, S. A., a subsidiary of Kern River Oil Fields of California, Ltd., was organized in Mexico in 1918, with 250 shares of 100 pesos par value. The company has leases on 28,500 acres under an agreement with Tampico Oil Company, Ltd., and other leases on 5,244 acres. Company's daily production averages 500 barrels.

"La Atlantica" Compañía Mexicana Productero y Refinadora de Petroleo, S. A., a subsidiary of Atlantic Lobos Oil Company of Philadelphia, was organized in Mexico in 1918, with a capitalization of 1,000 shares of $50 par value.

The Lagunita Oil Company, a subsidiary of Cities Fuel and Power Company, was organized in West Virginia in 1912, with a capitalization of 6,000 shares of common and 1,000 shares of preferred stock of $100 par value. The company owns the entire capital stock of the Tampascas Oil Company.

The Mexican Gulf Oil Company, a subsidiary of Gulf Oil Corporation of Pennsylvania, was organized in 1912 under the laws of Delaware, with a capitalization of 8,000 shares of $25 par value. The company owns oil-bearing lands in Panuco, Topila and in the southern fields of Mexico.

The Mexican Seaboard controls a pipe line subsidiary in Mexico known as the Compañía Nacional de Petroleo y Oleoductos, S. A. The company's operations are not very profitable and, for the first half of 1929, the net loss aggregated $13,281.

The Mexican Sinclair Petroleum Corporation, a subsidiary of Sinclair Consolidated Oil Corporation, owns and operates extensive oil-bearing lands in Mexico.

The Mexico Ohio Oil Company, a subsidiary of the Ohio Oil Company, was organized in Delaware in 1926, with a capitalization of 500,000 shares of no par value, of which 400,000 shares have been issued. The company owns all the stock of the Ohio Mexican

Oil Corporation, S. A., with the exception of directors' qualifying shares. The properties of the latter company consist of oil and gas concessions on 3,500,000 acres in West Central and North Central Coahuila. Additional acreage is being acquired in the State of Nuevo Leon.

The Mexico Oil Corporation was organized in 1919 under the laws of Maine, with a capitalization of 2,500,000 shares of $1 par value, of which 1,500,000 shares have been issued. The company has an interest in the Compañía Nueva de Petroleo Mexicana, S. A.

The New England Fuel Oil Company was organized in 1911 under the laws of Maine, with a capitalization of 25,000 shares of common of $10 par value. The company's Mexican properties produce about 750 barrels per day.

The Ohio Mexico Oil Corporation was organized in Mexico in 1926, with a capitalization of 500,000 shares of 20 pesos par value.

The Otontepec Petroleum Company, S. A., a subsidiary of the Venezuela Mexican Oil Corporation, holds leases on about 19,000 acres of land in the southern fields of Mexico.

The Panuco Boston Oil Company, a subsidiary of Atlantic Oil Producing Company, was organized in 1914 under the laws of Maine, with a capitalization of 10,000 shares of $100 par value. The company owns 511 acres near the Panuco Fields in Mexico, with nine producing wells and an average daily output of 650 barrels.

The Penn Mex Fuel Company, a subsidiary of the South Penn Oil Company, was organized in Delaware in 1912, with a capitalization of 400,000 shares of common of $25 par value. The company controls 160,000 acres under lease and in fee in the State of Vera Cruz, and it also has important holdings in the Paciencia Fields in Mexico.

The Southern Fuel & Refining Company, a subsidiary of Cities Fuel & Power Company, was organized in Delaware in 1911 with a capitalization of 99,500 shares of $10 par value. The company owns 441,000 acres of oil-bearing land in Mexico.

The Sun Oil Company operates in Mexico through its Mexican subsidiary, the Sun Oil Company of Mexico.

The Tal-Vez Oil Company, a subsidiary of the Southern Oil & Transport Corporation, was organized in Mexico in 1910 with a capitalization of 100 shares of 1,000 pesos par value. The company's properties have an average daily production of 10,000 barrels.

The Tamihua Petroleum Company, a subsidiary of Mexican Petroleum Company, Ltd. of Delaware, was organized in Maine in 1906 with a capitalization of $1,000,000.

The Tampascas Oil Company of Mexico, a subsidiary of Lagunita Oil Company, was organized in West Virginia in 1912 with a capitalization of 200 shares of $100 par value. The company's Mexican properties have an average daily production of 95 barrels.

The Texas Company of Mexico, S. A., a subsidiary of the Texas Corporation, was organized in Mexico in 1917, with a capitalization of 53,000 shares of 100 pesos par value, of which 35,000 have been issued. The company owns about 175,000 acres of leases and fee lands in the Gulf Coast area.

The Tuxpam Petroleum Company, a subsidiary of Mexican Petroleum Company, Ltd. of Delaware, was organized in 1906 under the laws of Maine with a capitalization of $1,000,000.

The Tuxpan Oil Company, a subsidiary of Producers Oil Corporation of America, was organized in 1907 under the laws of Delaware with a capitalization of 600 shares of common of $100 par value, and 300 shares of preferred of $100 par value. None of the preferred stock has been issued. The company owns 8,000 acres of oil lands in the State of Vera Cruz.

The Venezuelan Mexican Oil Corporation was organized in Virginia in 1917 with a capitalization of 1,500,000 shares of common of $10 par value, of which 719,250 have been issued, and 75,000 shares of 8% preferred of $10 par value, of which 24,414 have been issued. The company owns the entire capital stock of the Otontepec Petroleum Company, the California Investment Company, S. A., and the North American Leasing Corporation. The company owns properties in Mexico and concessions in Venezuela.

The Pan American Petroleum & Transport Company was organized in Delaware in 1916. It owns 98% in the Mexican Petroleum Company, Ltd., and 95% in Lago Oil & Transport Corporation. The Mexican Petroleum Company, Ltd., on the other hand, owns 99¼% in the Mexican Petroleum Company of California, 100% in the Huasteca Petroleum Company, 100% of the Tuxpam Petroleum Company, 100% of the Tamiahua Petroleum Company, 100% of the Mexican Petroleum Corporation of Louisiana, and 100% of the Mexican Petroleum Corporation. The fleet of oil-carrying steamers owned by the Pan American consists of 31 vessels totaling 273,333 tons, with carrying capacity of 1,800,000 barrels. These vessels are leased to the Huasteca Oil Company and, together with five vessels leased from outsiders, transport the company's oil from Tampico, Mexico, and Destrehan, Louisiana, to various stations of the company on the Atlantic and Gulf coasts of the United States, and in Panama and South America. The company's Mexican properties cover an area of about 1,500,000 acres and are located principally in the Tampico district. The output for 1927 was 24,000,000 barrels, against 33,000,000 barrels in 1926. It also owns and operates about 750 miles of pipe lines in Mexico with a capacity of 135,000 barrels per day, carrying oil from the southern fields to Tampico, and 90,000 barrels per day from the Panuco fields to Tampico. It also owns and operates at Tampico a complete refinery, with a capacity of 130,000 barrels of crude oil per day. The company further owns storage facilities in Mexico, of about 10,000,000 barrels, and a railroad 65 miles long running from San Geronimo to Cerro Azul.

The company's capitalization consists of $230,000,000, divided into 1,100,000 common shares of $50 each; 3,000,000 Class "B" common shares of $50 each; and 250,000 shares of preferred stock of $100 each. There are outstanding $7,487,500 of 10-year 6% convertible bonds offered in 1924 at 97, and due November 1, 1934; and $1,683,500 of 10-year 7% convertible bonds of an original issue of $10,000,000 offered in 1920 at 94½, and due in 1930.

The Union Oil of California was organized in 1890. It owns the entire capital stock of Union Oil Company of Mexico, Compañía Mexicana de Petroles "Union," and Compañía la Macarena. The area owned in Mexico amounts to 26,786 acres, and in Colombia to 405,524 acres.

The Kern River Oil Fields of California, Ltd., was organized under the laws of California, in 1910. In 1918, an arrangement was made with the Tampico Oil, Ltd., which owns 28,500 acres in the district of Panuco, Mexico, whereby Kern River has the right to take over the entire property subject to a royalty of 7½% of the production from such lands, and to the payment of expenses in Mexico as from April 1, 1918. In order to comply with Mexican laws, the company organized a Mexican subsidiary, known as the Kern Mex Oil Fields, S. A., with a nominal capital of $25,000, operations being directed to the properties leased from Tampico Oil, Ltd. Sub-leases of over 18,500 acres have been granted to the Mexican Gulf Oil Company. Further leases have been secured of about 5,244 acres in the State of Nuevo León, District of Los Aldamas. The company has also acquired properties in Trinidad; 3,651 acres free-hold, 145 acres lease-hold, and oil exploration license over 1,448 acres, subject to royalty from 1,284 acres free-hold. Of the 70 wells which have been sunk on the Trinidad property, 53 are producing. Capitalization consists of 3,000,000 shares of 10 shillings par value, which are quoted on the London Stock Exchange at about 7/6.

The Inter-Continent Petroleum Corporation was organized in Delaware in 1916 as the Mexican Panuco Oil Company. Through subsidiaries the company owns 2,000 acres in the Panuco Oil Fields in Mexico and controls more than 8,000,000 acres in Central and South America. It owns the entire capital stock of the English Oil Company, which owns 2,000 acres in the Panuco district in Mexico. Arrangements have been made for the Trans-Continental Petroleum Corporation, a subsidiary of Standard Oil of New Jersey, to take over and work the properties, without producing, paying for oil at the well. It is further interested in the British Guiana Oil Fields, Ltd., and the British Guiana Oil Syndicate, Ltd., which holds concessions in British Guiana covering 2,000,000 acres in the northeast coast extending from the Venezuelan boundary to the Pomeroon River. It also owns 80% of the capital stock of the Cachavi Syndicate, which owns about 300,000 acres of land in the Province of Esmeraldas in the northwestern part of Ecuador, between Colombia and the Pacific Ocean. The capitalization consists of 5,000,000 shares of $5 par value, of which 973,233 have been issued and fully paid. The shares are listed on the New York curb market and are traded in on the London Stock Exchange and on the Brussels Bourse. Recent quotations were at the rate of $2 per share.

The Marland Oil Company, a Delaware corporation organized in 1920, owns 94.9% of the Consolidated Oil Company of Mexico, and 50% of the stock of the Comar Oil Company.

The Mexican Seaboard Oil Company was organized in Delaware in 1919 and owns over 99% of the capital stock of International Petroleum Company of Maine, which owns directly or through subsidiaries about 308,817 acres in various parts of Mexico, sea loading terminals at Cherrera on the Gulf of Mexico connected by pipe lines with producing properties in the Panuco region. The company's output in Mexico has steadily gone down, amounting to 3,765,982 barrels in 1927, against 7,148,552 in 1926 and 13,381,015 in 1925. Capitalization consists of 1,000,000 shares of no par value, and an authorized issue of $15,000,000 of 7% 10-year debentures, of which $2,800,000 are outstanding, due for payment September 1, 1929. Shares of the company are quoted on the New York Stock Exchange.

The Ohio Oil Company was organized in 1887 under Ohio laws. It owns a 60% interest in the Ohio Mexico Oil Corporation, which was formed in 1926 to exploit properties in the State of Coahuila, Mexico.

The Penn-Mex Fuel Company was organized in 1912 in Delaware and controls 150,000 acres of oil-bearing properties in the State of

Vera Cruz, Mexico. The Trans-Continental Petroleum Company, a subsidiary of Standard Oil of New Jersey, has arranged to drill wells on the company's properties; expenses and profits to be shared equally. Capitalization consists of 400,000 shares of $25 par value, a considerable part of which is owned by the South Penn Oil Company. Shares are listed in New York, reported around $30.

The Pierce Petroleum Corporation was organized in Delaware in 1924 to acquire, *inter alia*, refineries at Tampico and Vera Cruz, Mexico.

The Standard Oil Company of California controls the Richmond Petroleum Company of Mexico, organized in Mexico; and the California Standard Oil Company of Mexico, organized in Delaware.

The Standard Oil Company of New York controls, *inter alia*, considerable area of prospective oil lands in the Panuco field in Mexico. Through a subsidiary, the General Petroleum Corporation of California, Standard of New York owns a topping plant at Tampico, Mexico, with water facilities on the Panuco River.

The South Penn Oil Company owns a controlling interest in the Penn-Mex Fuel Company, which operates in Mexico.

Texas Corporation owns 8,500 acres and refineries at Tampico with a daily capacity of 10,000 barrels.

The Rio Grande Oil Company of Delaware controls the Refineria Petrolera Occidental, S. A., which is not operating at present, existing only for the purpose of holding title to real estate in Mexico.

The Texas Corporation controls the Texas Company of Mexico, S. A. The Argentina subsidiary of the Texas Corporation is the Galena-Signal Oil Company, S. A. The Brazilian subsidiary is the Sociedade Anonima de Oleo Galena-Signal, also the Texas Company of South America. In Cuba the company operates through the Texas Company (West Indies), Limited. In Porto Rico, through the Texas Company of Porto Rico, Inc. The company's production in Mexico was 314,246 barrels in 1928, as compared with 386,819 in 1927. The Company's Colombian subsidiary has options on 428,644 acres of fee lands.

The Warner Quinlan Company of Maine owns 17,954 acres in the Panuco oil district of Mexico. It also owns and operates a loading terminal at Tampico, and 17½ acres of ground. On this property is a warehouse, pump station, two 55,000-barrel tanks, loading lines, etc.

Other American companies operating in Mexico include the following:

Port Lobos Petroleum Corporation;

Sinclair Consolidated Oil Corporation owns concessions on more than 1,000,000 acres. The company's Mexican subsidiaries include: the Freeport and Mexican Fuel Oil Corporation and International Petroleum Company;

Gulf Oil Corporation controls a number of companies, including the Mexican Gulf Oil Company, the South American Gulf Company and the Panama Gulf Oil Company.

The Mexican Gulf Oil Company was incorporated with a nominal capital of $25,000. Production in 1928 amounted to 2,500,000 barrels, as compared with 3,210,110 in 1927, and 5,930,704 in 1926;

New National Oil Company;

Cities Service Company, which controls the Cities Fuel & Power Company, which in turn controls the Empire Pipe Company of Mexico.

The Mexican subsidiaries of Cities Service Company reported for 1928 a production of 3,668,816 barrels. Earnings for 1928 showed a decrease over 1927, largely because of lower oil prices. Cities Service is also distributing its products through dealers in Argentina, Paraguay, Brazil and Uruguay;

Imperio Gas & Combustion Company;

"Imperio" Terminal Company;

"Imperio" Oil Lands Company;

"Imperio" Pipe Line Company;

Gulf Coast Corporation;

Holden-Evans Steamship Company;

Lagunita Oil Company;

National Petroleum Company;

Southern Fuel & Refinery Company;

Sentinel Oil & Gas Company;

Island Oil & Transport Company, which controls the Capuchinas Oil Company;

Port Lobos Oil Company;

Gulf Consolidated Oil Corporation;

East Coast Oil Company, which is controlled by the Southern Pacific Railroad;

Otontepec Petroleum Company, controlled by the Mexican Investment Company;

Gulf States Oil & Refining Company;

Caltex Oil Company;

Mexican Producing & Refining Company;

The Ammex Petroleum Corporation has a capitalization of 400,000 shares of common stock, $5.00 par, and has interests, rights and properties near Vera Cruz and Tampico;

Continental Mexican Petroleum Company, controlled by the General Petroleum Company;

Hidalgo Petroleum Company;

Noco Mexican Oil Company, which is affiliated with the Noco Petroleum Company;

Inter-Ocean Oil Company;

Curyon Oil Company;

Tex-Mex Fuel Oil Company;

The Eastern Oil Corporation;

Boston-Mexican Petroleum Trust;

Boston-Mexican Leasing Company;

Ventura Consolidated Oil Fields;

Lewis Oil Corporation;

New York-Mexican Oil Company;

National Oil Company;

Kumfort Oil & Gas Company;

Mexican Oil Company;

Federal Oil Company;

Equity Petroleum Corporation;

Casiano Petroleum Company;

Sun Oil Company, S. A., controlled by the Mexican Sun Oil Company;

Producers Oil Corporation of Mexico, which controls the Tuxpan Oil Company.

Other Interests. Next to petroleum, American capital has gone heavily into Mexican mining.

The largest amount of American capital invested in Mexican mining enterprises is represented by the American Smelting & Refining Company, a New Jersey corporation organized in 1899. The company owns five smelting and refining plants in Mexico and two in South America; also the Mines Lines of Mexico and the Mexican Union Railroad Company. The company's lead smelters are as follows:

AMERICAN SMELTING & REFINING COMPANY INTERESTS

	Daily Capacity (In Tons)	Furnaces
Monterey.	1,300	7
Chihuahua	1,500	8
Asarco.	500	3

AMERICAN SMELTING & REFINING COMPANY INTERESTS
– Continued

The company's copper smelters are as follows:

	Daily Capacity (In Tons)	Furnaces
Aguascalientes	1,600	6
Matchuala	1,300	4
Velardena	750	3
San Luis Potosí.	-	-

The company's zinc smelter is located at Rosita, Coahuila.

The mines owned by the company, together with location and the nature of mines, are presented hereunder:

NAME	Location	Metal
Asientos	Asientos	Silver
Dolores	Matehuala	Silver, copper
Bonanaza.	Bonanaza	Silver, lead
Parral	Parral	Silver, lead, zinc
Sta. Eulalia.	Sta. Eulalia	Silver, lead, zinc
Tecolotes.	Sta. Barbara	Silver, lead, zinc
Veta Grande & Veta Colorado . . .	Parral	Silver
Velardena	Velardena	Silver, lead, copper
Sierra Mojada	Sierra Mojada	Silver, lead, copper
Tiro General.	Charcas	Silver, lead, copper
Orizaba	Magistoal	– –
Prieta	Calera	– –
La Luz	Cordero	– –
Sta. Francisca	Asientos	Copper
Guadelupe	Parral	– –
Durango	Durango	Iron
Jesus Maria.	Sierra Mojada*	– –

*Operated under lease from the Negociacion Minera da Jesus Maria.

The company's capitalization comprises $50,000,000 of preferred; $60,998,000 of common stock; and a funded debt of $37,782,100. Total assets amounted on December 31, 1928, to more than $233,000,000.

In August, 1929, the R. C. A. Photophone, a subsidiary of the Radio Corporation of America, incorporated the R. C. A. Photophone of Mexico, Inc., under the laws of Delaware for the purpose of distributing its products in that country. Capitalization is given as 1,000 shares of no par value.

The subjoined table presents as complete a list as possible of all other mining companies operating in Mexico, which are controlled by or affiliated with American interests.

UNITED STATES INVESTMENTS IN MINING COMPANIES

NAME OF COMPANY	Common Stock	Affiliated with or Controlled by
Aguascalientes Copper Smelter.	–	Am. Smelting
Ahumada Lead	$1,192,018	– –
Cia. Minera de Plomo, S. A.	615,740	Ahumada
Cia. Minera la Corona, S. A..	–	– –
Cia. Minera Erupcion y Anexas, S. A. .	–	Ahumada
Cia. del Ferrocarril de Chihuahua y Oriente	592,500	Ahumada
Lamentation Syndicate.	–	Ahumada
Ahumada Silver Mining.	–	– –
Amajac Mines Co.	2,500,000	– –
American-Mexico Mining & Developing Co.	3,000,000	– –
American Mining & Refining Co.	3,000,000	– –
Ampara Mining Co.	2,000,000	– –
Cia. Minera la Mazata y Anexas, S. A. .	–	Ampara
Anita Copper Mines Co., S. A.	–	Douglas Copper Co.
Anita Hacienda		– –
Antimony Corporation.	1,000,000	– –
Cortez Associated Mines	–	Antimony Corp.
Arados Copper Co.	–	– –
Arizona Dearborn Mining Co.	–	– –
Asientos Mining Co..	1,000,000	– –
Aventura Mines Co.	–	– –
Aurora Silver Mines Corp..	1,000,000	– –
Aztec Consolidated Mining Co.	500,000	– –
Cia. Minera Consolida Los Aztecos, S. A.	–	Aztec Cons.
Sonora Exploration Co.	–	Aztec Cons.
La Cobriza Mining Co.	–	Aztec Cons.
Bank Mining Co..	–	– –
Batopilas Mining Co.[5]	8,931,980	– –
Belen Cabriza Mines.	–	– –
Blaisdell Coscotitlan Syndicate.	–	– –
Boston Montezuma Mining Co.	1,000,000	– –
Buena Noche Mine.	–	– –
Buffa Mining, Milling & Smelting Co. .	1,500,000	– –

[5]Funded debt, $366,500.

UNITED STATES INVESTMENTS IN MINING COMPANIES
– Continued

NAME OF COMPANY	Common Stock	Affiliated with or Controlled by
Butters Copala Mines	–	– –
Cadena de Cobre Mining Co.	$1,000,000	– –
Calera Mining Co.	–	– –
California-Mexico Mining Co..	–	– –
California Mine.	–	– –
Compañía Mine.	–	– –
Canario Copper Co.	9,000,000	– –
El Canario Copper Co., S. A.	–	Canario Copper
Mountain Cons. Copper Co., S. A. . . .	–	Canario Copper
Carmen Copper Co.	750,000	– –
Carmen Mines Co.	1,500,000	– –
Carnegie Lead & Zinc Co.[6]	2,000,000	– –
Calumet & Sonora of Cananea Mng. Co.	12,500	Carnegie Lead
Cerro de Oro Mine.	–	– –
Chihuahua Mining Co.	587,806	El Potosi
El Potosi Mining Co.	–	Howe Sound
Cieneguita Cons. Mines.	–	– –
Cinco Minas Co.	500,000	– –
Cia. Cobre Mexicana	–	– –
Cia. de Minas Santa Ana y Anexas, S.A .		
Real del Monte y Pachuca Cia	–	U. S. Smelting
Cia. de Minerales y Metales	2,500,000	American Metal
Cia. de Minera de Penoles, S. A	4,500,000	Cia. de Minerales
Cia. Exploradora de Chihuahua	–	
Cia. Exploradora de Santa Marta, S. A.	5,000[7]	– –
Cia. Exploradora de Sinaloa.	–	– –
Cia. Ferrocarrillero y Min. de Azufre. .	–	Sulphur Mng. & Ref.
Cia. Metalurgica de Torreon, S. A. . . .	2,000,000	Cia. Min. de Penoles
Cia. Metalurgica Mexicana[8].	1,750,000	– –
Sombrerete Mining Co..	–	Cia. Metalurgica
Mexican Lead Co.	–	Cia. Metalurgica
Montezuma Lead Co..	–	Cia. Metalurgica
Alvarez Lead & Timber Co..	–	Cia. Metalurgica
Mexican Mineral Railway Co..	–	Cia. Metalurgica
Potosi & Rio Verde Railway Co..	–	Cia. Metalurgica
Cia. Metalurgica Nacional	–	Am. Smelting
Cia. Minera de Palmarito.	–	Barnsdall Corp.
Cia. Minera Paloma y Cabrillas, S. A.. .	–	Cia. Min. de Penoles

[6]Funded debt, $244,000.
[7]Number of shares.
[8]Preferred stock, $2,250,000; funded debt. $2,774,700.

UNITED STATES INVESTMENTS IN MINING COMPANIES
– Continued

NAME OF COMPANY	Common Stock	Affiliated with or Controlled by
Sabinas Coal Mines	–	Cia. Min. Paloma
La Parena Metal Mine.	–	Cia. Min. Paloma
Mosqueteros Mine	–	Cia. Min. Paloma
Cia. de Combustibles Aguijita, S. A. . .	–	Cia. Min. Paloma
Cia. de Combustibles Nacional y Transp.	–	Cia. Min. Paloma
Cia. Minera el Refugio, S. A.	–	Alvarado Mining
Cia. Minera el Sacramento, S. A..	–	– –
Cia. de Minas de Mexico, S. A.	–	Potter Palmer Estate
Cia. Minera Nayarit de Cananea, S. A. .	$25,000,000	– –
Cia. Minera Nazareno y Catasillas, S. A.	2,000,000	– –
Cia. Minera Nazareno y Alicante, S.A. .	–	Cia. Min. Nazareno
Cia. Minera San Pascual de las Adargas, S. A..	10,000,000	– –
Cia. Metalifera Coadoro	–	– –
Concheno Mining Co..	–	– –
Conchita Mining & Development Co.. .	500,000	– –
Consolidada No. 2 Lease.	–	– –
Continental Mining Co..	1,000,000	– –
Jimulco Mining Co.	–	Continental Mining
Cepete Consolidated Copper Co.	1,000,000	– –
Melczer Mining Co.	25,000	Cepete Consolidated
Cori Gold Mines	711,206	– –
La Corona Mining & Milling Co..	100,000	– –
Cortez Associated Mines.	25,000	– –
Cia. Minera del Cubo, S. A.	175,000	Cubo Mng. & Milling
Cucharas Mining Co.	100,000	– –
Cusi Mexicana Mining Co.	2,600,000	– –
San Miguel Mining Co.	–	Cusi Mexicana
Cusi Mining Co..	–	Cia. Min. de Mirasol
De León Mining Co..	1,000,000	– –
Democrata Cananea Sonora Copper Co..	2,869,970	– –
Dinamita Mining Co.	–	– –
Dolores Esperanza Corp..	1,728,175	– –
Dolores Mines Co.	–	Dolores Esperanza
Consuelo Mining, Milling & Power Co..	–	Dolores Esperanza
Chihuahua Esperanza Gold Mining Co..	–	Dolores Esperanza
El Rayo Mines Co..	–	Dolores Esperanza
Creston Colorada Co.	–	Dolores Esperanza
La Dura Milling & Mining Co.	–	Dolores Esperanza

UNITED STATES INVESTMENTS IN MINING COMPANIES
– Continued

NAME OF COMPANY	Common Stock	Affiliated with or Controlled by
Cia. Minera Gloria y Fortuna Cons....	–	Dolores Esperanza
Duluth-Sonora Copper Co.........		– –
Durazno Mining Co..............	–	– –
El Paso Douglas Mining Co........	$250,000	– –
Emeralda Parral Mining Co........	1,000,000	– –
Espada Mines Co..............	–	– –
La Cia. Exploradora de Chihuahua ...	–	– –
El Favor Mining Co.............	3,500,000	– –
La Flor del Valle Mining Co........	200,000	– –
Fresnillo Co.[9].................	1,554,500	– –
El Fuerte Mining & Smelting Co.....	401,000	– –
Choix Consolidated Mining Co......	–	El Fuerte Mining
Los Platanos Mining Co...........	–	El Fuerte Mining
General Mines Corp..............	1,499,500	– –
Cia. Minera y Exploradora Azteca, S. A....................	–	General Mines
Giroux Consolidated Mines Co.....	144,142	Cons. Cop. M. of Nev.
Gulf Mining & Reduction Co.	–	Guggenheim Bros.
Great National Mexican Smelting Co. .	–	– –
Greene Cananea Copper Co........	50,000,000	– –
Superior Bonanza Mining Co.......	–	Greene Cananea
San Pedro Copper Co............	–	Greene Cananea
Guanajuato Cons. Mining & Milling...	3,000,000	– –
Carmen Guanajuato Gold Mining Co. .	–	Guanajuato Cons.
Guanajuato Reduction & Mines[10] ...	75,000	– –
Guatamo Lead Silver Co.	2,000,000	– –
Gueriguito Mining Co., S. A........	–	– –
Guerrero Development Co.........	75,000	– –
Guggenheim Smelting Co..........	–	– –
Gulf Copper Co...............	1,000,000	– –
Harrison & Co................	65,000	– –
Hileta Gold & Silver Mining Co......	–	Harrison & Co.
Hermosa Mining Co.............	300,000	– –
Humboldt Mining Co............	2,000,000	– –
Inde Gold Mining Co............	–	– –
Cia. Internacional Minera, S. A......	100,000	– –
International Mines & Development ..	2,400,000	– –
Neg. Minera de Jesus Maria, S. A.....	–	Am. Smelting
Cia. Minera Jesus Maria y Anexas	–	– –
Jimulco Mining Co..............	1,000,000	– –
Lane-Rincon Mines, Inc.[11]	3,000,000	– –

[9]Preferred stock, $484,900; funded debt, $187,000.
[10]Funded debt, $2,800,000.
[11]Funded debt, $431,000.

UNITED STATES INVESTMENTS IN MINING COMPANIES
− *Continued*

NAME OF COMPANY	Common Stock	Affiliated with or Controlled by
Cia. Minera Lepanto, S. A.	$2,500,000	− −
Leuvia del Oro Gold Mining Co.	−	− −
Cia. Minera de Loteria	−	Am. Smelting
Lucia Mining Co..	25,000	San Luis Mining
Lucky Tiger Combination Gold Mining.	7,153,370	− −
Tigre Mining Co., S. A.	−	Lucky Tiger
Magistral Ameca Copper Co.	1,255,300	− −
Cia. de Cobre Magistral Ameca, S. A.. .	500,000	Magistral Ameca
Las Moras Copper Co.	−	Cia. de Cobre
Manhattan Exploration Co.	1,806,000	− −
Maria Mining Co..	500,000	− −
Compania Metalurgica Mexicana.	40,000[12]	American Smelting
Sombrerete Mining Co..	−	American Smelting
Mexican Lead Co.[13]	862,500	American Smelting
Mexican Mineral Railway Co.	−	American Smelting
Montezuma Lead Co..	−	American Smelting
Alvarez Land & Timber Co..	−	American Smelting
Potosi & Rio Verde Railway Co..	−	American Smelting
Metatas Mining Co.	200,000	− −
Mexia-Kan Mining Co.	60,000	− −
La Mexicana Mines Co..	−	− −
Mexican Candelaria Co., S. A.	1,500,000	− −
Mexican Mines Co..	500,000	− −
Mexican Northern Mining & Ry. Co.[14]	600,000[12]	American Smelting
Alvarado Mining & Milling.	−	Mexican Northern
Cia. Minera El Refugio	−	Mexican Northern
Hidalgo Mining Co.	−	Mexican Northern
San Juanica Mining Co..	−	Mexican Northern
Consolidacion Minera de Parral	−	Mexican Northern
Mexican Premier Mines.	375,000	− −
Cia. Minera de San Jose, S. A.	−	Mexican Premier
Mexico Silver Mines Co.	2,000,000	− −
Caiman Mines, S. A..	−	Mexico Silver
Michoacan Ry. & Mining Co..	496,850	American Smelting
Michoacan & Pacific Ry. Co..	−	Michoacan Ry.
Cia. Minerales y Metales	1,250,000	American Metal
Las Truchas Iron Ore Co.	−	Bethlehem Steel
Montezuma Copper Co.	2,600,000	Phelps Dodge
Mololoa Mining Co..	3,000,000	− −

[12]Number of shares.
[13]Preferred stock, $1,250,000.
[14]Funded debt, $672,000.

UNITED STATES INVESTMENTS IN MINING COMPANIES
– *Continued*

NAME OF COMPANY	Common Stock	Affiliated with or Controlled by
Monte Cristo Mining Co...........	$1,500,000	– –
Cia. Minera Monte Cristo	–	Monte Cristo
Monte Cristo Mining Co. of Sonora...	500,000	– –
Monterey Mining, Smelting & Ref. Co.....................	3,000,000	Cia. de Minerales
Mosqueteros Mining Co...........	1,500,000	– –
National Metallurgical Co.........	–	American Smelting
Nacozari Consolidated Copper Co. ...	20,000,000	– –
Novidad Mines & Reduction Co......	1,000,000	– –
Novidad Development Co., S. A.	100,000	American Smelting
North American Development Co. ...	10,000,000	– –
North American Lead Corp.[15]......	4,500,000	– –
El Orito Mining & Milling Co.	432,500	– –
Pasadena El Monte Silver Mines	300,000	– –
Cia. Minera de Penoles, S. A........	4,500,000	Cia. de Minerales
Cia. Minera Paloma y Cabrillas, S. A...	–	Cia. Min. de Penoles
Sabinas Coal Mines	–	Cia. Min. de Penoles
La Parrena Metal Mine	–	Cia. Min. de Penoles
Cia. Metalurgica de Torreon, S. A. ...	2,000,000	Cia. Min. de Penoles
Suriana Mining & Smelting Co.......	–	Cia. Min. de Penoles
Jimulco Mining Co..............	–	Cia. Min. de Penoles
Cia. Minera de Natividad y Anexas ...	–	Cia. Min. de Penoles
Inglaterra Mining Co.............	–	Cia. Min. de Penoles
San-Toy Mining Co..............	6,000,000	Cia. Min. de Penoles
Cia. Minera La Constancia........	–	Cia. Min. de Penoles
Cia. Combustibles Aguijita, S. A.	–	Cia. Min. de Penoles
Cia. Minera y Beneficiadora de Norte .	–	Cia. Min. de Penoles
Naica Mines of Mexico	–	Cia. Min. de Penoles
Candelaria Mining Co.	–	Cia. Min. de Penoles
Perla Mining Co.	1,500,000	– –
Pilares Extension Mining Co.......	1,000,000	– –
Pinos Altos Mines Co..	200,000	Barnsdall Corp.
Pintas Mines Co.	2,500	Buffalo-Arizona Mines
Piquito Mining Co..	1,000,000	– –
Pittsburgh Bote Mining Co., S. A.....	50,000	Carnegie Metals Co.
Pittsburgh Vetagrande Mining	150,000	Carnegie Metals Co.
El Potosi Mining Co.	60,000	Howe Sound
Chihuahua Mining Co.	–	El Potosi Mining
Promontorio Mines Co.[16]........	250,000[17]	– –

[15]Preferred stock, $500,000.
[16]Preferred stock, $310,000.
[17]Number of shares.

UNITED STATES INVESTMENTS IN MINING COMPANIES
—Concluded

NAME OF COMPANY	Common Stock	Affiliated with or Controlled by
Cia. Minera Explotadora de Promontorio, S. A..	—	Promontorio Mines
Puebla Smelting & Refining Co.[18] . . .	$5,000,000	— —
Cia. Real del Monte y Pachuca	2,554[19]	U. S. Smelting
Cia. de Minas Santa Ana y Anexas . . .	2,000,000	Cia. de Real del Monte
U. S. Smelting, Ref. & Mng. Explor. Co.	50,000	U. S. Smelting
Arevalo Mines.	1,250,000	U. S. Smelting
Reforma Mining & Milling Co.	—	Lewisohn Interests
La Regina Mining Co.[20]	1,000,000	— —
Revosadero Mining Co.	1,000,000	— —
Rio Plata Mining Co.	1,872,590	— —
San Cayetano Mines, Ltd.	256,950	General Dev. Co.
San Geronimo Mines & Metals Corp. . .	—	— —
San Luis Mining Co.	3,000,000	— —
Lucia Mining Co.	—	San Luis Mining
San Pablo Mining Co.	2,500,000	— —
Cia. Minera de San Patricio, S. A.	50,000	— —
Santa Eulalia Mining Co.	300,000	— —
Sinaloa Exploration & Dev. Co.	50,000[19]	— —
Sinaloa Power & Development Co. . . .	1,425,000	— —
Smith Cananea Mining Co.	1,021,345	— —
Sonora Development Co.	500,000	— —
La Suerte Mining Co.	750,000	— —
Superior Bonanza Mining Co.	749,230	Cananea Consol.
Bonanza Mining Co., S. A.	—	Superior Bonanza
Tecolote Copper Corp.[21]	9,386,593	— —
Tecolote Copper Co., S. A.	—	Tecolote Cop. Corp.
Towne Mines, Inc.[22]	40,000[19]	Towne Securities
Transvaal Cop. Mines Co. (Utah)	4,000,000	— —
United Mines Co..	2,500,000	— —
La Ventura Metals Co.	500,000	— —
La Ventura Mining Co., S. A.	1,500	La Ventura Metals
Washington Mines Development Co. . .	1,300,000	— —
Ysleta Sonora Mining Co.	50,000	— —

[18]Funded debt, $1,000,000.
[19]Number of shares.
[20]Funded debt, $62,000.
[21]Preferred stock, $554,220; funded debt, $1,000,000.
[22]Preferred stock, $4,000,000; funded debt, $1,250,000.

The Portrero Sugar Company of Delaware owns all the stock of the Cia. Manufacturera del Portrero in the state of Vera Cruz. Capitalization comprises 200,000 shares of common stock of no par value, and $2,000,000 first mortgage 7% bonds, due in 1947.

The Tabasco Plantation Company was organized in 1901 in Delaware to engage in the production of bananas and rubber and the refining of sugar. Properties are located at Santa Lucrecia, Vera Cruz, and are operated under lease by the Latin American Sugar Co., Ltd. Capitalization consists of $3,500,000 capital stock and $500,000 of first mortgage 7% bonds, due in 1943.

The Mexican Telephone and Telegraph Company belongs to the International Telephone and Telegraph Corporation system and had 32,000 telephones in service in 1928. The company's capitalization consists of 70,000 shares of common, 30,000 shares of 5% preferred, both of $10 par value, and 3,375 shares of $7 prior preference stock of no par value. There are also outstanding $1,500,000 10-year notes due in 1935.

Light and power plants in Mexico represent an investment of $103,043,536, according to a study prepared by the Bureau of National Statistics of Mexico. Of this sum, American capital has invested $37,758,192, British $11,684,134, Mexican $8,933,003, French $6,032,625. Canadian, German, Italian, Japanese and Spanish capital is also represented in this industry to a small extent.

The American & Foreign Power Company, Inc., reported gross earnings for the year 1928 of $1,653,744 from its Mexican public utility properties. The company's operating subsidiaries in Mexico supply electric power and light and other public utilities service in 89 communities, and also operate electric street railways in 6 communities. Important subsidiaries include the Tampico Electric Light, Power & Traction Company; the Puebla Tramway Light & Power Company, S. A.; the Central Mexico Light & Power Company; the Guanajuato Power & Electric Company; the Vera Cruz Electric Light, Power & Traction, Ltd.; and the Compañía de Electricidad de Merida, S. A. Total population of the territory served is estimated at 1,135,000. In April, 1928, American & Foreign Power acquired control of the Mexican Utilities Company through the acquisition of common stock, preferred stock and collateral gold bonds of that company in exchange for its $6 preferred stock. The Mexican Utilities Company had outstanding 35,000 shares of common stock, 30,812 3/5 shares of $7 preferred stock, and $1,550,000 of 8% gold bonds due in 1955. The basis of the exchange was as follows: For each common share, 35/100 of a share of $6 preferred; for each preferred share, 75/100 of a share of $6 preferred; and for each $100 bond, 9/10 of a share of $6 preferred. As of September 30, 1928, 33,560 shares of common, 25,847.2 shares of preferred, and $1,367,600 of bonds had been acquired. In October, 1928, American & Foreign Power acquired from the Whitehall Electric Investments, Ltd., of London the electric power and light systems in Vera Cruz, Tampico, Puebla and Orizaba; street railway properties in Vera Cruz and Puebla; and wholesale power and light business in Cordoba. The Mexican properties are owned by Compañía de Luz Electrica Fuerza Motriz de Orizaba, S. A.; the Compañía Electrica de Tampico, S. A.; the Compañía Hidro Electrica; the Compañía Electrica de Cordoba, S. A.; the Puebla Tramway Light & Power Company; and the Vera Cruz Electric Power & Traction, Ltd. The capitalization of the Puebla Tramway Company consists of 65,000 shares of $100 par value. There are also outstanding $3,721,800 of prior lien gold 5% bonds, $3,123,500 of first mortgage 5% gold bonds, and 136,480 pounds of 8% notes. The Vera Cruz Company is capitalized at 350,000 shares of 1 pound par value, and has outstanding 181,960 pounds of first mortgage debentures due in 1960.

In December, 1928, American & Foreign Power made an offer to purchase at $125 a share the outstanding $10,000,000 of common stock of the Northern Mexico Power & Development Company, Ltd. The Guanajuato Power & Electric Company, which is controlled by the Mexican Utilities Company, is capitalized at $3,500,000 of common stock, and $1,500,000 of 6% cumulative preferred stock, both of $100 par value. There are also outstanding $989,000 first mortgage 6% gold bonds due in 1932. The company controls the Central Mexico Light & Power Company, capitalized at 15,000 shares of common, and 9,000 shares of 6% cumulative preferred stock, both of $100 par value. Funded debt consists of $1,432,000 first mortgage 6% gold bonds due in 1940. The Guanajuato Company also controls the Michoacan Power Company, capitalized at 10,000 shares of common stock of $100 par value, and $535,100 of first mortgage 6% gold bonds due in 1937. The Northern Mexico Power & Development Company has outstanding, in addition to the $10,000,000 of common stock referred to above, 30,000 shares of 7% cumulative preferred stock of $100 par value, and $490,000 of first mortgage of 7% gold bonds due in 1933.

In 1929, the National City Bank of New York established a branch in Mexico City with a capitalization of 550,000 pesos.

Details of Four States. In view of the disturbances which broke out early in 1929, reference to the extent and nature of American investments in the states most affected by the upheaval should be of especial interest. According to data furnished by the United States Department of State, American investments are heavier in four of the states which were wholly or partly in the hands of the revolutionists than in any other part of Mexico. These states are Sonora, where there are important copper mines; Vera Cruz, where Americans have invested in oil fields and banana plantations, and Chihuahua and Coahuila, where there is a great number of American cattle ranches. Although some of the companies mentioned hereunder have been briefly referred to above, the information is presented in somewhat greater detail and because of the official character of the date.

Reports emanating from Mexico are to the effect that Henry Ford had ordered suspension of plans for expansion of the Assembly Plant in Mexico City, pending the study of proposals for new federal labor legislation.

The location of some of the most important American property in these areas follows:

In the State of Coahuila, the American Metals Company, 61 Broadway, New York, leases the Compañía Metalúrgica de Torreón, S. A., a lead smelting concern at Torreón, operating six blast furnaces, with a total investment of $2,500,000 and employing 900 men.

The Continental Mexican Rubber Company, with offices at 1,776 Broadway, New York, operates a rubber factory at Torreón employing 150 men and having a production of 225,000 pounds per month and a total investment of $350,000.

The Methodist Church (South) of Nashville, Tenn., maintains a hospital at Torreón with property valued at $60,000.

Otto Kahrnud of San Antonio, Texas, owns a copper mine at Jimulco, with an investment of $200,000.

Property in the State of Sonora includes:

The Montezuma Copper Company, owned by the Phelps Dodge Corporation, 99 John Street, New York, operates a mine at Nacozari valued at $16,000,000, which produces about 1,778,000 pounds of copper, 42,200 ounces of silver and 198 ounces of gold per month. It owns a power plant, hotel, office buildings, workmen's homes and has been operating continuously since 1899.

The Nacozari Railroad, owned by the Southern Pacific, operates about 100 miles of track between Douglas, Ariz., and Nacozari and is valued at $2,000,000.

El Tigre Mining Company, owned by the Lucky Tiger Mining Company of Kansas City, operates a copper, gold and silver mine at El Tigre, which is valued at $5,005,000 and which has a monthly output of more than 250,000 pounds of copper.

The Nacozari Consolidated Copper Company operates a copper and gold mine at the city of that name, valued at $1,000,000.

The San Pablo Mining and Milling Company has a $500,000 investment near Pilares de Nacozari which produces high-grade copper.

The Southern Arizona Edison Company supplies water, light and power to the population of Agua Prieta.

Three retail drug stores, owned by American druggists in Douglas, Ariz., are operated in Agua Prieta, Nacozari and Pilares de Nacozari.

The Transvaal Mine, owned by the Transvaal Copper Company of Salt Lake City, owns a mine at Cumpas which once was one of the most important mining properties of the district, but has not produced since 1919.

Ranch properties in the Agua Prieta consular district are valued at about $250,000.

American property in the State of Jalisco includes:

An $8,000,000 investment by Morrison and McCall of San Antonio and St. Louis in the Compañía Hidro-Electrica Irrigadora del Chapala which operates lighting, heating and street car lines in the city of Guadalajara and vicinity. American investments in ranches at Piedras Negras, Coahuila, total $1,902,500, while the coal producing properties of Americans there are valued at $16,975,000. They are owned by the American Metals Company, the American Smelting and Refining Company and Spencer Trask & Co.

The State of Chihuahua contains some of the largest cattle ranches in Mexico, most of them owned by American and British interests. Among these are the ranch at Madera, belonging to William R. Hearst, valued at $2,000,000; the Three Oaks Ranch of E. K. Warren & Son in the Galeana district, valued at $200,000; the Cudahy ranch at Ahumada, valued at $120,000; the Morris and Company ranch in northeast Chihuahua, valued at $300,000; the Palomas Land and Cattle Company's ranch at Palomas, valued at $600,000; the Corralitos Land and Cattle Company in Galeana, valued at $200,000; and the Grove ranch at Ahumada, valued at $425,000.

In addition, the holdings of small ranchers, chiefly in the Galeana district of Chihuahua, are valued at $3,825,000, of which Mormon holdings alone total $2,900,000.

Other important properties in the State of Chihuahua are:

The Dolores Esperanza silver and gold mine, employing 300 men, near Madera, valued at $1,250,000.

The Ahumada Lead Company, employing 668 men, at Los Lamentos, valued at $1,900,000.

The Erupcion Mining Company, mining lead and some silver, at Los Lamentos, valued at $1,400,000.

Liquidation was ordered in August, 1929, of the Chihuahua Investment Company, which had operated for many years as a bank owned by J. B. Dale and associates, as a result of financial distress caused by the raid made by order of one of the Mexican generals. The Liquidation Committee reported that assets amounted to 1,699,659 pesos, and liabilities to 1,241,701 pesos. It is expected that certificates will be issued to the creditors for semi-annual payments, and that liquidation will be completed by July 1, 1931.

The Chihuahua y Oriente Railway operates 47 miles of track between Lucero and Los Lamentos, valued at $6,000.

The Mexico Northwestern Railway Company (partly Canadian) is valued at $37,500,000.

American property in Vera Cruz:

The Cuatotolapam Sugar Company, operating at the city of that name, valued at $1,500,000.

The Mexican-American Fruit and Steamship Corporation, operating banana farms at El Hule and Santa Lucrecia, valued at $1,500,000, and one of the most important new industries established in Vera Cruz.

The Cuyamel Fruit Company, operating fruit farms near Vera Cruz, valued at $200,000.

The Jantha Plantation Company, operating banana farms at Tuxtepec, with an investment of $200,000.

The Mexican Cable Company operates cables to Galveston and New Orleans.

The Cruchilla sugar plant is valued at $300,000.

A UNITED STATES GOVERNMENT OFFICIAL
TESTIFIES ON MEXICAN INVESTMENTS

MONDAY, MAY 10, 1920.

UNITED STATES SENATE,
SUBCOMMITTEE ON FOREIGN RELATIONS,
Washington, D. C.

The subcommittee met, pursuant to call, at 11 o'clock a.m., in room 128, Senate Office Building, Senator Albert B. Fall, presiding.

The CHAIRMAN. The committee will be in order.

TESTIMONY OF HON. FRANKLIN K. LANE.

(The witness was duly sworn by the chairman.)

The CHAIRMAN. Will you please give your full name to the reporter?

Mr. LANE. Franklin K. Lane.

The CHAIRMAN. Mr. Secretary, what official position with the United States Government have you held during the last few years until a recent date?

Mr. LANE. Recently, until the last couple of months, I was Secretary of the Interior.

The CHAIRMAN. As Secretary of the Interior have you been and are you now familiar with the laws of the United States relating to the public domain?

Mr. LANE. Yes, sir.

The CHAIRMAN. Have you had anything to do with shaping the

policy of the United States with reference to its public domain during your incumbency of that office?

Mr. LANE. I have made recommendations to committees of Congress and to the President with respect to that policy.

The CHAIRMAN. Following your recommendations, has legislation been enacted along the lines suggested by you and along other lines?

Mr. LANE. There has been legislation along those lines.

The CHAIRMAN. Has your attention at any time been called to the testimony of Mr. John Lind, taken before this committee at a recent hearing?

Mr. LANE. I saw his testimony as stated in the papers.

The CHAIRMAN. In answer to questions Mr. Lind testified as follows, the question leading up to it being:

Do you think that the oil companies have any just ground of complaint on that score?

That is, of the President's decrees with reference to the exploitation of oil lands in Mexico.

To which Mr. Lind answered:

In Mexico, the same as with us, originally the State owned all the minerals. You know, the Government of the United States owned all of the minerals, I think, until in the forties Congress released the minerals. We have recently —

That is, in the United States —

We have recently resumed the oil and coal and minerals of that character in the public lands. The State in Mexico owned the oil until some time during Diaz's administration, when Lord Cowdray discovered oil. Then they secured an act of the Mexican Congress relinquishing the State's claim to the oil and the real property.

The committee wants to direct your attention to Mr. Lind's statement, practically to the effect that the United States in resuming control or ownership of a claim of oil in the public domain of this country was not only following the example of Mexico but was resuming the control of property which it had theretofore exercised control or ownership of, and apparently which it had not exercised such control of for some period of time. What has been the policy of the United States with reference to oil upon private lands in this country and oil upon public lands?

Mr. LANE. The policy of the United States with respect to oil upon private lands is that the oil goes with the surface. As to public lands, there has been no other policy until recently, when the Congress has seen fit to pass a law under which the Government will directly lease oil lands. It was only within the last month that that law has gone into effect, although it has been advocated for some seven or eight years.

The CHAIRMAN. The United States Government, to your knowledge, has not attempted by legislation, executive or administrative order, or action in any other way, to assume control as against the individual owners of the subsurface products of privately owned land?

Mr. LANE. Never.

Senator BRANDEGEE. Is that true also of the oil on the lands of the Five Civilized Tribes in Oklahoma?

Mr. LANE. Yes.

Senator BRANDEGEE. The same policy?

Mr. LANE. The same policy. The Indians own the oil. All that the Government does is make leases as trustee for the Indians.

The CHAIRMAN. Even upon the Indian lands, if the United States desired to acquire the subsurface product — that is, the oil — it could only do so as any other purchaser?

Mr. LANE. Precisely.

The CHAIRMAN. Then Mr. Lind's statement is not accurate with reference to the policy or the law, is it?

Mr. LANE. No; Mr. Lind evidently was mistaken.

The CHAIRMAN. So far as the laws of the United States are concerned or in so far as the policy is concerned?

Mr. LANE. Yes.

The CHAIRMAN. Are you familiar with the laws of Mexico and the old Spanish laws?

Mr. LANE. In a very rough and general way.

The CHAIRMAN. I understand that we have a witness here who is thoroughly familiar with that subject.

What, in your judgment, Mr. Secretary, would be the effect of allowing to go out to the public unchallenged a statement such as made by Mr. Lind, as to informing or misinforming the people of the United States concerning the oil question, as we generally understand it between this country and Mexico?

Mr. LANE. Oh, I think the people of the United States are so generally familiar with the law as to public lands and private lands that much attention would not be paid to it.

The CHAIRMAN. The people are not generally familiar with Mexican law, though, are they?

Mr. LANE. No, sir.

The CHAIRMAN. So that when he undertakes to say that the Mexican creeds or laws are along the lines of the laws and policy of the United States such a statement, if allowed to go unchallenged, would create a false impression, would it not?

Mr. LANE. That statement might have that effect in Mexico, but not in the United States.

The CHAIRMAN. Might it not affect the public sentiment in the United States, as to feelings with Mexico, by creating an erroneous impression with reference to law, practice, and procedure in Mexico?

Mr. LANE. Yes.

Senator BRANDEGEE. It would produce the impression, would it not, that if Mexico, by its decrees in relation to oil, was confiscating American rights that this Government would do the same?

Mr. LANE. Yes; it certainly would. I think this point ought to be clearly understood, Senator, that there never has been any protest made by anybody, so far as I ever heard, against Mexico or any other country following the policy that the United States is now pursuing, which is a policy of leasing its own national lands upon a royalty basis. There is an impression in the United States that the land held by American corporations has been obtained by grants similar to our large railroad grants in this country; that they have been given the lands by Mexico; whereas the fact is that Americans went to Mexico and bought their land from the private owners, and the title that they got carried with it the right to drill for oil. That is exactly as it has been and as it is in the United States.

Senator BRANDEGEE. You say there is a prevalent impression in this country that Americans got their oil rights in Mexico by a grant. The word ordinarily used instead of "grant" is "concession," is it not?

Mr. LANE. Yes; that is a word that has been misconstrued in this country.

Senator BRANDEGEE. Yes.

Mr. LANE. Because "concession," as we understand it, means something granted by the Government in the way of land, whereas the concessions that are made by the Mexican Government are simply an agreement that for a certain period those who introduced a new industry into Mexico would be relieved of taxation upon what they brought in or took out. That period, so far as we are concerned, long ago expired, and there was no land whatever obtained by concession or grant from the Mexican Government to the oil companies.

Senator BRANDEGEE. I have read quite a number of articles from time to time in magazines and newspapers to the general effect that those American citizens who went into the oil business in Mexico had, by corruption or other improper means, secured from the Mexican Government concessions for these oil rights, which they claimed to own, and that, having secured them corruptly, they are now engaged in an attempt to make the United States Government guarantee them in the peaceful possession of corruptly obtained rights. Have you read articles to that effect?

Mr. LANE. I have.

Senator BRANDEGEE. So the situation is, as you describe it, that Americans engaged in the oil business in Mexico went there and bought their oil rights from individual proprietors, just as they have done in this country, and are simply demanding that their rights as Americans be protected against confiscation by the Mexican Government. That places a different face upon the question with reference to these attacks to which I have referred, it seems to me. Does it not to you?

Mr. LANE. It does. The Americans who have gone into Mexico and have been complained of as you describe have done just as they would have done if they had gone into California; just as if a Pennsylvania oil driller had gone into California and bought a ranch and drilled his well. Under the laws of Mexico he had precisely the same title to the petroleum that is discovered upon that land as he would have in California.

Senator BRANDEGEE. Possibly I was mistaken, but I understood you to say there had been no protest made on account of violations by the Government of Mexico of these American oil rights. Did you mean there had been no protest made by the owners of those rights to the department, or no protest made by the State Department to the Mexican Government? I do not know whether I understood you correctly or not, but you did say something about protests, and I would like to have that made clear?

Mr. LANE. The point I was making was this: That we ought to be consistent in the United States, and that we are thoroughly consistent. We have no objection whatever to a law being enacted in Mexico or any other country by which they would take the lands that are still in public ownership, held by the Government, and lease those upon terms to the citizens or to any others; that that is the policy adopted in the United States as to the lands that still remain in the hands of the Government. And there was no protest whatever on the part of the oil men of the United States against such a policy being adopted by Mexico or any other country, but there was a serious protest against a policy being adopted by which the American owners, who had gone to Mexico, under Mexican laws, and obtained property, for which they had paid cash, from the individuals who owned the land, to having that property taken from them.

You said something a moment or two ago as to certain propaganda being presented to the country on this matter, and one of your points was that it was given out to the public that Americans had gone down there and obtained concessions of land from the Government, and that it was the policy of the Mexican Government itself to resume possession. Now, the fact is that the law under which these lands were obtained — remember always that these lands were purchased from private individuals — was a law passed by Mexico before there had been any discovery of petroleum in Mexico, recognizing the general principle that these lands, such as coal and asphalt and clay lands, were the exclusive property of their private owners. There was a more positive declaration in the Mexican law than there was at that time I believe in our own law that the petroleum lands were the exclusive property of the man who had the title.

Senator BRANDEGEE. My suggestion was also based to a certain extent upon what I had heard had been substantially the statements of Mr. Bryan, when he was Secretary of State, to American citizens who protested to the State Department against the lack of protection accorded to them and their property in Mexico, although it was stated that he had told parties making such protests that they had gone there voluntarily for the purpose of making money, had simply gone there to exploit the resources of Mexico, and as such were entitled to no protection by this Government; if they did not like the treatment, their business was to come back here.

I was trying to get at whether it was your notion that American citizens who went there and bought property, as you have described, as you have stated these oil men have done, from private people, and who are developing their own private property, were entitled to any protection from our Government?

Mr. LANE. Yes; they are entitled to protection; not only because of their own interests but because of our interests and the interests of the world in the development of those resources.

Senator BRANDEGEE. I do not know what line Senator Fall is going to inquire about, but this may be as good a place as any to ask this question:

What importance do you think the development of the Mexican oil fields has to this Government and to the necessities of our people? By that I mean the development of those oil fields by our citizens, and in our interests, rather than the development by some foreign interests.

Mr. LANE. Foreign interests other than Mexican, perhaps you mean?

Senator BRANDEGEE. Yes.

Mr. LANE. Of course, I would not contend for a moment that Mexico did not have the first claim on her own resources. She undoubtedly has, and there is no contention to the contrary so far as this Nation is concerned or our people; but we — who have gone in there and developed that property, discovered the oil there, found that Mexico had a resource of which she had no knowledge herself, and had invested our money in the development of that resource under the smile and approval of the Mexican Government — certainly will contend that she should allow that that product shall be used for the benefit of the United States, if that did not conflict with Mexican interests.

Now, we must have more oil in this country. Last year we produced 1,600,000 automobiles. We have got over 8,000,000 interior-combustion engines upon the lands of the United States. We have got to use oil in our merchant marine. What that demand will be two or three years hence is impossible to say, but an estimate has been made within the Shipping Board of a requirement of 100,000,-000 barrels within four years. Our Navy has come to rely upon it. We are using 400,000,000 barrels a year in the United States; increasing rapidly. Last year we used between thirty and forty million barrels more than we produced. All of which means there has got to be an increase in the supply. We do not know where that is coming from within this country, although it is regarded as so serious a matter that Congress has hastened legislation to meet our need. There is a great supply along the Caribbean Sea and the Gulf of Mexico. It is needed for the industries of this country. It is near to us. The geologists who have made a study of the maps of the world indicate there are two great bodies of oil; one near the eastern end of the Mediterranean, running from the Caucasus to the Persian Gulf and back to the Mediterranean; the other around the Caribbean Sea and the Gulf of Mexico.

If we are to have a supply of oil immediately, and we have a great need arising immediately, we must get our supply from either one of those two sources. One is at hand, and is one in which American capital is interested. The other is distant, and no American capital, except to a very small extent, is interested. So that, if we are in a petroleum period in our power history, it is essential to us that the flow of oil from Mexico and other countries to the United States shall continue, for the development of our foreign trade and building up of our merchant marine, the upbuilding of our Navy and the development of our industries.

Senator BRANDEGEE. When you say you recognize the right of

the first claim by Mexico to her own resources, I do not suppose you mean they have a right to confiscate that American capital that has been invested down there in oil enterprises without compensation?

Mr. LANE. No; hardly.

Senator BRANDEGEE. You mean, of course, that they have that right as to what they own, their public lands?

Mr. LANE. Yes; but I was talking generally of the product. They have undoubtedly the right to that.

Senator BRANDEGEE. Oh, yes.

Mr. LANE. And they have the right, I think, to protect themselves in the matter of seeing that their industries would have a sufficient supply.

The CHAIRMAN. By an embargo, or otherwise, if their national interests demanded.

Mr. LANE. Certainly.

Senator BRANDEGEE. I have seen a statement in the last few weeks, and it has been referred to on the floor of the Senate, as having been made by, I think, some Member of the British House of Commons, stating if not boasting of the fact, in reference to the oil fields that some of the companies had acquired in Mesopotamia and Syria and around the Mediterranean, and stating that we would soon have to call upon them for an enormous quantity of oil, and stating practically that they controlled the oil supply.

Mr. LANE. I have seen that statement.

Senator BRANDEGEE. It made me apprehensive, and upon the floor of the Senate, Senators commented upon the fact. I think Senator Jones, of Washington, in relation to the merchant marine shipping bill, referred to it, calling the attention of the country to the danger of that situation, and unless we get our own supply from the Gulf of Mexico base.

Mr. LANE. Our people in the United States, who are the pioneers in the oil business, who know how to drill oil wells and handle such property better than any other people alive — our people who are capable and who have the money are able and are willing to protect the United States in that respect. We can get the oil we need provided our people can be assured that in going to another country, where they acquire property under the laws of that country and in strict conformity with them, they will be protected. Protection of our rights is all we need. I do not know what statement you refer to, but I have seen various statements made by English authorities on that question of British control of the petroleum supply. I hope those statements are not true. I do not believe there is any reason why they should be true.

They have got possession pretty generally of the whole Persian field and the field extending from Persia to the Mediterranean, but there is a vast amount of territory that can be had to the south of the United States, upon terms perfectly fair to those people and agreeable to them, which will give us all the oil that we need, and we can get it if it is understood that the United States is sufficiently interested to see that no unfair thing is done to those people there, and that no unfair thing is done to us here.

Senator BRANDEGEE. I think the Democratic platform, either four or eight years ago, pledged the protection of the United States to its citizens and their property everywhere, and our platform did also.

Mr. LANE. No oil property has been actually taken from any American citizens that I know of, although efforts have been made in that direction, I believe.

Senator BRANDEGEE. I think the testimony before this committee shows that, whether property has been taken or not, the Government has forbidden those who have obtained the right to drill oil fields from drilling them.

Mr. LANE. That is true.

Senator BRANDEGEE. The use of the property, or the prevention of its proper use, is the equivalent to its confiscation.

Mr. LANE. Very true.

Senator BRANDEGEE. This has been more or less of a diversion. I think Senator Fall desired to examine on another branch.

The CHAIRMAN. No; I had concluded the examination. I have been very much interested in the examination as it proceeded.

You speak of the claims of Great Britain. This oil field, as far as it is developed around the Gulf and the Caribbean Sea, is known to extend to the Island of Trinidad, off the coast of Venezuela in South America, is it not?

Mr. LANE. Yes.

The CHAIRMAN. To whom does the island of Trinidad belong?

Mr. LANE. I understand it belongs to Great Britain.

The CHAIRMAN. Do you know whether any American can acquire oil lands or permits or drilling rights to develop oil in the Island of Trinidad under the British law?

Mr. LANE. I understand not, and I think it goes still further, that the general policy of Great Britain is that no foreigner shall be in possession or control of an oil property that is on their soil.

The CHAIRMAN. As far back as 1882, by order from the council or legislature, or executive order, the Standard Oil Co. of the United States was prohibited from going into India.

Mr. LANE. I am not familiar with that fact, but England undoubtedly has seen for some time that this is a new source of power, and has been forehanded and foresighted.

The CHAIRMAN. England has pursued a policy of encouraging her citizens in every way in the acquisition by such citizens of oil rights all over the world, has she not?

Mr. LANE. Undoubtedly. Of course, we have never recognized ourselves as promoters of commerce.

The CHAIRMAN. No. During this war, within the last few years, have the English gone further than they had before, to this extent: That the English Government itself has acquired a majority interest in a great oil development company or its subsidiaries?

Mr. LANE. I understand that is true. I made a report when I was Secretary of the Interior, which came eventually to the Senate, upon that question.

The CHAIRMAN. That policy is being developed through what is known as the Dutch Shell Co.?

Mr. LANE. Yes.

The CHAIRMAN. Do you know whether that company is interested in oil development in Mexico?

Mr. LANE. I understand it is.

The CHAIRMAN. Do you know whether it is interested in the field in Colombia?

Mr. LANE. I understand it is also there.

The CHAIRMAN. Do you know anything about the American syndicate, the Tropical Oil Co., and other American companies doing business in South or Latin America?

Mr. LANE. I understand there are two American companies in Colombia doing business of a very large character and having producing wells.

The CHAIRMAN. Do you know whether or not those companies which have acquired that interest have transferred the majority to the Dutch Shell and its subsidiary company?

Mr. LANE. I do not. I think that is not true.

The CHAIRMAN. I am afraid it is true, that a three-fourth interest in a large concession for a tract of oil land obtained by American companies has been transferred recently to the Dutch Shell syndicate.

Mr. LANE. That is a menace to the United States in that we must get an outside supply of oil, and if it continues something like what Senator Brandegee says may come true, that we may be compelled to buy from them.

The CHAIRMAN. And yet there is an enormous amount of ready

capital in the United States which could be employed in the development of these American properties. Then there must be some reason to induce American companies to part with majority interests in their property to an English company.

Mr. LANE. I think, perhaps, I can say one of the reasons is the uncertainty as to the security — the sureness or safety of the investment in the other country.

The CHAIRMAN. Do you understand that the English in their developments entertain the same apprehension?

Mr. LANE. They evidently have not to the same extent.

Senator BRANDEGEE. You spoke about the number of barrels of oil. How many gallons are there in a barrel of oil?

Mr. LANE. Forty-two.

Senator BRANDEGEE. I ask permission to put in with my remarks an excerpt read by Senator Jones of Washington describing the statement of this Englishman as to this oil situation.

The CHAIRMAN. Certainly, that may go in.

(The exhibit referred to is as follows, being from the Congressional Record of April 28, 1920, pp. 6719, 6720:)

Mr. JONES of Washington. I have here a clipping from the Public Ledger of Philadelphia under date of April 9, dated at London, a special cable dispatch:

"Writing in the Times, Sir E. Mackay Edgar, in explaining Great Britain's control of the oil resources of the world, says that within a few years the United States will be paying British oil interests $1,000,000,000 annually for oil for the American Navy and for American home consumption.

"With the exception of Mexico and to a lesser extent of Central America, the outer world is securely barricaded against an American invasion in force, he said. There may be small isolated sallies, but there can never be a massed attack. The British position is impregnable."

If our administrative officers, if our State Department, who should know more about this situation than we can know or than anyone else in the country can know, are satisfied that the only way we can protect our interests in the acquirement of oil concessions and in securing oil to meet our future needs, is through a corporation or company, as suggested by the Senator from California, it seems to me that it is the duty of those administrative officers to say so, and to recommend to Congress legislation along those lines. If they will come to Congress and do that, I, for one, will stand by them.

Mr. KING. Will the Senator permit an interruption right there?

Mr. JONES of Washington. Yes; although I had not expected to take so much time.

Mr. KING. I will wait until the Senator concludes the article and then I will propound the question.

Mr. JONES of Washington. It is rather lengthy, and the Senator can proceed.

Mr. KING. Very well. I have thought for some time, particularly in view of the information which the Senator from California (Mr. Phelan) furnished to the Senate several months ago, that it is the duty of the Navy Department of the Government to acquire oil lands for naval purposes and uses in remote parts of the earth where our fleet will be called, and I should be glad to see an appropriation made, to be placed in the hands of the President, for the purpose of acquiring oil lands in those countries to which our fleet may go and when oil might be needed for our Navy.

I should be very glad if the Committee on Naval Affairs would consider that question, or if some other committee of the Senate would take up the matter. If it is not done I shall offer an amendment to the pending bill or introduce an independent bill, so that the whole subject may be considered by the Senate.

Mr. JONES of Washington. I would welcome something along that line, but I want to emphasize the statement I made. I am not criticizing the administration or the department, but it seems to me that, they being more familiar with the details of the needs and the difficulties that they face, it is their duty to recommend to Congress what they think ought to be done. We can not know these facts and the details except as we get them in a general way. They run right up against them in the conduct of their affairs.

Just as the Senator from Utah (Mr. King) has said, the Secretary of the Navy and the officials of the Navy know exactly what are the needs of the Navy; they know the difficulties that they have in supplying those needs; they know the facts at the different points of the compass in the world that we do not know, and about the only way that we can get the information is that they call them to our attention and make recommendations to us, based upon their knowledge of the situation and the facts.

Reading further from this article:

"Sir Mackay declares that all known oil fields and all likely or probable oil fields outside the United States are in British hands or under British management or control or financed by British capital.

" 'We shall have to wait a few years before the full advantages of the situation shall begin to be reaped,' he said, 'but that that harvest eventually will be a great one there can be no manner of doubt. To the tune of many millions of pounds a year America before very long will have to purchase from British companies and to pay for in dollar currency in progressively increasing proportion the oil she can not do without and is no longer able to furnish from her own store. I estimate that, if their present curve of consumption, especially of high-grade products, is maintained, Americans in 10 years will be under the necessity of importing 500,000,000 barrels of oil yearly at $2 a barrel, a very low figure, and that means an annual payment of $1,000,000,000 per annum, most, if not all, of which will find its way into British pockets. If there are pessimists left in the United Kingdom, I confidently invite them to put that in their pipes and smoke it.' "

And, Mr. President, in this connection I desire to suggest that now is the time for us to begin to lay our plans to meet any such situation as that. There are different ways by which we can meet it.

Mr. WATSON. Mr. President, does the Senator understand that the Mexican oil fields are in control of the British?

Mr. JONES of Washington. No; I do not understand that they are entirely so.

Mr. WATSON. The all-sweeping declaration the Senator has read would lead one to conclude that such was the case.

Mr. JONES of Washington. No; just preceding that statement – probably the Senator from Indiana did not notice it – I think he says that, outside of Mexico and one other field, the British practically control the oil of all the world.

However, what I want to suggest is this: This is the time for us to unshackle ourselves so that we can do whatever we think along different lines will be for the protection of our interests. We may in a few years be dependent upon the British Empire for oil, as Sir Mackay Edgar says; but, Mr. President, they are dependent upon us in this country for many things, and we ought to prepare ourselves so that we can use their needs to secure just treatment in the satisfaction of our needs. There ought to be some reciprocity in these matters to our advantage as well as to theirs. Concessions ought not to go always from this country to other people; and we are in a position, in my judgment, to insist that when we make concessions along certain lines, or when our needs must be supplied from other countries, that we shall also get concessions because of needs of theirs which we must meet.

There are treaties now that prevent us from doing what we ought to do for ourselves and for our own interests. Those treaties ought to be abrogated, so that we shall be in a position to look after our own interests. Our administrative officers — and I am not saying that they are not doing it — ought to see to it when advantages and concessions are secured by other countries, especially along commercial lines, that we also get concessions and advantages for our benefit.

Mr. PHELAN. Mr. President, will the Senator allow me to interrupt him?

The VICE PRESIDENT. Does the Senator from Washington yield to the Senator from California?

Mr. JONES of Washington. I yield.

Mr. PHELAN. The Senator has observed that the United States has been asked to take the mandate for Armenia?

Mr. JONES of Washington. I hope we shall not get the League of Nations up today.

Mr. PHELAN. I will spare the Senator, because I was about to observe that if we have a representative in that body we might make terms, but now —

Mr. JONES of Washington. We do not have to have such a representative. I can not yield to the Senator for that, because I do not want to go into its discussion. However, Mr. President, we have administrative representatives and diplomatic agents abroad who can look after the interests of this country, and it is not necessary to make the excuse that we need some representative on the council of the League of Nations to deal with mandatories or anything like that to look after the interests of this country, and the Senator from California knows that as well as I do.

UNITED STATES GOVERNMENT ON QUI VIVE.

"That this view is not exaggerated is indicated by the fact that four departments of the American Government — War, Navy, State, and Commerce — have instructed their representatives throughout the world to watch all oil developments with the greatest care and report to Washington fully."

Mr. President, I am glad that that has been done. What use is being made of these reports? This is right in line with what I suggested awhile ago, that they get information which we can not get unless they give it to us. If there is information which they have secured or that they shall secure, that shows the need of action by Congress, it is their duty to come to Congress and tell us what they want and then ask us to enact the legislation.

Mr. SMOOT. We are locking the stable door after the horse is stolen.

Mr. JONES of Washington. The quotation continues:

"During the last week several important conferences have taken place both in Paris and London, between American officials, when the oil situation was discussed because of the persistent reports that British interests are about to close big oil deals in Mexico and Peru with companies now operating there or owning concessions."

Mr. President, if there are companies and corporations, for instance, in Peru, that hold great oil concessions there, why is not our Government trying to get similar concession or to get an interest in them? If they need authority, if they need legislation that is important to enable them to do so, let them ask Congress and the authority will be granted.

"If this deal goes through, Britain's control of the oil resources of the world will be equal to a strangle hold.

" 'Apart from Mexico,' Sir Mackay Edgar continues, 'it is almost a case of the British first and the rest of the world nowhere. I should say that two-thirds of the improved fields of Central and South America are in British hands. In Guatemala, Honduras, Nicaragua, Costa Rica, Panama, Colombia, Venezuela, and Ecuador a decisive and really overwhelming majority of the petroleum concessions are held by British subjects. They will be developed by British capital.' "

Why is it, Mr. President, that American citizens can not get oil concessions in South American countries? In my judgment, they can if our Government will take the proper steps, diplomatic and otherwise, with those countries. Quoting further:

EXTENT OF BRITISH CONTROL.

"The Alves group, whose holdings encircle practically two-thirds of the Caribbean Sea, is wholly British, working under arrangements which insure that perpetual control of its undertakings shall remain in British hands. No American citizen and no American group has acquired or ever could acquire any such position in Central America as that which enterprise and personality have secured for Mr. Alves."

I believe, Mr. President, that we have men in this country who have just as fine personality and just as much enterprise as has any British subject or citizen, and, with the encouragement that our Government ought to give them, I believe we could accomplish just as much as the British citizens have accomplished.

"Or, take again that greatest of all oil organizations, the Shell group. It owns exclusive or controls interests in every important oil field in the world, including the United States, Russia, Mexico, the Dutch East Indies, Roumania, Egypt, Venezuela, Trinidad, India, Ceylon, the Malay States, North and South China, Siam, the Straits Settlements, and the Philippines."

It looks to me as though we ought to be able to have some little control at least over the Philippines and the interests of the United States there.

Mr. LANE. You will find in the *New York World* some extracts from those statements. One of them was from Walter Long, I think, and another by Jepson Smith.

Senator BRANDEGEE. Do you remember what proportion of the oil that is produced in the United States is produced in California?

Mr. LANE. Two or three years ago it was about one-third, about 100,000,000 barrels out of 300,000,000. I think there is a larger yield now from Texas than from California. Probably California yields now about one-quarter.

Senator BRANDEGEE. Do you not think that, in view of what you have intimated as to the needs of our proposed merchant marine and of our naval vessels, both of which are governmental and both of which may involve the protection of this country and of its outlying possessions, the Government itself has an interest, irrespective of the commercial use of oil in this country, to at least, whether it promotes or not, protect private citizens who are trying to promote an adequate supply of oil to this country?

Mr. LANE. Undoubtedly so, Senator. I made specific recommendations upon that proposition in my last annual report, and in a report which I approved which was sent to Congress over a year ago.

Senator BRANDEGEE. I am glad to refer to that. That is all I care to ask.

The CHAIRMAN. We thank you very much, Mr. Secretary.

A RAILROAD ENTREPRENEUR TESTIFIES

THURSDAY, MARCH 4, 1920.

UNITED STATES SENATE,
SUBCOMMITTEE ON FOREIGN RELATIONS,
New York, N. Y.

Testimony taken at New York City, N. Y., March 4, 1920, by Francis J. Kearful, Esq., in pursuance of an order of the Subcommittee of the Committee on Foreign Relations of the Senate.

STATEMENT OF MR. EDWARD N. BROWN.

(The witness was duly sworn by Mr. Kearful.)

Mr. KEARFUL. Please state your name.

Mr. BROWN. Edward N. Brown.

Mr. KEARFUL. And your post-office address?

Mr. BROWN. 120 Broadway, New York.

Mr. KEARFUL. Mr. Brown, you have been subpoenaed by the subcommittee to give the committee the benefit of your knowledge of railway conditions in Mexico. What has been your opportunity to know about the railway interests in Mexico?

Mr. BROWN. I was, of course, quite well informed up to the time I left there, Judge, but that is six years ago. Since that time I have been brought into direct contact but very little with the railway operations. All I know since that is from information that I have received through various and sundry people coming from Mexico, with whom I was acquainted or intimate with, and so on.

Mr. KEARFUL. Have you retained an interest in ascertaining the conditions since you left there?

Mr. BROWN. Yes, sir. In fact, it is rather a keen interest, because I consider that the railways — what is known as the National Railways and their subsidiaries — as largely my work in Mexico for some 26 or 27 years.

Mr. KEARFUL. Will you please relate the positions that you held and the work that you did in connection with the railways of Mexico?

Mr. BROWN. I went to Mexico in the spring of 1887, with an arrangement to build the line south from Saltillo to a connection with San Miguel, 252 miles, which was a gap remaining to complete the line from Laredo, Tex., to the City of Mexico. I was first assistant chief engineer of that. Very shortly afterwards I was made superintendent of construction, and had charge of the construction of that piece of line. I lived in Saltillo for some 15 months, until the line was nearly completed, and then moved to San Luis Potosi. When the line was connected I was, in addition to my other duties as superintendent of construction, made superintendent of the operation of that piece of that road. I remained there for some 18 months in that capacity. I was then transferred to Mexico City as superintendent of the whole road out of Mexico City, and remained in that position for some three years. I was then put in charge of the physical operation of the entire road, known as the National Railroad at that time, embracing about 1,400 miles of road.

Mr. KEARFUL. Between what points?

Mr. BROWN. The main line between Laredo, Tex., and the City of Mexico, with several branches, and a Texas line from Laredo to Corpus Christi, Tex. I remained in charge of the physical operation of that road until 1900, when I was made third vice president and general manager. In 1901 I was made second vice president and general manager, and began the work of standard gauging the system. About that time, and partly at my suggestion, the Mexican Government acquired a 47 per cent interest in the stock of that company and very shortly after that we acquired control of the Mexican International Railway, the line between Eagle Pass and Durango. At the end of 1902 I was made president of the company, and just at that time they acquired a controlling interest in the Interoceanic Railway, and took that under the operation of the National Railways.

Mr. KEARFUL. Between what points did the Interoceanic run?

Mr. BROWN. Mexico City, via Puebla, to Vera Cruz, with some short branches.

Mr. KEARFUL. That was a narrow-gauge road?

Mr. BROWN. Yes, sir. I remained in that capacity until 1907, when they undertook to merge all those properties with the Mexican Central, which was accomplished during the first part of 1908, and just about that time we acquired the stock which gave control of the Vera Cruz and Pacific Railroad, from Vera Cruz, via Cordova, to Santa Lucrecia, on the Isthmus of Tehuantepec. Very shortly afterwards, by the same method of acquiring the stock, we acquired control of the Pan-American Railway.

Mr. KEARFUL. Where does the Pan-American run?

Mr. BROWN. I can not just now think of the name of the town. It is from that town on the Tehuantepec National Railway, skirting the Pacific coast, to Mariscal, on the Guatemala frontier.

Mr. KEARFUL. Did you describe what is called the Mexican Central?

Mr. BROWN. No, sir; I did not. The Mexican Central had for its main line the railroad from El Paso to Mexico City, and across the continent from Tampico, via San Luis Potosi and Guadalajara, to Manzanillo, on the Pacific coast; also the important line from Tampico, via Monterrey, to Torreon, and several branches. The reasons leading up to the merger of those properties was that all the railways had exhausted their right to issue bonds to secure additional capital under their mortgages, and most of the mileage was in bad physical condition, with a shortage of rolling stock.

Mr. KEARFUL. That condition did not apply to the National Railways, did it?

Mr. BROWN. In part only. In organizing the National Railways of Mexico, in 1907, the Mexican Government undertook to guarantee, both as to principal and interest, all of the general mortgage bonds of the first preferred and second preferred stock issued by the new company. It also gave a reasonable margin, with the Government approval, for new bond issues to secure new capital for improving the existing lines and furnishing additional rolling stock, as well as building new lines. In lieu of that Government guarantee, $75,000,000 United States money, of common stock was issued to the Mexican Government to give them voting control, the different issues of stock ranking on a parity in the votes, and with this common stock the Government secured about 50½ per cent of the total voting power.

Mr. KEARFUL. Was that stock paid for by the Mexican Government?

Mr. BROWN. No. The Mexican Government paid nothing for that common stock. They did, however, own some stock in the old

Central and National Railroads, for which they paid approximately $9,000,000, United States money, or, in other words, a total investment, not counting subsidies, given to the various railroads, of the Mexican Government in these railways of approximately $9,000,000 United States money.

Mr. KEARFUL. You have not yet completed the statement as to the positions that you held.

Mr. BROWN. Let us go back. At the end of 1902 I was made president of the National Railroads, which position I retained until the merger in the beginning of 1908, when I was made president of the merged systems, representing about 7,500 miles of main line. This position I continued to occupy until October, 1914, when I severed my connection with all the companies. I think that covers it, does it not?

Mr. KEARFUL. Yes. Under what circumstances did you sever your connection, after giving practically your life to that work?

Mr. BROWN. I left Mexico City during the first days of March, 1914, in answer to a telegram from the bankers, asking me to join them here to consider renewing and financing certain notes that were falling due, some $27,000,000, expecting to be away some three or four weeks, coming via Vera Cruz and boat directly to New York. I had engaged my passage for the return trip by boat when, on April 22, 1914, the troops were landed at Vera Cruz, and Gen. Huerta, who was then exercising the powers of President, issued a proclamation, removing all of the foreigners from any connection with the railway work in Mexico. At the insistance of the bankers, however, I continued to exercise the functions of president from the New York office until the next annual meeting of the shareholders, which was during the first days of October, 1914, when they did not reelect me as the president or a director of the company.

Mr. KEARFUL. At that time Mexico City, the seat of government, was in the hands of the Carranzistas?

Mr. BROWN. Yes, sir. I failed to be elected as a director and president in October, 1914.

Mr. KEARFUL. You remember that Huerta left the country in July, 1914, and the forces of Carranza entered Mexico City in August, 1914?

Mr. BROWN. That is right.

Mr. KEARFUL. So that the stockholders' meeting, of which the Mexican Government had the controlling votes, was held under the auspices of the Carranzistas in October?

Mr. BROWN. Yes, sir. In July, 1913, seeing conditions so bad that the properties were apparently demoralized and disorganized, due to Government control, I resigned as president; but on telegrams received from New York and Europe I went to London and Paris to see committees of bankers and bondholders, who persuaded me to withdraw my resignation, which I stated I would do if I could satisfactorily arrange with the Mexican authorities. That was afterwards done, and I withdrew my resignation.

Mr. KEARFUL. You are an American citizen, born in the United States, are you not?

Mr. BROWN. I am an American citizen, born in Alabama.

Mr. KEARFUL. In what business are you now engaged?

Mr. BROWN. I am chairman of the board of the St. Louis & San Francisco Railway Co. and also of the Pere Marquette Railway Co.

Mr. KEARFUL. What was the reason for the demoralization of the railroad business in 1913?

Mr. BROWN. With the Government control recognized by practically all of the citizens of the Republic, they had the erroneous impression that the Government owned the railway properties, and they should be operated by Mexican citizens only. In fact, they seemed to think that their political friends should have preference, and the officials were flooded with requests from mayors, governors, and other officials to give positions to their friends, many of whom had had no railroad experience.

Mr. KEARFUL. Was it possible for you and those under your direction to comply with those requests and operate the roads efficiently?

Mr. BROWN. In a large majority of instances we had to decline to entertain the requests at all, for the reason that the applicants had no experience. Naturally, that was not pleasing to the different officials who had made the requests, and in a large number of instances they would go over the heads of the railroad officials in an effort to get the Cabinet or even the President to intercede and order their friends given positions.

Mr. KEARFUL. In order to maintain friendly relations with the officials did you find it expedient at times to comply with their requests?

Mr. BROWN. Only in a few instances. We felt that the service was such and the safety of the public was such that we were justified in ignoring many of those requests.

Mr. KEARFUL. What railroads are there in Mexico that are not included in this merger?

Mr. BROWN. The merger represented about 8,000 miles when I left there of actual main line under operation and some 500 miles under construction, which was approximately one-half of the total.

The principal lines not included in the so-called merger, known as the National Railways of Mexico, was, first, the Southern Pacific of Mexico —

Mr. KEARFUL. Running down the west coast?

Mr. BROWN. Running down the west coast from Nogales via Guaymas to Manzanillo and Tepic; the Mexico Northwestern, between El Paso and Chihuahua; the Kansas City, Mexico & Orient, two pieces of lines, disconnected, but running both ways out of Chihuahua, and a piece of road on the Pacific coast from Topolobampo; the Mexican Railway, from Mexico City to Vera Cruz, with several branches; the Isthmus & Tehuantepec Railway; and various short lines, industrial lines, etc.

Mr. KEARFUL. Was there also a road in Yucatan?

Mr. BROWN. Yes; that is right. The United Railways of Yucatan. That is another.

Mr. KEARFUL. Who built the railways of Mexico?

Mr. BROWN. Practically all of them were built under concessions from the Mexican Government, with some subsidies or help in their construction. This subsidy amounted usually to six to ten thousand pesos per kilometer, equal to three to five thousand dollars United States money. With the exception of the subsidies the money was practically all furnished by foreign investors, principally from the United States, Great Britain, France, and Germany.

Mr. KEARFUL. What class of people did the actual construction work of these roads?

Mr. BROWN. All of the construction of which I have had any knowledge or anything to do with was done by foreigners, principally Americans, except the laboring people, who were mostly or very nearly all native peons. During the latter days of construction, however, there were some Mexican engineers and trainmen, with a few train masters and superintendents, used in connection with the construction and operation.

Mr. KEARFUL. Had these men been educated in that work by the Americans previously in operation?

Mr. BROWN. Practically all of them. In fact, we established schools for that purpose and would take in any of the young men who could read and write and who looked physically fit and put them under apprentice contracts on most of the work.

Mr. KEARFUL. Were those contracts oppressive on those young people or otherwise?

Mr. BROWN. We started them out in the different shop crafts, as a rule, boys of 14 or 15 years old, under a four-year contract at 62½ cents per day for the first year, increasing it gradually up to the end of four years when they received 3½ pesos per day. We retained from them 25 cents per day as a guaranty of faithful performance of the contract. At the end of the four-year period they drew from the treasury about 176 pesos in cash, and were given a certificate of service, constituting them what is known as journeymen. They were also allowed to continue in the service, if they so elected, at the standard rates of pay for work performed by the different crafts of which they were members.

Mr. KEARFUL. How did those wages compare with wages that the Mexicans were accustomed to receive before the railroads were projected?

Mr. BROWN. They were very much higher. In fact, they compared favorably with pay on the United States railways for similar service.

Mr. KEARFUL. Can you give the number of such Mexican boys or young men who were educated in that manner annually from the time of the institution of that school?

Mr. BROWN. I put the apprentice contract into service in 1890, on the old National Railroad. At that time they had some 1,400 miles of road, and I should say at the end of the first year we probably had 300 of those contracts in existence. As the mileage increased, and the number of men employed increased — and naturally the number increased very materially — until about the year 1912 it was estimated there were some 2,000 of these contracts in existence. I think it is safe to say that practically all of the skilled mechanics and other craftsmen on the railways in Mexico had been trained by the railways.

Mr. KEARFUL. Can you give an estimate of the entire number of men who were trained in this way during the time that you were making a survey of railways?

Mr. BROWN. From 1890 until 1912, covering a period of 22 years, I would estimate that under my jurisdiction there were trained fifteen to eighteen thousand.

Mr. KEARFUL. Was a somewhat similar system employed by the other railways?

Mr. BROWN. Not so far as I know.

Mr. KEARFUL. What, if anything, did the effect of the training of these men have upon other industries of the country, as to being beneficial or not?

Mr. BROWN. Many of these boys and men — and such number is not included in the above estimate — after becoming rather proficient in certain crafts, especially the boiler work and machine work, would be taken by mining industries, smelting industries, factories, and other people requiring such help, as stationary engineers, machinists, etc., and at the end of probably two or three years they would leave the service, abandon their contract, and go with these other industries at a much increased wage.

Mr. KEARFUL. Did you endeavor to prevent them going when they pleased?

Mr. BROWN. Never. We always encouraged it.

Mr. KEARFUL. They simply forfeited the 25 cents per day?

Mr. BROWN. Whatever had been retained under that 25 cents per day.

Mr. KEARFUL. You made no opposition to their going when they could better their condition?

Mr. BROWN. When they could get better wages.

Mr. KEARFUL. So that the training school that you maintained was the source of supply to various industries of the country of trained mechanics and engineers?

Mr. BROWN. All the different crafts. Some were boiler makers and some were machinists. Even many of the clerks that worked in the railroad offices were taken away to keep books in different plantations and stores, and so on.

Mr. KEARFUL. Did you find these young men apt to learn?

Mr. BROWN. Yes; as a rule those that were educated were quite apt to learn.

Mr. KEARFUL. To become capable mechanics and proficient in the various crafts?

Mr. BROWN. I should say quite the average. We had very satisfactory results from our efforts.

Mr. KEARFUL. Were any complaints ever made of unfair treatment of these people on the part of your company?

Mr. BROWN. You mean the contract?

Mr. KEARFUL. By the people or the Government or by the men themselves?

Mr. BROWN. Never; except in some individual cases, and those were very few, and were always carefully investigated and righted if they had been injured or done a wrong. During the last five years of my service, or between 1907 and 1912, we established 15 schools to educate the different men and train them in the operating service, so as to make them proficient on train rules, air signals, air brakes, and other mechanical appliances, and they had lectures given periodically, for which the company paid, by experts in these lines, principally Americans. There was also apparatus installed in these schools to demonstrate the appliances.

Mr. KEARFUL. Did the Mexican Government contribute anything to the maintenance of these schools?

Mr. BROWN. No, sir. They gave their approval to it, and were quite favorable to it, looked favorably upon it, but the railways company maintained it.

Mr. KEARFUL. The men themselves were not assessed?

Mr. BROWN. Not at all. It was free.

Mr. KEARFUL. According to the figures about subsidies in construction that you gave a while ago, how did those figures compare with the actual cost of construction?

Mr. BROWN. I should say normally it was probably 15 to 18 per cent of the total cost of construction, but most of these subsidies were paid in partial payments and extended over a period of time. It was not all cash, but it was ultimately collected.

Mr. KEARFUL. Were there any other special privileges or grants made to the railroads to aid construction?

Mr. BROWN. The importation of construction material was, as a rule, free of duty.

Mr. KEARFUL. And was privilege given upon certain conditions to be performed, which conditions had to be secured?

Mr. BROWN. Well, it was in compliance with concessions, which provided that the company had to construct certain mileage and furnish certain equipment and other things, and that the material which was to be imported for that purpose would come in free of duty, for construction only.

Mr. KEARFUL. You are familiar with the history of railroad building in the United States, are you?

Mr. BROWN. To a certain extent.

Mr. KEARFUL. Do you know something about the grants of public land that have been made by Congress for building railroads across the western country?

Mr. BROWN. Yes, sir; I know something of it in a general way.

Mr. KEARFUL. The policy was to grant 20 odd numbered sections on each side of each mile of construction through Territories, and 10 sections through States, there being at that time very few States, and in the case of some of the roads their obligations were guaranteed by the Government. How did those privileges and grants made to aid in the construction of railroads in the western part of the United States compare with the concessions and subsidies you have spoken of that were granted to aid in construction of railroads in Mexico, as to liberality?

Mr. BROWN. We had on this line in Texas, belonging to the merger, the very same condition of land grants, and from my knowledge of the situation it is not easy to draw a comparison. At the time those land grants were made the land was not supposed to be very valuable, but as the construction of these roads progressed, they brought in immigrants and settled those lands, and in some instances, before the railways disposed of the balance of the lands they had, they brought fancy figures. But taking the thing as a whole, and comparing it in a general way, the only way I can make a comparison, my impression is that the subsidies given in Mexico, which was a money consideration, were on the whole less than was ultimately secured by these railroads in the United States.

Mr. KEARFUL. So that the statement which is frequently made that foreign capital has been engaged in exploiting the Mexican people and Mexican resources under iniquitous concessions obtained by fraud and bribery of Mexican officials, if it is true in any respect, has no truth in reference to railroads?

Mr. BROWN. That is my belief. In fact, I think it is perfectly safe to say that for many years after the first construction of these railways they did not pay interest on the capital invested, after having deducted the subsidies by the Mexican Government.

Mr. KEARFUL. Was there any overcapitalization for the purpose of stock operations or fraudulent practices?

Mr. BROWN. That is not easy to answer, but so far as my knowledge goes the stock issued represented only the cash put into those properties, except the stock issued to the Mexican Government without payment for voting purposes in the merger in 1907, and in a few minor instances where rights of way or some other grants were given, and the value of that right of way supposed to have been capitalized, but on the whole I think it is of negligible quantity.

Mr. KEARFUL. You think if there was any overcapitalization it was practically negligible?

Mr. BROWN. Yes, sir.

Mr. KEARFUL. You mentioned the amount of money, in addition to the subsidies, that was put into the roads by the Mexican Government. About what percentage would you say that would be of the actual investment?

Mr. BROWN. 15 to 18 per cent would be my estimate.

Mr. KEARFUL. How was it possible for the Mexican Government, with that small investment, to obtain actual voting control of the road?

Mr. BROWN. Through the guarantee of principal and interest on the general mortgage bonds, and first preferred and second preferred stock of the company.

Mr. KEARFUL. Which was necessary in order to raise money?

Mr. BROWN. Yes, sir; in order to get a bond issue that would enable us to do that financing.

Mr. KEARFUL. When did the roads, of which you have knowledge, first begin to make profits on their actual investment?

Mr. BROWN. The amount of dividends paid or profits made were negligible until 1908. At that time the merged roads began to pay interest on their first preferred shares, and continued until 1913 to pay 4 per cent on $30,000,000.

Mr. KEARFUL. Has any interest been paid since that time?

Mr. BROWN. Not since the beginning of 1914. In fact, Mr. Carranza commandeered the railways known as the National Railways of Mexico in August, 1914, and since that time there has been nothing paid, either as dividends or interest, and, if my information be correct, the companies have had no earnings since that date — not a cent.

Mr. KEARFUL. What is your information as to condition of the roads since they were taken over by the Carranza Government?

Mr. BROWN. The first three years or so after they took them over there seemed to be very little repair work done on the physical part of the roads or rolling stock. Most of the important bridge structures on the northern half of the National Railways, for some 4,000 miles, were greatly damaged or destroyed by the different revolutionary forces, and most of those structures have only been repaired temporarily, using, as a rule, trestles for the purpose. Ties and rails are very seriously needed, and no rail repairs made. Probably one-half of the rolling stock is not serviceable, either having been damaged or worn out to such an extent as to need repairs. During the last two years or so there have been some repairs made to rolling stock, and a good many ties renewed. The track between Laredo, Tex., and the City of Mexico, is said to be in very fair condition, with the exception of needing a small percentage of the ties renewed. Very few of the station buildings remain between San Luis Potosi and Laredo, and the same applies to the line between Zacatecas and Mexico City, and between Manzanillo and Irapuato. Most of the branch lines are said to be seriously in need of repairs. It is estimated that some 15,000,000 ties are necessary to be replaced in order to bring the track up to normal condition as regards ties.

Mr. KEARFUL. What is your information as to the condition of the rolling stock?

Mr. BROWN. Generally speaking, in very bad shape, with only about one-half of it available for service. In 1913 the National Railways and the subsidiary lines had some 22,000 freight cars in service, and 729 locomotives. I am told that about half of that are in service today, many of those, however, needing repairs.

Mr. KEARFUL. Do you know anything about cars or locomotives from railroads of this country being in Mexico at the time they were taken over and not returned?

Mr. BROWN. Yes; there were quite a few, but I have no definite information as to the number. I should say, as a guess, probably 1,000 freight cars, no locomotives.

Mr. KEARFUL. Can you give an estimate of the amount of money that would be required to place the railways in the condition they were in normal times?

Mr. BROWN. Including repairs to rolling stock, bridges, stations, and other destroyed property, together with making good arrears of repairs, I should estimate sixty-five or seventy million dollars United States money would be required.

Mr. KEARFUL. That would not include overdue interest on bonds?

Mr. BROWN. No, indeed. On the merged lines the interest charges in 1913 were approximately one and a quarter million dollars per month, and if seven years interest is due, with interest on interest, it would probably be a total of something in excess of ninety million dollars United States money, including that interest.

Mr. KEARFUL. Do you have the figures of the amount of the outstanding bonds?

Mr. BROWN. I have not those figures before me now.

Mr. KEARFUL. Do you know what has become of the money that has been received from the operation of the lines by Mexico?

Mr. BROWN. No; I do not; but I understand, from what I consider competent authority, that for the last year and a half or two years the Mexican Government has required the railway operating officials to deliver to the treasurer of the nation a million and a half pesos per month, allowing the use of the balance in repairs and upkeep of the property.

Mr. KEARFUL. The condition of the roads and rolling stock which you have mentioned, does that indicate that a sufficient amount has been left to the railroad officials by the Government for the purpose of upkeep?

Mr. BROWN. No, sir; my impression is that they have not had sufficient.

Mr. KEARFUL. Do you know of any legal right of the Mexican Government to require the railroads to pay to the Government a certain amount, leaving their interest charges and operating expenses unpaid?

Mr. BROWN. If I understand correctly, Mr. Carranza issued a decree when he commandeered the railways, saying it was for war purposes. Under the concessions of practically all the railroads the Government has the right to commandeer the railways when public necessity or enemy operations require it.

Mr. KEARFUL. But is it your understanding that the Government can do that, without any responsibility to pay damages?

Mr. BROWN. No, sir. If I remember correctly the law specifically provides that they shall indemnify the railway companies by allowing them the same rate of earnings that they were making for a certain period prior to the time they were taken over. That is clearly stated in the law as the basis of responsibility assumed by the Government in taking over the roads, commandeering them.

Mr. KEARFUL. Then, in addition to the amount of about $90,000,000 due for interest, and some $75,000,000 necessary for reconstruction, the Government is under legal obligations to reimburse the railroads in accordance with their earnings of previous years? Is that your understanding?

Mr. BROWN. Yes, sir. But, of course, you will have to take into account the interest charges there as a part of their previous condition, because their previous net earnings would probably have been applied in part to interest payments.

Mr. KEARFUL. At any rate, there is an additional obligation on the part of the Government to compensate the railroads for their use since they have been taken over, in addition to the damage that has been suffered, represented, by the amount necessary to reconstruct them, and the interest charges?

Mr. BROWN. That is my understanding.

Mr. KEARFUL. Can you give an estimate of about what that would be?

Mr. BROWN. No; but it would be quite a little in excess of the damages and interest charges.

Mr. KEARFUL. Combined?

Mr. BROWN. Combined, and, of course, the upkeep must also be taken into consideration. In other words, when the Government uses those properties they are supposed to maintain them and return them in as good condition as when taken over.

Mr. KEARFUL. That would be accounted for in the item for reconstruction?

Mr. BROWN. Yes, sir.

Mr. KEARFUL. What do you consider the necessity of the railroad systems in Mexico to the general development of the country?

Mr. BROWN. That country has about 750,000 square miles of territory, and two-thirds of it is on an elevated table-land, leaving only the fringe around the Pacific and Gulf coasts subject to water transportation. Most of the industries, farming, mining, and so on, are on that table-land, where water transportation is lacking. I know of no country where railway transportation is so essential to the proper work and development of mines and smelters and farms and timberlands and other things as in Mexico. It is, from my point of view, the first and most important feature, to reestablish their transportation before they can reestablish their industries in proper shape.

Mr. KEARFUL. Most of these railroads were projected and completed during the time of Porfirio Diaz, were they not?

Mr. BROWN. Practically all of them.

Mr. KEARFUL. And were in accordance with his constant policy toward the development of the country?

Mr. BROWN. Yes, sir.

Mr. KEARFUL. What was his attitude toward foreign investors and capital?

Mr. BROWN. I think very liberal and favorable, so far as I know. I think he gave protection in every practical way to foreigners and their investments.

Mr. KEARFUL. Did he exact tribute from them by way of graft for himself or his favorites?

Mr. BROWN. In the early days of railroad construction there were rumors that something of that kind was done by the authorities. I never heard anything applied to Gen. Diaz himself personally, but during the latter 10 years of his régime I think it is safe to say that whatever might have been the case in the early part of his régime had disappeared, and things were going along in a proper way during the last 10 years of his incumbency. That is my impression and information.

Mr. KEARFUL. During the latter part of the rule of Porfirio Diaz what was the condition throughout Mexico as to security for life and property and safety of travel by individuals?

Mr. BROWN. Until the last years of his régime it was considered more than satisfactory. In fact, I have heard many, including the ambassador from this country, say they considered life and property as safe in Mexico as any place they knew of, not excepting the United States.

Mr. KEARFUL. You are more or less familiar with the history of Mexico?

Mr. BROWN. Yes, sir.

Mr. KEARFUL. Has there ever been any period in Mexico's history in which there has been substantial progress, except during the rule of Porfirio Diaz?

Mr. BROWN. No; I believe it is safe to say that its progress came with his assuming power.

Mr. KEARFUL. And what happened when he fell?

Mr. BROWN. The Madero revolution overthrew him in 1911. Things then were fairly quiet during the six months or so that De la Barra occupied the presidency, prior to the May election. During the first year of Madero's régime they were satisfactory. It then began to be noticeable that he was losing control, and these revolutionary factions began to be active again. Prior to that time there were none of them that I know of that were serious at all, except in that country south of Mexico that Zapata was operating in. Immediately after Madero's overthrow in February, 1913, the revolutionary troubles began to be more serious, culminating in Gen. Huerta leaving the country, and finally in Mr. Carranza assuming power. Since Mr. Carranza assumed power there has been more or less trouble in various sections of the country, and still is. He probably controls 60 per cent of the country, but possibly 80 per cent of its income.

Mr. KEARFUL. When you speak of the control of 60 per cent, do you mean such control that the territory can not be entered by rebel forces?

Mr. BROWN. No. There are various gangs at work in some of those, but he is recognized as having more or less authority over 60 per cent of the country.

Mr. KEARFUL. And you would say that in about 40 per cent he has no authority?

Mr. BROWN. I would say that in about 40 per cent he has no authority. I believe that is approximately correct.

Mr. KEARFUL. What would you say as to the tendency of the progress of Mexico, even since the time of the fall of Diaz, as to being upward or downward?

Mr. BROWN. Taking the country as a whole?

Mr. KEARFUL. Yes, sir.

Mr. BROWN. Well, since that time their finances have been wrecked; they have paid no interest on the Government debt, many of the districts have been depopulated, many of the cattle ranches and farms and sugar plantations have been damaged or abandoned, and I believe it is safe to say that the present production of the country is probably not more than two-thirds of what it was in 1913.

Mr. KEARFUL. According to your information, have the conditions since the time of Diaz been growing steadily worse?

Mr. BROWN. Up to a year or so ago, yes. I think that during the last year or possibly 18 months that it has been more or less at a standstill. In a few localities, like the City of Mexico, Tampico, the coal mining district, and a few of the mining districts, there have been some improvements. As against that there have been gradually worse conditions elsewhere.

Mr. KEARFUL. Do you know about some trips that Mr. William Jennings Bryan made to Mexico while you were there?

Mr. BROWN. Shortly after his defeat in the first presidential race I knew of his coming there; in fact, met him there.

Mr. KEARFUL. And then again, shortly after his second defeat, he made another trip. Do you remember that?

Mr. BROWN. I do not recall that.

Mr. KEARFUL. After he returned from the second trip he prepared a lecture, which is in the form of an article and was printed in *the Commoner,* a paper owned and published by him, in the issue of January 30, 1903. In that article he speaks of Porfirio Diaz in these terms:

The third great man produced by the Mexican Republic is the present President. With the exception of one term he has been President since 1876, during which time he has shown wonderful ability, and it is doubtful if there is in the world today a chief executive of great capacity or devotion to his people. Certainly no people have made greater relative progress than the Mexican people have made under the administration of Porfirio Diaz. Education has been promoted, law and order established, agriculture developed, commerce stimulated, and nearly every section of the country connected by railroad with the capital.

Would you regard that as a fair statement with reference to the character and policies and success of Porfirio Diaz?

Mr. BROWN. I would. I do not think it is overdrawn.

Mr. KEARFUL. Do you think that anything like that could be said of the present incumbent of the presidency of Mexico?

Mr. BROWN. No; I do not think he has succeeded in firmly establishing himself, certainly not throughout the whole country.

Mr. KEARFUL. If Mr. Bryan had anything to do with the success of the present incumbent, as against the régime of Porfirio Diaz, do you think he made a mistake or not, according to his own description of Diaz?

Mr. BROWN. Yes, sir; I would think so. There is this to be said, however, that Gen. Diaz, while a very successful administrator of the affairs of that country, had grown to be a very elderly man and was gradually losing contact with the people, and about the time of his overthrow it was pretty generally thought that his age had practically destroyed his ability to fulfill properly the administrative functions of president.

Mr. KEARFUL. Without regard to the personality of Diaz, what would you say in reference to the policies of the present system as compared with the policies of his system?

Mr. BROWN. For any country like Mexico I doubt if the present policies, as I understand them to be, are such as will succeed in establishing justice, law, and order there.

Mr. KEARFUL. What do you understand to be the present policies of the administration?

Mr. BROWN. If my information be correct, they are more or less socialistic; and with so small a percentage of education in the country, it is doubtful if they are as yet capable of conducting a purely democratic form of government, as we understand it here.

Mr. KEARFUL. There is a class which has been designated as the "submerged 80 per cent." What is that class?

Mr. BROWN. I think it is safe to say that those represent entirely Indians who could neither read nor write, who are indifferent as to what the form of government is or who is at the head of it; and all they want is to be left alone in peace and quiet to till their little pieces of land and pursue the customs and traditions as originally brought down by their forefathers.

Mr. KEARFUL. What other classes are there in Mexico?

Mr. BROWN. There is what they call the Mexican class, which is more or less a mixed breed. I should say they represent probably 10 or 12 per cent of the total population — might be called the middle class. Those are the people that are doing things there. They are as a rule aggressive, intelligent, and brave, and when properly directed could be made good citizens in any country.

Mr. KEARFUL. What is the difficulty in reference to their direction, as you understand it?

Mr. BROWN. My information is and my experience was that they are more or less sentimental and easily led. They are wonderfully brave, and a leader can influence them to do things that, probably, on mature consideration they would hesitate to do, but do it on the spur of the moment.

Mr. KEARFUL. What effect does the dissemination of socialistic doctrines have upon them?

Mr. BROWN. I think they are temporary, Judge, and I am sure they have some effect. That was not very much in evidence up to the time I left Mexico. I am told that since that, with the German propaganda that has been going on there, that that is very much in evidence during the last two or three years.

Mr. KEARFUL. What third class is there in Mexico?

Mr. BROWN. The owners of the farms and factories and so on. The majority of those are of either Spanish blood or a mixture.

Mr. KEARFUL. They are generally referred to as the "intelligent class"?

Mr. BROWN. Yes, sir.

Mr. KEARFUL. The "intellectual class"?

Mr. BROWN. The "intellectual class." Those are the property owners, as a rule, and I should say represent less than 10 per cent of the total.

Mr. KEARFUL. It has been testified by prominent Mexicans before the committee that approximately 80 per cent of that class have been compelled to live in exile from Mexico and are now living outside the country. Is that in accordance with your information?

Mr. BROWN. I should say that was a fair estimate.

Mr. KEARFUL. What State did you say you were from?

Mr. BROWN. I was born in Alabama.

Mr. KEARFUL. Alabama is largely populated by negroes, is it not?

Mr. BROWN. Yes, sir; forty-odd per cent are negroes, as I understand.

Mr. KEARFUL. And quite a percentage is known as mulattoes, mixed with the white?

Mr. BROWN. Yes; I guess 10 or 12 per cent of the so-called negroes.

Mr. KEARFUL. What do you think would be the situation in Alabama if 80 per cent of the intellectual class were excluded from the State and the affairs of the Government were in the hands of the mulattoes?

Mr. BROWN. I certainly would not look for much progress, and I think probably, as is supposed to be the case in Mexico, things would go backward instead of forward.

Mr. KEARFUL. Do you think such a situation as I have described in Alabama would be somewhat parallel to that in Mexico?

Mr. BROWN. Yes, sir. Certainly it is comparable, but in view of the fact that a large percentage of all the classes are such as can read and write, it might not be quite so extreme.

Mr. KEARFUL. Since you have returned to this country, or while you were living in Mexico, did you ever have any talk with Mr. Bryan when he was Secretary of State, or other officials of the State Department?

Mr. BROWN. Yes, sir. During the early part of Mr. Bryan's incumbency as Secretary of State I had two or three different talks with him, one of which covered probably an hour and a half, but the others were short.

Mr. KEARFUL. What was his attitude with reference to the

protection of Americans and their interests in Mexico, if you could judge of it from your conversation with him?

Mr. BROWN. I questioned him to know what the administration's policy would be, and also what would be the policy about the so-called dollar diplomacy. His answer in each instance was that while that had been discussed some no decision had been reached by the President or the Cabinet, so he made no reply to either of them.

Mr. KEARFUL. Did you ever receive any information in regard to Mr. Bryan's attitude toward American citizens operating in Mexico, that correct information could not be obtained from them because they were interested parties?

Mr. BROWN. I have heard that from various sources, Judge, but personally I never received it from Mr. Bryan. That is the impression that practically all those who have lived in Mexico and have spoken to me have of the situation. Some of them say they have been told that. Whether Mr. Bryan told them personally or somebody else, I do not know.

Mr. KEARFUL. What was Mr. Bryan's attitude in reference to getting information from you?

Mr. BROWN. At first he seemed rather listless, indifferent, but at the end of an hour or so when I got up to leave, and that conversation had lasted some considerable time, he seemed to be quite interested, and asked me to stay and give him further information. He further said that the President wanted to see me, and said he was having luncheon with him that day and wanted to know where he could reach me at 2:15 that afternoon. I told him at the Shoreham, and he did call me up over the phone, and said he was sorry but it would not be convenient for the President to see me then, but he was going to see him again during the afternoon and wanted to know where he could reach me again at 7:30, I think it was, just after the dinner hour, that he wanted to talk with me further at that time. He called up over the phone again promptly at the time specified, but regretted that the President thought it best not to see me.

Mr. KEARFUL. During the time that you were in Mexico, and during the rule of Porfirio Diaz, did you have any knowledge of invitations extended to American citizens to make investments in Mexico and to go there to develop the country, on the part of the Mexican Government or of this Government, for the extension of trade and friendly relations?

Mr. BROWN. Yes, sir. I think it is safe to say that I know of many instances. That is evidenced by the fact that most of the railroad companies there were chartered in States of this country. In addition to that, I know in connection with the establishment of the oil industry and smelting and mining industries, certain rubber interests, cattle ranches, factories for the manufacture of various products, including steel and iron and so on, where it was currently reported, and the newspapers published the concessions and the contracts, that American interests were not only solicited, but supposed to have been given some satisfactory concessions.

Mr. KEARFUL. Did you know about the attitude of this Government and its officials with reference to its citizens going to Mexico?

Mr. BROWN. Not specifically, but so far as I know that was the impression I gathered when I went there, going down to build a railroad in Mexico under concessions from the Mexican Government in the first instance, under a charter from a State in the United States in the second instance, that it was what was wanted and was looked upon favorably and in a friendly way by both this and the Mexican Government.

Mr. KEARFUL. Were you in Mexico at the time of the visit of Secretary Root?

Mr. BROWN. Yes, sir.

Mr. KEARFUL. Do you remember Mr. Root's attitude with reference to the necessity for the extension of foreign trade and friendly relations with Mexico and South America?

Mr. BROWN. Yes, sir; I think so. In fact, I read everything that was published about that time, and I gathered the impression that that was the object of his trip there, as well as to other Latin-American countries.

(Thereupon, at 1 o'clock p.m., an adjournment was taken until 2:30 o'clock p.m.)

AFTER RECESS.

The hearing was resumed at the expiration of the recess.

STATEMENT OF MR. EDWARD N. BROWN — Resumed.

Mr. KEARFUL. What did you understand to be the position of Secretary Root with reference to citizens of this country going to Mexico and other Latin-American countries in order to extend our foreign trade with those countries?

Mr. BROWN. Well, I do not know that I heard him make any specific declaration, but I am certainly under the impression that that was largely the object of his visit, not only to Mexico but to other Latin-American countries about that time.

Mr. KEARFUL. Do you believe it possible to extend our foreign trade with Mexico and other countries without our citizens going to those countries, to any large extent?

Mr. BROWN. Certainly it could not be done in a satisfactory or large way. It would be very much curtailed, at any rate.

Mr. KEARFUL. Do you think it would be feasible for our citizens to go to Mexico for that purpose and accomplish anything unless they could call upon the protection of this Government in case they were persecuted?

Mr. BROWN. It would certainly be very discouraging to them, and most of them would not consider it at all.

Mr. KEARFUL. Mr. Bryan's article in *The Commoner*, before referred to, has this to say on the subject:

> I am sometimes asked whether I would advise people to invest in Mexico.

Then he goes on to enumerate the various investments, amounting to over $500,000,000, that had been made in Mexico, citing railroad investments, mining investments, agricultural investments, manufacturing investments, and investments in city realty. He cites a large number of instances of Americans who have operated successfully in various lines, including coffee, sugar, railroads, law, plantations, and concludes by saying:

> There are many opportunities in Mexico for the man who goes there with capital and with knowledge of an industry to bring out the latent possibilities of soil and climate. There are also opportunities for those who go as skilled laborers to oversee industries in the process of development, although these opportunities lessen with the increase of education among the Mexicans.

Do you consider that a fair statement of the conditions at that time?

Mr. BROWN. Yes, sir; I would say so.

Mr. KEARFUL. Did you have an opportunity to ascertain the position of Mr. Bryan with reference to the protection of Americans who had gone there subsequent to this article?

Mr. BROWN. He did not give me a definite answer to my question, but the impression which I got from the conversation, coupled with what others told me was his attitude, gave me the idea that no protection was to be expected.

Mr. KEARFUL. No protection was ever given, to your knowledge, was there?

Mr. BROWN. None whatever.

Mr. KEARFUL. The first thing that Bryan did when trouble began down there was to order Americans to leave Mexico, was it not?

Mr. BROWN. It was among the early stages of his incumbency in Washington and was repeated two or three times. I think some of the people I know have left there at least three times under orders from the State Department in Washington to get out.

Mr. KEARFUL. How were those orders considered? What deduction was made as to what was going to be done when those orders were first given?

Mr. BROWN. The first time, I think, it was expected there might be trouble between the United States and Mexico, and that this had some relation with what the United States might do; but the last time or two they were issued I do not think they were given very much consideration, further than carrying out the orders of the representatives of our country. That was the impression I got from those who left there.

Mr. KEARFUL. Do you know whether Americans generally consider that such an order would not be given unless the United States intended to go into Mexico?

Mr. BROWN. Yes; I am sure that impression prevailed. I do not think that some of those who left there were at all sure that anything would be done. At least, that was what some of them told me, that they left under the mandate, but they then doubted that anything would be done. They did not think it was necessary for them to leave there.

Mr. KEARFUL. Was it generally considered that it was not necessary to give such an order unless the American Government was going in to stabilize the country.

Mr. BROWN. I think you might go further and say that they considered it folly to call them away from there unless something of that kind was anticipated.

Mr. KEARFUL. Did you ever have an opportunity to discover the attitude of President Wilson on the subject of protecting Americans in Mexico?

Mr. BROWN. Personally, no. I never have seen President Wilson.

Mr. KEARFUL. Have you a fixed opinion, based upon information you have gathered, as to what his attitude was toward Americans operating in Mexico?

Mr. BROWN. Nothing, except through hearsay and reading in the papers. My personal knowledge is only through those channels.

Mr. KEARFUL. Did you make an effort to see him and impress upon him the necessity of doing something in Mexico?

Mr. BROWN. No, sir; I never asked for an interview with the President.

Mr. KEARFUL. Are you familiar with the results of requests made by other Americans for interviews?

Mr. BROWN. I know of a committee having been appointed at one time to take the general question up with the authorities in Washington, on which I was appointed without my knowledge and consent. It so happened that I could not go. Several of those committeemen told me they got no encouragement when they saw the President.

Mr. KEARFUL. Can you state what reasons, if any, the President gave in regard to not taking action for the protection of Americans?

Mr. BROWN. I am not positive. I am not sure just what they did say, but as I recall now he personally made the statement that it would not be convenient for them to do anything at that time, without assigning a reason.

Mr. KEARFUL. Mr. Bryan makes another statement in his article which seems to be almost prophetic. He says, in reference to railroads:

The Mexican railroads employ Americans for conductors and engineers almost to the exclusion of the natives. The reason given me by one of the conductors was that there is not so large a middle class to draw from there as in the United States. In Mexico the peons are not competent to fill these positions and the well-to-do Mexicans prefer the professions. With the increase in education, however, it is probable that the Americans will not long be able to monopolize this branch of the service.

What happened under your observation in reference to the elimination of Americans from railroad service?

Mr. BROWN. We gradually trained the natives to fill practically all the positions in agencies and shops and train service, and during the last few years of my connection with it, it was very satisfactory; but it takes time and a great deal of careful attention to bring them up to that point. It was done gradually during these twenty-odd years.

Mr. KEARFUL. That was, of course, a benefit to the Mexicans?

Mr. BROWN. Well, I am sure I considered it so, and I think they did.

Mr. KEARFUL. What was the character of the concessions, if you know, granted for the development of other enterprises than railroads?

Mr. BROWN. My knowledge of that is so superficial that I do not think it would be of any service to you.

Mr. KEARFUL. It has been said that Americans operating in Mexico were not entitled to consideration at the hands of the Government, as they were a class of speculators operating under concessions obtained by bribery and graft and thus oppressing the Mexican people. Do you believe that is so?

Mr. BROWN. It certainly is not so in those that I know of. I am surprised at the statement.

Mr. KEARFUL. That statement has emanated at times from persons in high authority. What do you know generally about the character of Americans operating in Mexico?

Mr. BROWN. I think it is safe to say that during the early days of the construction of railroads a great many of them were not all they should have been. Some of them were criminals from this country who went down there and followed the construction of the railroads to get positions. As soon as the construction or the bulk of it was over those objectionable characters gradually migrated further south to Guatemala and other Latin-American countries.

I believe that it is safe to say that from about the year 1890 to the present time the average American who went there to work was an average of this country, without any reason other than seeking profitable employment. I further think that in the representation of many of the industries and companies operating there they selected the highest intelligence they could find, and the representatives of many of the industries and commercial and banking institutions was a superior class.

Mr. KEARFUL. Superior to a similar class in this country?

Mr. BROWN. Well, above the average.

Mr. KEARFUL. Were there in Mexico among the Americans there or in the American colony any of what is called the lower class in this country?

Mr. BROWN. Of the Americans living there?

Mr. KEARFUL. Yes, sir.

Mr. BROWN. A few of the laboring class, but very few. About the lowest class were brakemen and firemen on the Mexican International Railroad, which were taken from similar positions in the Middle West of this country down there to occupy those positions, and they did occupy them until 1904. At that time those positions were all filled by Mexicans, and those men were relieved and returned to the States. So far as my knowledge goes, that was the lowest class of American laborers or other people that went there.

Mr. KEARFUL. They would not be considered a low class of people, would they?

Mr. BROWN. I would not say so. They were brakemen and firemen of average intelligence, and as a rule good citizens.

Mr. KEARFUL. What do you consider the principal difficulty with Mexico?

Mr. BROWN. Today?

Mr. KEARFUL. Yes.

Mr. BROWN. The different factions there have been brought into a very severe and antagonistic feeling, growing out of these revolutionary troubles, and it has grown largely into personal differences with the chiefs of these factions. They started out, of course, with the idea that they were going to ameliorate the condition of the people, and I suppose, incidentally, to better their own condition, by taking the chief places in these movements, and they built up around them a certain contingent with promises of bettering their condition, as well as bettering the condition of the country. They have never succeeded in settling the differences among themselves, so there are a number of different factions headed by different people with their satellites and followers. That condition not only exists today but has grown into feuds and personalities, apart from the general political question, and it is difficult from my point of view to see how, without some help, they can compose those differences. I believe that in some of these instances the principles enunciated that caused them to get into revolutionary troubles were very good, and probably the people who took the lead were conscientious in the belief and hope that they could better the country, better the condition of all the people of the country; but I think they were mistaken in seeing just what was necessary and what their ability was to do it, to accomplish it. I think they overlooked the condition of the country as a whole, the illiteracy and other conditions of the people which would affect their success.

Mr. KEARFUL. To what extent do you think they were controlled by the desire to help themselves?

Mr. BROWN. I am sure that many of them had that question foremost in their minds, but I am of the opinion that a few of them started out originally with the idea that they were doing it only through patriotic motives.

Mr. KEARFUL. The condition of factional strife that you mentioned — does that indicate to you that the leaders have been actuated by personal ambitions rather than patriotic motives?

Mr. BROWN. I think originally most of the leaders had patriotic motives, but I fear that having once tasted the full authority of leadership their personal ambitions got the better of them.

Mr. KEARFUL. Do you think the fact that the country has been so devastated that there is perhaps not enough to go around, and they have begun to fight among themselves over what remains, has anything to do with it?

Mr. BROWN. No, sir; I do not think that has had so much to do with it. I think that had a good deal to do with it in the beginning. I think it is the personal feeling between them and the fear or reluctance to acknowledge the authority of the other that is keeping them going to a very great extent today.

Mr. KEARFUL. What class of people had control of the Government during the time of Porfirio Diaz?

Mr. BROWN. I think it is safe to say that 90 per cent of them were the best people there.

Mr. KEARFUL. They were what you spoke of a while ago as the intellectual class?

Mr. BROWN. Yes, sir; the intellectual class, who were people of not only native birth, but whose interests were solely and only those of Mexico. The other 10 per cent, I think, were, as in most other countries, people that had been put into positions from the States, or from their own countries.

Mr. KEARFUL. Do you believe there is any hope for Mexico from the inside, except through this intellectual class?

Mr. BROWN. I do not. I think that is the only hope in the immediate future, and when I say "the immediate future" I mean the present generation.

Mr. KEARFUL. With 80 per cent of that class excluded from Mexico do you believe there is any hope at all from the inside?

Mr. BROWN. No; I do not, unless it be a long drawn out procedure, and another generation brought in.

Mr. KEARFUL. I mean for the immediate future?

Mr. BROWN. No; I do not.

Mr. KEARFUL. What is your opinion as to what this country ought to do, if anything, in reference to correcting the conditions in Mexico?

Mr. BROWN. I always felt a most friendly interest in Mexico, and still feel it, and what I should like to see done would be this country, either alone, or in conjunction with some of the European countries, to offer their assistance, first financially. I suppose in doing that they would have to have, as is usual, some understanding that they were to have a commission to supervise the income and expenses of the country, and see if through that channel they could not work out some satisfactory proposition with reference to rehabilitating the country, not only with reference to finances, but its transportation and industries and educational institutions, and so on. I believe that is the first thing to consider. I am not sure, but I had hoped that Mexico would not look with an unfriendly feeling on such a proposition. It seems to me that through that or some similar channel the effort should first be made.

Mr. KEARFUL. Do you know of any effort having been made by the present Government of Mexico to borrow money with which to rebuild the railroads and establish banks, etc.?

Mr. BROWN. I have been told they made two or three efforts through some of the bankers here, but that their efforts were not successful.

Mr. KEARFUL. Do you know the reason why bankers would not lend the money?

Mr. BROWN. Well, first, the lack of guaranty; second, I understood the Mexican authorities were not willing to accept the idea of a commission to supervise the expenditures.

Mr. KEARFUL. In case an arrangement should be made with the Mexican Government for the furnishing of sufficient money to finance the country and rehabilitate it, under supervision of a commission named by the financiers, and either the present Government or some other Government that might come into power through a revolution would repudiate that agreement, then what do you think would have to be done?

Mr. BROWN. I think it would be up to this or such Government as might be represented on that commission to protect the property.

Mr. KEARFUL. Do you believe that any banker or group of bankers would undertake to finance Mexico without some assurance that if an arrangement made was not carried out this Government would insist upon carrying it out by force if necessary?

Mr. BROWN. Certainly not, unless the United States Government alone or in conjunction with other Governments would underwrite the issue through which the bankers made the advance.

Mr. KEARFUL. You mean by underwriting the issue that it would undertake, not to guarantee the payment of the money, but to enforce conditions of security?

Mr. BROWN. Either one or the other. Certainly one or the other would be necessary. Otherwise, I do not see how the bankers' group could raise money. You see, the Mexican Government, for a loan that had been made some years ago, pledged 62 per cent of the customs duties as guaranty for those loans. Then about 1904 they made additional loans through Speyer & Co. and other bankers, guaranteeing the remaining 38 per cent of the customs duties. Therefore, all the customs duties are pledged to these different loans. Subsequently, and I think during Gen. Huerta's time, there were certain securities issued for which the stamp taxes were pledged, and, if I understand correctly, those are the two things that are usually given by small governments as guaranties for loans.

Mr. KEARFUL. Since the time of Huerta, have the customs duties been collected and appropriated, and nothing paid on any of these securities?

Mr. BROWN. It is certainly the case that nothing has been paid on account of either government or railway indebtedness, no interest.

Mr. KEARFUL. A portion of the railway bonds are secured by guaranty of the Government?

Mr. BROWN. Yes, sir.

Mr. KEARFUL. You mentioned the possibility of an arrangement by means of financial commission. What alternative is there, if such an arrangement can not be carried out?

Mr. BROWN. Well, either to let them go ahead with their internal troubles indefinitely, or else some friendly help to put their house in order.

Mr. KEARFUL. What course do you think that help would necessarily take?

Mr. BROWN. Well, I should say it ought to be offered from a friendly point of view, and only a friendly point of view, but with force of arms sufficient to maintain and keep the authority in power that the Government, by itself or through this representation of the commission, might decide upon.

A MINING ENTREPRENEUR TESTIFIES

THURSDAY, APRIL 1, 1920.

UNITED STATES SENATE,
SUBCOMMITTEE OF THE
COMMITTEE ON FOREIGN RELATIONS,
Washington, D. C.

Testimony taken at Washington, D. C., April 1, 1920, by Francis J. Kearful, Esq., in pursuance of an order of the subcommittee of the Committee on Foreign Relations of the Senate.

TESTIMONY OF MR. MICHAEL J. SLATTERY.

(The witness was duly sworn by Mr. Kearful.)

Mr. KEARFUL. Please state your full name.

Mr. SLATTERY. Michael J. Slattery.

Mr. KEARFUL. What is your present place of residence?

Mr. SLATTERY. 830 North Sixty-third Street, Philadelphia.

Mr. KEARFUL. Are you an American citizen?

Mr. SLATTERY. Yes, sir.

Mr. KEARFUL. Where were you born?

Mr. SLATTERY. Philadelphia.

Mr. KEARFUL. What is your profession?

Mr. SLATTERY. I am a mine operator.

Mr. KEARFUL. What opportunities have you had to observe conditions in Mexico?

Mr. SLATTERY. Recently?

Mr. KEARFUL. At any time.

Mr. SLATTERY. First of all, my close contact with the people;
I went into Mexico in March, 1901, coming out when we were
forced out by the invasion of Vera Cruz by the United States Government, in April, 1914. Living all those years in Mexico gave me a
splendid opportunity of knowing the people, becoming acquainted
with them, their customs and mode of living; and, after my coming
out of Mexico, keeping up the friendship with most of the friends
that I had made down there. I think, therefore, I am in a position
to say that I know something of Mexico.

Mr. KEARFUL. What was your business in Mexico?

Mr. SLATTERY. My business was being engaged in mining.

Mr. KEARFUL. In what part of the country?

Mr. SLATTERY. I was in charge of many operations in the State
of Zacatecas, the State of Colima, and the State of Jalisco, particularly Jalisco. I was in charge of a number of big properties down
there, and not only in charge of a number of properties, but I
owned considerable property of my own.

Mr. KEARFUL. Will you proceed to state in your own way the
nature and extent of the operations with which you were connected
in Mexico?

Mr. SLATTERY. I do not quite get that question; in how large
a way?

Mr. KEARFUL. Yes.

Mr. SLATTERY. For instance, in one property we were operating a mill of 200 tons capacity and were considering the advisability
of further adding to that mill. We employed close on to 1,100 men.

Mr. KEARFUL. What kind of a mine was that?

Mr. SLATTERY. That was gold mining. At another place we
had about 350 men and were building and constructing a mill. At
a number of other places we had anywhere from 50 to 75 men at
work prospecting and doing development work.

Mr. KEARFUL. Can you make an estimate of the amount of
money invested in these enterprises with which you were connected?

Mr. SLATTERY. Yes. The actual capital invested I would imagine would be in the neighborhood of $7,000,000. Aside from that
there were a number of properties in which I have been directly interested, properties that I have owned myself, for instance, where I
have taken considerable money out of the ground and put it back
into the property; that is to say, in the development work I took
this money that we received for the sale of bullion and concentrate
returns and put it right back into development and improvements.

Mr. KEARFUL. Are you familiar with the condition of mining

in Mexico prior to the time that the Americans went in there to engage in mining?

Mr. SLATTERY. My experience with mining only dates from March, 1901; but from talking with the natives themselves about the mining prior to that time and comparing it with the conditions of the succeeding years, say from 1901 to 1910, I should say that I was familiar with those conditions.

Mr. KEARFUL. About what time in the history of mining in Mexico did the Americans go into that country?

Mr. SLATTERY. I do not know exactly. I do not know when Porfirio Diaz — one of the most wonderful Presidents that Mexico has ever had — issued that famous proclamation of his, which, among other things, if my memory serves me correctly, said:

> Recognizing that the economic condition of Mexico can not be developed from within, I hereby invite the nationals of the world to come into Mexico and develop the resources of Mexico, guaranteeing to them the same rights and privileges as are now enjoyed by Mexican citizens, excepting, of course, the right of suffrage.

When I came into Mexico that was one of the first — in fact, before I went into Mexico that was one of the first things that was called to my attention. It was called to my attention for the reason that Mexico to me was a strange country and I was anxious to understand the conditions which would safeguard a man, his life, and his property while in that country; and it was while I was in the City of Mexico talking to one of the most prominent members of the legal profession that that proclamation was shown to me, and of course I have always understood and during my years under Diaz I realized that that proclamation was being carried fully into effect, namely, that Americans as well as all other nationals were given every right and privilege to engage in the mining industry.

Mr. KEARFUL. You regard that as practically the beginning of American mining operations in Mexico?

Mr. SLATTERY. I believe that that was the beginning of the American entry into Mexico on a large scale in mining.

Mr. KEARFUL. Diaz was president first in 1876, and again in 1884.

Mr. SLATTERY. Yes.

Mr. KEARFUL. So that it was near the beginning of his administration?

Mr. SLATTERY. No; that I can not say, because I never took the trouble of looking it up. I am only familiar with it because it appears on the first page of the constitution.

Mr. KEARFUL. What was the fact in regard to the mining

prospects of Mexico when the Americans went in? Were there great bonanzas ready to be developed at little cost, or were they problematical and expensive?

Mr. SLATTERY. In my entire experience in Mexico, my long years in Mexico, I never saw in any part of Mexico and never met any American or Britisher who ever ran across one of those so-called bonanzas. Personally I was always on the lookout for that kind of a proposition; but in my 18 years professional prober connections in Mexico I never knew of such a thing. Bonanzas only come where there is an intersection of veins, and those intersections of veins are usually not found on the surface; they are usually found very deep down in the ground, and it requires a great deal of development work to locate such bonanzas.

Mr. KEARFUL. What was the condition with respect to the surface prospects having been worked out when the Americans went in there?

Mr. SLATTERY. Mexico is known as the land of antiguas. That is to say, there are a number of old mines, some of them going back to the time of Carlos V of Spain; but the way those mines have been worked, those antiguas, have been such that in nearly every case every piece of ground that has been worthwhile has been practically, you might say, worked all over again, for the reason that there were very narrow passageways. We mining men developing the ground call them rat holes. They simply followed the pay streak. The development work was not carried on as we carry it on. They simply gouge and follow the streak. If it is a foot wide they will just drive the width of a man's body; so you can readily see that when any Americans came across these antiguas that were supposed to be very rich mines in the days gone by, it required considerable money to open up and develop them; and there are very few antiguas that are in actual operation.

Mr. KEARFUL. Was it a fact that all of the rich prospects had been worked out and abandoned at the time the Americans went in there?

Mr. SLATTERY. I should like to answer your question in this way: Every big mine in Mexico today that is worthy of the name of being called a big mine has been developed by American enterprise or British engineers. In other words, when those men first went in there and took hold of these properties they were merely prospects, and today they are the most wonderful properties in Mexico, and those mines were developed by American and British capital. I want to say that the reason why I say "American and British capital" is this: It is a strange thing that the American people have never realized. We fellows in Mexico have been dubbed, you might say, back here, as being soldiers of fortune. It has been said that we have gone down there and that we have grabbed the lands, and that we have stolen the mines, and in other words that we have taken these things away from the Mexican people, when as a matter of fact Americans in Mexico have only been engaged in things that have required nerve, patience, and sacrifice. That is to say, they have been engaged in mining, and every man knows that a man who lives in the mining country is away from civilization; he is out in the lonely hills. He does not develop a mine overnight. It takes time to do that. Every shot he puts into the ground does not produce ore, and he has his disappointments. Then we have the railroad men, engaged in building railroads. The Americans built all the railroads. When we talk about the progress of Mexico during the years prior to Mr. Diaz, and we say that nearly every section of Mexico has been connected with the capital by railroad, we can also say that these same railroads have been built by Americans. Our dams, waterworks, ports of entry, our beautiful harbors at Vera Cruz and Manzanillo, and all big things like that, Americans have been asked to go in and do these things.

Mr. KEARFUL. What about the paving of the streets?

Mr. SLATTERY. We are laying out the sewers in the different cities. Americans as a class have not gone into the commercial enterprises. The thought I want to convey to you is that we did not take away any opportunity from the native people. We developed the opportunity.

Mr. KEARFUL. Is it a fact that the Americans went in there and did the things that the Mexicans themselves would not do or did not do?

Mr. SLATTERY. That is the truest statement that has ever been made.

Mr. KEARFUL. Is that especially true with regard to mines?

Mr. SLATTERY. Absolutely so. I have been in contact with a great many Mexicans and I have never known a Mexican in my entire experience in Mexico to ever invest a dollar in what we would call a prospect — that is, what we fellows would consider a good gamble that we would be willing to sink our own money in to help to develop. I never knew of a Mexican in my entire experience that would be willing to invest in that prospect with you.

Mr. KEARFUL. In getting control of mining prospects in Mexico, did you ever know of Americans who had special concessions that they obtained from the Mexican Government that gave them any special privileges over the Mexicans?

Mr. SLATTERY. Do not make me laugh. As to these so-called special concessions, I have only heard of the term since I have been back in the United States. Anything our people got in Mexico, we bought and we dearly paid for.

Mr. KEARFUL. Did you or your associates have any special privileges that you got from anybody?

Mr. SLATTERY. I not only did not have any special privileges, but I can cite many occasions where they have attempted to take away from me what I really secured in the proper and legal way, after I developed them from a prospect into a paying proposition.

Mr. KEARFUL. Has it been true with many other operators, as it has been with you that when profits were made from the mines, those profits were reinvested for further development?

Mr. SLATTERY. Oh, yes; that has been our general policy. That has been the general policy of many of our American mine operators.

Mr. KEARFUL. What effect did the operation of American capital and enterprise in the mining industry have upon the laboring classes of Mexico? Did it tend to oppress them?

Mr. SLATTERY. It seems to me — and of course I am only going to speak of my own experience — that we put life into the whole country where Americans were engaged in an enterprise. Speaking for myself, I can recite to you three places where practically a blade of grass did not grow. When I say "a blade of grass," you know what I mean — developed in the proper way; there was nothing but a little prospect, little indications, superficial indications that there was ore in the ground. We developed those three places, so that in time we built practically towns around those mines with the people engaged in the development of our work.

Mr. KEARFUL. Did you employ natives exclusively?

Mr. SLATTERY. Natives. When I went to Mexico first, the average wage of the peon, the laborer, was 6 cents a day, Mexican money. The first crew of men I ever employed I paid 50 cents a day. That was the beginning, you might say, of the hatred that sprang up between the mining men and the hacienda men.

Mr. KEARFUL. The Mexican hacienda men?

Mr. SLATTERY. The Mexican hacienda men. They were paying their men 6 cents a day and allowing them so much of the corn and beans that they would raise on the hacienda. Sometimes they got what was coming to them, and sometimes they did not. In any case, we began at 50 cents a day. We raised that to 75 cents a day. We have been paying from a dollar for common labor up to two and three dollars a day.

Mr. KEARFUL. You are speaking in terms of Mexican money?

Mr. SLATTERY. In terms of Mexican money. I never operated nor would I operate a company store, but I always saw to it that in dealing with storekeepers that were in my village or in the place where I was operating, we bought those goods for cash. You know Mexico is a country of long-time credits, but by paying cash for everything you can buy things considerably cheaper.

Mr. KEARFUL. What was the system of company stores that operated to oppress Mexican laborers as it was operated by the Mexicans?

Mr. SLATTERY. The company store was a store where the peon or the laborer could go to the store on what they called a ticket, and on this ticket everything that he was given out of the store was put down. At the end of two weeks, or at the end of a quincena — two weeks' time — or a month, or whatever the time or period of employment was the amount that he was supposed to receive every day was then placed opposite what he received, and it was always found that that man was in debt. No matter how it was figured, the peon was always in debt. In addition to that, the prices in the company store were always higher for everything than he could buy them for right out in the open market.

Mr. KEARFUL. Provided he had the cash?

Mr. SLATTERY. Providing he had the money. I saw the dangers of that system, and I always desired to have the confidence of the Mexican laborer, and in order that he would not think we were trying, as we use the term nowadays, to profiteer, we did not operate a company store, but we did control every storekeeper in our village. That is to say, every man, every storekeeper who sold a piece of goods higher than what the price was that we fixed on it, we practically took the privileges of the store away from that man. In other words, what I mean by that is that we would not honor our time-cards in his store.

Mr. KEARFUL. That is, if he sold on credit to your workmen and charged them an exorbitant price you would see that he did not get paid?

Mr. SLATTERY. We would not honor those cards, and in that way our laboring men, our miners, were able to buy in these stores articles of wearing apparel and also edibles for less than they could buy these same articles for in the smaller towns, because of the opportunities we afforded them, by paying cash for everything and buying at wholesale prices.

Mr. KEARFUL. What other benefits accrued to the Mexican natives by reason of the operations, besides this doing away with the company-store system and the wage scale? What about their habits of living and their clothing, etc.?

Mr. SLATTERY. That would have to be answered with a long story, which I do not like to go into.

The average American who has gone to Mexico has been practically the judge and jury and doctor and everything else for his laborers. Once an American obtained the confidence of the native, that native would bring and did bring his domestic troubles, his family troubles, all his troubles to him. In case of any quarrels or anything of that sort he would never think of going into the town to the jefe politico or to the judge to settle them. He would bring them up to his American patron and have him adjust them. We Americans moved among those Mexicans; we were practically their doctors; many of us took up a course of medicine, you might say by correspondence, through the Parke-Davis system, just to learn the general symptoms of diseases and have some pills and things around about the place, so that in case of little ills and all that sort of thing we would be able to administer to them.

What the Americans have done for their laborers and for the people connected with their work, no man is in a position to give a real statistical account. For instance, those of us that knew their habits, we celebrated their own fiestas right on our own grounds; we gave them their own entertainments; we gave them their own music; everything that they would have by going to the big towns we gave them right on our own place.

Mr. KEARFUL. Without assessing them for it?

Mr. SLATTERY. Without charging them a nickel.

Mr. KEARFUL. What about the matter of education?

Mr. SLATTERY. In the matter of education, we always saw to it — of course, that was never carried on in a systematic manner, because, after all, the word "education" is a misnomer in Mexico. Although I have read so many beautiful things about the educational system of Mexico, I never came in direct contact with it; at least, I never saw it, although I searched for it — this wonderful educational system that was said to be going on in Mexico. Without speaking for anybody else, we had a rural school — you might call it — out our way, that we had two or three hundred children attending, and we practically paid 50 per cent of the expenses of maintaining that school.

Mr. KEARFUL. Was the system that you describe, of gaining the confidence of the Mexican workmen, generally followed by American mining operators?

Mr. SLATTERY. Generally; yes.

Mr. KEARFUL. What was the attitude of the Mexicans toward the American operators during the time of Porfirio Diaz?

Mr. SLATTERY. The attitude was, I would say, of the most friendly kind.

Mr. KEARFUL. Were they grateful for the things that were done for them, or otherwise?

Mr. SLATTERY. Well, yes; but that word "grateful" is a peculiar word in Mexico. A Mexican very seldom — I suppose it is a trait that is unexplainable — shows gratitude, but if we could use the word in its broadest sense, they would go out of their way to appreciate what was done for them by their American patrons.

Mr. KEARFUL. Were they trustworthy, as a rule, and faithful?

Mr. SLATTERY. Absolutely. That is a thing that I should like to describe for you, because it has been asked of me so many times. The most faithful individual that I have ever met is the Mexican peon. He will stick with you, if he has a responsibility, 24 hours of the day, if it is necessary.

Mr. KEARFUL. Do you not call that gratitude for good treatment?

Mr. SLATTERY. You have asked me another question, now.

Mr. KEARFUL. Very well.

Mr. SLATTERY. You asked me if they were trustworthy. You can put on your desk $10,000 in money in all denominations, and go out; go down to the mill, or go somewhere else, and come back, and not a nickel of that money will be touched; but some old rivet or some old bolt or something that is absolutely of no use to the Mexican himself, but may, perhaps, be of some use to you, will be taken by him simply because it is lying around. Now, that is almost indescribable.

Mr. KEARFUL. You are talking now of a period that is past, are you not?

Mr. SLATTERY. I am talking now of the Mexican.

Mr. KEARFUL. The characteristics of the Mexican generally?

Mr. SLATTERY. I am talking now of the Mexican of today, as well as the Mexican of 1901 that came under the direct influence of the Americans. When I say that, I do not include in that a single member of the outfit that has taken up arms with one faction or another. I describe him as nothing more than a bandit — members of that outfit.

Mr. KEARFUL. Do you include in the term "bandit" the government army?

Mr. SLATTERY. I include in the term "bandit" every man that has been in the Carranza army, the Villa army, the Obregon army, all the factional strife; every one of those fellows I include in that term.

Mr. KEARFUL. Which predominated in the mining business in Mexico — Americans or British?

Mr. SLATTERY. Oh, we were way ahead, both in money and men and development of mines, of British capital.

Mr. KEARFUL. Did you have any troubles at all during the time of Porfirio Diaz in your operations?

Mr. SLATTERY. Never. We never worried a minute. I rode all over Mexico during those good old days on horseback, and I felt as safe as if I were back in my own home town. The thought of danger never occurred to me. In fact, at night at the mine we slept with our doors and our windows wide open.

Mr. KEARFUL. You never had any feeling of insecurity?

Mr. SLATTERY. We never had any feeling of insecurity during all of those years.

Mr. KEARFUL. How is it now?

Mr. SLATTERY. As it is now, we are not even permitted to spend a night in our own place.

Mr. KEARFUL. At what point did this change begin to take place?

Mr. SLATTERY. It started in 1910. In September, 1910, Mexico was celebrating the one hundredth anniversary of its independence from Spain. Everyone who was within the gates of Mexico at that time would think that she was the greatest country in the world, everybody seemed to be so happy and lovely with one another. Two months afterwards, if you will recall, Pancho Madero hoisted his flag of revolt, and then started the anti-American riots. From some of the men who were closely connected with Pancho Madero, I was given to understand that these anti-American riots were inaugurated or initiated to convey to the American people and the world at large outside of Mexico that Porfirio Diaz was not capable of protecting life and property; so in nearly all the cities of the republic these riots started.

Mr. KEARFUL. What result did they anticipate, upon showing to the world that Porfirio Diaz was incapable of protecting life and property?

Mr. SLATTERY. It appeared to Madero, and it appeared to a great many of the other malcontents, who were few in number at that time, that Porfirio Diaz had such a hold on the world at large that it would be a very unpopular thing to start anything in a regular way that would tend to defeat Diaz for reelection as president, so they took the other method of — as we use the word nowadays

— propaganda, but it was armed propaganda. By having an outrage here, and another one there, and another one somewhere else, the impression would get out eventually that Diaz, after all, was not doing what he was supposed to be doing; namely, protecting life and property.

To get back to that period, I recall very vividly what happened in Guadalajara in September of 1910. We Americans were asked to get up some kind of a show. In fact, there was a day set aside for us, and we put on a set of athletic events. It was something new to them. They never had had them before. In fact, it was the first athletic meet that was ever held in Mexico. I was the chairman of the committee. I invited the governor out. The governor said, "Oh, well, it is going to be like all the rest of these festivities. You will say you will start at 2:30 and you will not get started until 4 o'clock." I told the governor we would start at 2:30, and that a pistol shot would be fired, and that the motorcyclists — which was to be our first race — would start at that time.

The governor was eating his dinner when he heard the motorcyclists go by. He immediately rushed out, got into his automobile, and came out to the races. He asked me to call him, notify him, at 5 o'clock, as he had another engagement to keep. He sat and watched those races, and at quarter of 5 I notified him. He said: "I am not going to leave here; I am so interested," and he remained.

The day after the races were over the governor sent for me and told me that he was so much interested in what he saw the day before that he wanted some of us to go into his schools at Guadalajara and arrange to have an athletic course, as he called it, and he could then understand why it was that these things appealed so much to the American people. As a result of the work at that time I received a medal from the Mexican Government, showing that at that time we Americans were not what we are considered to be today by the present Government.

Then, two months later, followed the anti-American riots. For two days and two nights the mobs just ran riot. Every American house was stoned. My house was stoned, and was not only stoned but was shot into. We got into a little trouble, for the reason that we met at the American Club, and we notified the governor that if he did not stop the rioting we Americans would take the streets ourselves that night, and we would stop it for him. This was after the second day. So the governor, knowing his American friends, and knowing they would carry out anything they threatened to do, saw to it that the rioting was stopped that night. In other words, there was no more rioting.

Mr. KEARFUL. What, if any, patriotic pretext was there for this rioting?

Mr. SLATTERY. Absolutely none at all.

Mr. KEARFUL. Was there no slogan or cry that they used?

Mr. SLATTERY. Well, of course, in some places it was "Viva Madero!" and "Mueran los Gringos!" — in other words, "Long live Madero!" and "Death to the Yankees!"

Mr. KEARFUL. What were your next troubles?

Mr. SLATTERY. Then came the four bad years. What I mean by the four bad years was that this life of security that I have spoken of suddenly disappeared. The flag of revolt seemed to be hoisted, and everybody in arms became nothing more than a downright bandit. You will recall that I said I consider the term "bandit" as used in that connection as meaning one who served in the armies of the various factions. There was never an outfit that rode into my place that did not have with them, flying, the flag of the Republic of Mexico.

A UNITED STATES SENATOR TESTIFIES

TESTIMONY OF SENATOR ALBERT B. FALL.

(The witness was duly sworn by Dan M. Jackson, Esq., clerk of the subcommittee, duly authorized.)

Senator FALL. I am going to make a statement for the record and for the public; I am going to break the silence of eight years. From time to time my colleagues and friends have insisted that I should make public a statement as to my interests in Mexico, rumors concerning which have been constantly circulated by Mexican propagandists and those possibly sincere or otherwise, knowing or unwittingly assisting in the circulation of such propaganda.

I went to Mexico in 1883; I went on horseback through eight States of the Republic. I located at Nieves, in the State of Zacatecas, about 60 miles from the station of Cañoncitos on the Mexican Central Road. I became interested in mining at Nieves. My associate in some of the mining interests was Don Jesus Peñeri, a member at that time of the Mexican Congress. I was a practical miner, a timber man — I educated certain of Mexican laborers in timbering mines under the American system of mining; I worked with my hands with them; I had 600 men, Mexicans, the majority of whom I paid 12½ cents a day, Mexican money, and the highest paid labor at that time — *picadero* received 50 cents a day, Mexican money; they boarded themselves. I quit Mexico in 1906, and I had for the company's control, under my charge, 8,000 men on my pay roll, the maximum wage paid to either, if my recollection serves me, was $1.50 — from that to $5 or $6, and $7 per day, for Mexican labor.

I never had a concession of any kind in my life in Mexico, and knew nothing about concessions, except that in agreeing to erect public smelters or reduction works where one might be treated for the Republic — for the public as well as for our private enterprises — I had agreements with the Mexican authorities in more than one instance that machinery for such purposes might be introduced into Mexico free of import duty, and in each instance a bond was required of me that I should faithfully perform my portion of the contract, and the prices for which ores were to be reduced or handled were fixed by the Mexican Government — the maximum price. I was interested in Mexico from 1883, in a greater or less degree, until July 12, 1906. In the latter years my interests consisted entirely of stock interests in American companies only, one the Sierra Madre Land & Lumber Co., owning and controlling some acres principally in the State of Chihuahua; in certain railroad companies being developed in connection with the lumber companies and mines; in certain large mining companies which invested very heavily in Mexico. The nucleus of the mining companies were the mines which myself and an old Texan, my partner, located ourselves — found, discovered in Mexico in two or three different places in the Sierra Madres. I spent a great deal of time, both alone and in company with this partner, camping out, prospecting, and mining throughout the Sierra Madres along the line of Sonora and Chihuahua. I assisted in organizing some large companies and merged my industrial interests with them, took stock for my interest and holdings. I became, of course, well acquainted with the Mexicans in the Republic. I went there during the administration of Gonzales as President. I knew Mr. Diaz personally very well, and am proud to say that I had his friendship and his very material assistance in the various enterprises with which I was connected.

Of course I knew the prominent Mexicans, and I was in camp with and associated with the men who worked for the companies which I had control of, and came in contact with the Mexican worker or peon or laborer, and knew him as very few Mexicans of the higher class ever knew the Mexican lower class, or peon, or pelado. In July, 1906, I severed my connection with every company or interest which I had in Mexico except that I retained a personal power of attorney for my partner, who had a great many million dollars invested there, and who was to me much more than a business associate or partner. In 1907 and 1908 this partner became very deeply involved in Mexico, largely through indorsements for the companies in which we had been jointly interested. His health was very bad, he was compelled to leave the United States and take a sea voyage to Japan, and all his property was deeply involved, and I arose from a sick bed and went down to take charge of his business, without remuneration, for the purpose of saving something of the business for his family of little children. He died shortly afterwards. In winding up his business affairs I became personally interested in certain mining claims in the district of Jesus Maris de Ocampo in the State of Chihuahua. I disposed of those interests for his account and mine and that of a large number of Mexican creditors, to an American syndicate, and formed what is known as the Sierra Mines Co. (Ltd.). So, disposing of my interests I received $75,000, par value of the stock of the company. I yet have that stock in my possession. That is my only interest in Mexico of any kind or character.

In my operation in Chihuahua I became very well acquainted with Gen. Luis Terrazas, who was the war general of that State, the man who had driven Maximilian out of the State and who had enabled Benito Juarez to make headway against the French when Juarez was a fugitive in El Paso, Tex. I have always been proud of the acquaintance and friendship with Gen. Terrazas. After the battle of Chihuahua, when Mercado was driven from that State, came through Ojinaga and took refuge with his soldiers in this State, I received from Gen. Luis Terrazas, who came out through Ojinaga with Mercado, a telegram asking me to meet him in the city of El Paso. I did so, and would have gone to meet him under any circumstances. He spoke to me of conditions in Mexico and particularly of the incarceration of his son, Luis, Chico, as I know him and had known for 20 years or more, by Villa; that Villa was demanding $500,000 ransom for him, and asked me to assist if possible in securing his release. He had some business disagreements with an American in El Paso touching a cattle contract, and at the same time a suit was brought against him there for a large amount, I think $185,000. He asked me to assist in the settlement of that suit. I did so, paying to the American, I think, $26,000 in full settlement, and taking his receipts in favor of Gen. Terrazas for that amount. I was never the attorney for Gen. Terrazas; I was never interested with him in any business transaction of any kind or character, nor with any member of his family, nor with Governor Creel, who was his son-in-law, nor with any member of his family. I never, as an attorney, represented any American interests in Mexico except those which I had assisted in organizing, and in which I had the stock interests which I have referred to. I never owned a dollar of oil stock in my life. I never represented an oil company in Mexico. I worked for $3.50 a day on the hammer in quartz mining with Ed Doheny. I think very highly of him, and personally I would do anything possible to assist him. I have many friends who have been interested in Mexico, who are in the United States, for whom I have the same feeling. I have very many friends among the Mexicans who are fugitives and are being protected under our flag here, for whom I have the very warmest feeling.

I represent a constituency, the majority of whom, more than 55 per cent, are of the Mexican blood. Any prominence which I may have achieved politically I owe to Mexican people. I am their one representative in the Congress of the United States. I have a very great and sincere, deep and abiding affection for the Mexican people in general. Since I have been in the Senate I have had in my office at one time representatives of Huerta, of Carranza, of Villa, and of the old Cientifico element, all consulting me, and I think telling me everything that they knew or thought, and asking advice. I should have said, in speaking of the Cientifico element, representatives of Gen. Felix Diaz himself personally.

As to my ideas as to what should have been done with reference to Mexican affairs, it is not necessary for me to mention them now. Any recommendation hereafter made by this committee as to what shall be done with reference to Mexico, if anything, such recommendation will be made upon the record of this case, in so far as I am concerned. This committee was appointed by the Foreign Relations Committee of the United States Senate, of which I am a member, upon a resolution introduced in the Senate by Senator King, of Utah; he is not a member of the Foreign Relations. It was reported back unanimously from the Foreign Relations Committee, and I was directed to make such verbal report to the Senate. I did so, and the resolution providing for the appointment of the committee was adopted unanimously by the United States Senate, without dissenting voice. I may say that it was understood that in any committee that was appointed that I would be a member of it, because of my long knowledge of Mexico and of the Latin American, my familiarity with the language and the laws. I devoted five years of my time to the civil law of Mexico, and had seven prominent Mexican attorneys on my staff for more than seven years there.

I was appointed without any division of sentiment, political or otherwise, just as I have been appointed by the same authority as the chairman of the committee on Colombian affairs, handling the Colombian treaty and Colombian oil matters, etc., at issue between the United States and Colombia. No question of politics has ever arisen in any of these things. After this committee was appointed I was directed to formulate a resolution providing for its procedure, and giving me authority to use any amount of money whatsoever necessary, not limiting the amount. The two resolutions are the broadest which the Senate has ever adopted in authorization of any investigation. The committee is authorized to go anywhere and has all powers that the Senate of the United States can vest in a committee. Except by propagandists, or those knowingly or unknowingly influenced by certain propagandists, no question has ever been raised of the good faith of this committee. I have had my attention called to an editorial recently appearing in one of the great papers of the State of Texas under date of January 13, and I want to say now that what has occurred here today with reference to the newspaper story which was attempted to be sent out, concerning myself — not that, but rather more, this editorial has caused me to make the statement which I have just made, and which is my last word on this subject. It is an astounding thing to me that any great American paper would reflect upon the American people and the American Congress by questioning the motives of a committee appointed as this commmittee has been appointed. It is hard for me to understand it. But my resentment is not because of personal criticism — that I have never replied to until this moment — but it is because such an editorial, and such efforts as have been made from time to time to attack this committee, are, under the circumstances, a reflection upon the Senate of the United States and upon the departments of this Government with which this Government is so cordially cooperating. I have no personal resentment in a matter of this kind. I do not propose to be drawn into any further controversy in this matter, but I made this statement for the benefit of the public.

The CHAIRMAN. The committee will go into executive session now to hear some of these witnesses who desire to testify. No further public hearing today.

AN OIL ENTREPRENEUR TESTIFIES

SATURDAY, DECEMBER 6, 1919.

UNITED STATES SENATE,
SUBCOMMITTEE ON FOREIGN RELATIONS,
Washington, D. C.

Testimony taken at Washington, D. C., December 6, 1919, by Francis J. Kearful, Esq., in pursuance of an order of the Subcommittee of the Committee on Foreign Relations of the Senate.

STATEMENT OF MR. WILLIAM FRANK BUCKLEY.

(The witness was duly sworn by Mr. Kearful.)

Mr. KEARFUL. You have stated your name. What is your present address?

Mr. BUCKLEY. Mexico City.

Mr. KEARFUL. Your present address in this country?

Mr. BUCKLEY. My present address in this country is Bronxville, N. Y.

Mr. KEARFUL. What is your birthplace?

Mr. BUCKLEY. San Diego, Tex.

Mr. KEARFUL. What is your profession?

Mr. BUCKLEY. I used to be an attorney.

Mr. KEARFUL. In what business are you now engaged?

Mr. BUCKLEY. Real estate and oil leases.

Mr. KEARFUL. In Mexico?

Mr. BUCKLEY. In Mexico.

Mr. KEARFUL. How long have you been acquainted with Mexico?

Mr. BUCKLEY. I have lived in Mexico since 1908.

Mr. KEARFUL. Are you thoroughly familiar with the Spanish language?

Mr. BUCKLEY. Yes.

Mr. KEARFUL. Are you able to talk with the natives of Mexico freely upon any subject?

Mr. BUCKLEY. Yes.

Mr. KEARFUL. Have you made a study of Mexican conditions during the time that you were in Mexico and during the last few months in this country?

Mr. BUCKLEY. Yes; I have.

Mr. KEARFUL. What have been your facilities for gathering information with respect to the conditions in Mexico?

Mr. BUCKLEY. I have been associated socially and in a professional way with a number of Mexicans of prominence. I was counsel for the Mexican delegation to the Niagara Conference, and in connection with this conference and subsequent events that have transpired in Mexico I have maintained my association with these gentlemen.

In July of this year, with the idea of gathering facts with regard to the Mexican situation that might be susceptible of proof, I induced seven or eight friends, all Americans, who have lived in Mexico for a number of years and who are intimately acquainted with the situation in that country, to work with me in this connection, with the result that during the last four months we have gotten together a mass of material on every phase of the Mexican situation, which is at the disposal of the committee whenever the committee desires to have it presented. We have had a great many prospective witnesses interviewed and will be glad, whenever the committee desires, to present detailed information through competent witnesses of economic conditions in Mexico, including the railroad situation, the Henequen and Yucatan situation, the mining and oil situation; information with regard to the activities of the Carranza government, its methods; outrages on American citizens and the destruction and confiscation of American property, in which connection we have the names and addresses of many witnesses that are willing to appear before the committee, those residing in the States being willing to appear in public session, whereas those residing in Mexico, in their majority, insisting on executive session because of fear of reprisals by the Carranza government.

Mr. KEARFUL. Where is the headquarters of your organization?

Mr. BUCKLEY. The Murray Hill Hotel in New York.

Mr. KEARFUL. Have you any connection with the Association for the Protection of American Rights in Mexico?

Mr. BUCKLEY. No.

Mr. KEARFUL. Have you any connection with the oil companies operating in Mexico? Are they contributing in any way toward your organization?

Mr. BUCKLEY. No oil company or any other corporation is contributing in any way to this organization. The only oil company I am connected with is a small company owning some leases and a terminal property in Mexico. The total investment of this company does not exceed a few hundred thousand dollars and it is not a member of the oil association.

Mr. KEARFUL. The committee has heretofore had testimony showing in a fragmentary way various incidents which go to make up a picture of Mexican conditions. I understand that you have made such a study of Mexico as to be able to give a more or less complete picture of the situation from the time of the overthrow of the Madero government up to the present time. Such a complete statement would naturally be divisible into various heads. Will you proceed in your own way to make a statement of the conditions covering the entire period mentioned beginning with the overthrow of the Madero government?

Mr. BUCKLEY. To understand the Mexican situation it must be understood in the beginning that the present is more or less the normal condition of Mexico; the era of peace during the Diaz régime from 1876 to 1910 was an abnormal period in the history of that country. All revolutions in Mexico work along conventional lines and the present series of revolutions are in no material sense different from those that beset that country from 1810 to 1876; the abnormal element of the present series of revolutions is the active participation in them by the American Government. During the pre-Diaz period there were hundreds of revolutions and over 50 rulers. All of these revolutions, like the present revolution, promised everything to the people, including universal suffrage, independent judiciary, division of lands, democratic form of government, etc. To the average American the present situation in Mexico is a novel one; to the man who has studied Mexico's history there is not much novelty in it.

There is a distinction between the Madero revolution and the Carranza revolution; the former had for its object the establishment in Mexico of a democratic form of government; the latter had as its object social, and not political, reforms — the principal reforms being the destruction of private property and the expulsion from the country of the Americans. The former revolution was dominated by Mexicans of the old Liberal type and included in its ranks some of the finest men in Mexico. These men were soon disillusioned, quit the revolution, and were succeeded by radicals of an inferior social type who directed the Carranza revolution and now control the Carranza government. The only political reforms that the leaders of the Carranza revolution sought were for the purpose of vesting political power in themselves, and not in the Mexican people. Control of the political machinery would enable them, first, to enrich themselves by graft, and second, to force through their social reforms.

When Madero was President, Carranza was governor of the State of Coahuila. Carranza, as well as other governors, received from the Federal Government an allowance of a large sum of money each month for the support of the State constabulary to put down local revolutions. Limantour had left 63,000,000 pesos in the Mexican treasury, and this was one of the favorite methods used by the groups surrounding Madero to loot the treasury. Of course, troops were not maintained in the several States, or, at least, not more troops than were necessary to cover appearances, and the Governor of the State divided up his monthly allowance with the grafters in Mexico City.

It is stated that because of a disagreement between Carranza and the group surrounding President Madero, Carranza's monthly allowance was cut off and this led to friction between Carranza and Madero and to the formulation of plans by the former to revolt against his chief. It is generally understood that Carranza invited Alberto Garcia Granados, a noted Liberal in Mexico, who formed a part of Madero's cabinet, to join him in his revolt. Garcia Granados had become dissatisfied with Madero, and Carranza thought that he would be friendly to such a suggestion. It is stated that Garcia Granados declined to join in the revolt. After Carranza entered Mexico City Garcia Granados was executed.

Madero was overthrown before Carranza's alleged plans matured. Huerta, the successor of Madero, conducted negotiations with Carranza for some time looking toward recognition of his government by Carranza, but the latter finally broke off negotiations and revolted.

When Madero was killed the agents of Carranza advised him of the bad impression that this outrage had produced in the United States, whereupon Carranza realized his opportunity and proclaimed loudly, especially where Americans could hear, that his purpose in revolting was to avenge the shameful murder of his beloved chief. Carranza's agents in the United States played this up with great effect on the American people. The Mexican point of view with regard to this assassination has never been understood by the Americans. The Mexican people were not as a rule shocked by the assassination of Madero; you seldom hear reference in Mexico to this crime. As a rule Mexicans who favored Huerta maintained that if Huerta did kill Madero it was good politics; the followers of Madero, while protesting that they were sorry their chief had been killed, admitted that they could understand the attitude of the opposition as constituting good politics.

Mr. KEARFUL. What have you to say with reference to the attitude of Mexicans towards Huerta?

Mr. BUCKLEY. The mass of the Mexican people have no preferences in politics, for they know nothing about politics. The middle-class and upper-class Mexicans favored Huerta, principally because they were anxious for peace and order and because they had been satiated with the advanced political doctrines announced by Madero and satiated with the shameless graft that surrounded his administration.

Carranza propaganda in the United States, very ably assisted by the American Government, succeeded in instilling into the public mind certain erroneous impressions that have been the basis of American public opinion, where there has been any public opinion, for the last six or seven years.

The Carranzista press explained that there were three classes of people in Mexico — the lower classes, representing what Mr. Wilson has termed "the submerged 80 per cent," the middle class, comprising probably 10 per cent, and the upper class. It is stated that the middle and lower classes were trying to wrest political power from the Cientificos, a so-called party composing the upper classes, that it was alleged had governed Mexico for their own exclusive benefit and the benefit of foreign capital during the Diaz régime.

The peace and order established by the Diaz Government, and maintained for 35 years, enabled the middle class to form. There was no such thing as a middle class in Mexico before the Diaz régime, and the people of the middle class were the strongest advocates of the Diaz régime, for without peace and order it could not subsist.

The "submerged 80 per cent" has no political ambition; does not know how to read or write; lives from hand to mouth, and has no political ideas or preferences; all it wants is to be let alone and be allowed to live in peace and receive those material necessities that are indispensable for the maintenance of life. This class has never received any consideration or protection in Mexico except during the régime of Porfirio Diaz.

I do not contend that this is all that the 80 per cent of the population is entitled to, but I do contend, and history shows, that material benefits must come first and that a people does not concern itself with the niceties of government or universal suffrage until after it is provided with bread and clothes.

The educated Mexican, the type that governed Mexico for 35 years, and gave it the only decent Government that it ever had — the Mexican whom the American Government has driven out of that country — did not sympathize with Huerta and was not a partisan of Huerta's. To him Huerta was the lesser of several evils; he preferred Huerta to either Carranza or Villa, and subsequent events have demonstrated the wisdom of his choice. The cultivated Mexican, however, would never have chosen Huerta for president of his own free will.

Mr. KEARFUL. We have often heard the term "Cientificos" and it has been many times stated that the Cientificos consisted of a party of political grafters who surrounded Porfirio Diaz and with whom he was in full accord for the purpose of exploiting and oppressing the Mexican people. Will you please elucidate that matter and give a description of and state who the Cientificos were and what they did?

Mr. BUCKLEY. The Cientificos were not grafters. As a matter of fact, they did not constitute a party in Mexico, as is erroneously believed to be the case in the United States, but consisted of nine Mexican Liberals who tried to force upon Porfirio Diaz a Liberal régime. The story of the Cientificos is as follows:

In 1892 a national convention was held in Mexico City for the nomination of a candidate for President. This convention was dominated by a group of young and cultured men, nearly all Congressmen. Gen. Diaz was proclaimed the candidate of the convention and this group of young men prepared a manifesto to the Nation which served as a platform of the convention. In this manifesto certain principles were advocated which had for their purpose committing Gen. Diaz to a program of reform, two principles being mentioned in particular — first, life tenure of the judges of the Supreme Court for the purpose of assuring the independence of the administration of justice, and, second, the creation of the office of Vice President to minimize the chances of revolution in the event of the death of Gen. Diaz.

Gen. Diaz viewed with suspicion the activities of this independent group, and his unconditional adherents in the Chamber of Deputies derisively gave them the name of "Cientificos." This name was coined in connection with the discussion of a bill prepared by this group in which Francisco Bulnes, one of the group, in answer to an objection by a member of the House, stated that this bill had been prepared after much study and after a scientific investigation of the matter had been made, to which a member retorted that the group then were "Cientificos." This word translated into English does not mean a scientist; it means a man learned in any branch of knowledge.

The Cientificos constituted a minority of the Congress and their adversaries, who were popularly called the Jacobins, were in the majority. The Jacobins were always submissive to Gen. Diaz, whereas the Cientificos, although friends of the President, endeavored to force upon him a policy of political reform giving a larger measure of control to the people, which Diaz refused to accept. The Cientificos presented a bill in Congress providing for life tenure of Federal judges, which was passed in the lower House, but was defeated in the Senate by order of Gen. Diaz. (This necessary reform was revived by the independent Senators in 1912, under the Government of the so-called apostle of liberty, Madero, but was defeated through the influence of the latter.)

In 1893 President Diaz appointed as minister of finance the scientific Jose I. Limantour, the great financier, who raised the finances of Mexico and the credit of the nation to a high place among the great powers of the world. Limantour abandoned his political activity to accept this position, and the rest of the Cientificos, in order not to embarrass him, because of their inability to cope with Gen. Diaz, desisted somewhat from their activities thereafter.

When Ramon Corral became vice president in 1904, although he endeavored not to indulge in activities that would arouse the suspicion of Gen. Diaz, he favored the Cientificos, because he sympathized with their ideas of reform and recognized their talent, and this led the enemies of Corral to also attack the Cientificos.

The so-called Cientifico Group was composed of but a few persons, who always refused to form a political party. The Cientificos were as follows:

Jose I. Limantour. The great minister of finance, under whose direction Mexico's public credit was founded. He enjoyed a worldwide reputation and is today consulted by financial institutions in France and England. He was born a millionaire and in public and private life was a model of honesty.

Rosendo Pineda. A lawyer of great talent and a noted orator; he was most persistent in advocating the political reforms opposed by Gen. Diaz. He was the only one of the Cientificos who in the last seven years of the Government of Diaz dared to oppose his indications, and upon several occasions opposed him in the chamber of deputies. He was never a man of wealth and died in absolute poverty.

Justo Sierra. He was among the most notable orators and litterateurs produced by Mexico. He was minister of instruction from 1902 to 1911 and founded the National University. He lived and died in poverty.

Joaquin D. Casasus. An attorney of American and British interests who became wealthy. He was an orator and litterateur and at one time served as ambassador to Washington.

Pablo Macedo. A lawyer who became distinguished in his youth and amassed a fortune before becoming one of the Cientificos; he represented many English and American business enterprises and was well known abroad; an honest and highly educated man; the author of the project that Limantour approved for the establishment of the gold system in Mexico. He never held any other public office outside of being a Congressman and director of the School of Jurisprudence.

Francisco Bulnes. Probably the most finished orator that Latin America has produced, the author of many splendid works on the political history of Mexico and a man of great and varied learning. He has never been a man of means and is now living in exile in Cuba.

Miguel Macedo. One of the most distinguished lawyers in Mexico; who is still living in Mexico City and enjoys a reputation for great intelligence and integrity. He was a national senator for one year and a subsecretary of the department of Gobernacion (Interior) during the last five years of the administration of Gen. Diaz. He has a modest fortune, which he has accumulated in 40 years through intelligent and constant labor.

Emilio Pimentel. A member of Congress; a lawyer of good reputation and of recognized probity of character; Governor of the State of Oaxaca during the last eight years of Diaz's administration. A man of moderate wealth.

Roberto Nuñez. A lawyer, who occupied many public offices, and after 1893 was subsecretary of the department of finance; always regarded as an honest man. Died in Paris, leaving a small fortune.

The Mexican public never referred to anybody outside of these men as Cientificos. Mr. Bryan and other American politicians have always thought that the Cientificos constituted a national party. As is seen from the above statement, only three of these men were wealthy and only one of them made his money after he had become a Cientifico. Gen. Diaz was always suspicious of their ideas, and never yielded to their influence.

The Mexican revolutionaries, to give them a pretext to persecute the men in Mexico who were distinguished for their talent, or for their wealth, called all those whom they wished to victimize "Cientificos." The American Government, accepting this version, has popularized in the United States the alleged crimes of the Cientificos and has given the name of Cientifico to all those men in Mexico who were, in fact, useful to Mexico, and stood in the way of designs of the revolutionaries.

A UNITED STATES AMBASSADOR TESTIFIES

FRIDAY, APRIL 16, 1920.

UNITED STATES SENATE
SUBCOMMITTEE ON FOREIGN RELATIONS,
Washington, D. C.

Testimony taken at Washington, D. C., April 16, 1920, by Francis J. Kearful, Esq., in pursuance of an order of the Subcommittee of the Committee on Foreign Relations of the Senate.

TESTIMONY OF HENRY LANE WILSON.

(The witness was sworn by Mr. Kearful.)

Mr. KEARFUL. Please state your full name.

Mr. WILSON. Henry Lane Wilson.

Mr. KEARFUL. What is your present post-office address?

Mr. WILSON. 2712 North Meridian Street, Indianapolis, Ind.

Mr. KEARFUL. What is your profession?

Mr. WILSON. Lawyer, I suppose, although I do not practice.

Mr. KEARFUL. You have been in the Diplomatic Service?

Mr. WILSON. Seventeen years.

Mr. KEARFUL. What has been your experience in the diplomatic service?

Mr. WILSON. I was appointed minister to Chile in 1897 by President McKinley; minister to Greece and Belgium in 1905 by President Roosevelt; and ambassador to Turkey and Mexico in 1909 by President Taft.

Mr. KEARFUL. Has your diplomatic service been continuous from the time of your appointment as minister to Chile in 1897?

Mr. WILSON. Until December, 1913, under President Wilson.

Mr. KEARFUL. What was the period of your service as ambassador to Mexico?

Mr. WILSON. I was appointed in November, 1909, and my term extended from that time until November, 1913.

Mr. KEARFUL. How long were you minister to Chile?

Mr. WILSON. Eight years; five in Belgium and four in Mexico. My diplomatic service, I believe, is the longest continuous service as chief of a mission in the history of this Government.

Mr. KEARFUL. When was it that President Diaz abdicated and left Mexico?

Mr. WILSON. In June, 1911, as I remember.

Mr. KEARFUL. You had then been ambassador to Mexico for about a year and a half? Is that correct?

Mr. WILSON. Yes.

Mr. KEARFUL. Will you please describe for the benefit of the committee the conditions of business and the situation as to law and order under President Diaz?

Mr. WILSON. When I arrived in Mexico, and for probably a year thereafter, the government was in full control of the situation in Mexico in the remotest parts, and life was as safe upon a Mexican highway as upon one of the great thoroughfares of New York City. The Government's finances were in a highly flourishing condition, with one hundred millions in the treasury. Immigration was increasing rapidly, especially from the United States, and American capital during that year was seeking investment in Mexico to a greater extent than ever before. Everything indicated a highly prosperous future for Mexico.

Mr. KEARFUL. What were the inducements for the investment of capital in Mexico?

Mr. WILSON. American capital as it went with Mexico took the form of investment in mines, in farms, in public utilities, and in oil.

Mr. KEARFUL. What, if any, special inducements were offered by the Government for the investment of capital?

Mr. WILSON. Land was purchased at extremely low valuations, a policy that was encouraged by the Government for the purpose of enlarging the taxable resources of the country. The Government pursued the same policy with reference to investments in the oil country and in mines and public utilities, it being the well settled principle of the Diaz Government that the investment of foreign capital in Mexico led constantly to the creation of taxable resources.

Mr. KEARFUL. And how was that policy realized?

Mr. WILSON. It was realized very successfully.

Mr. KEARFUL. You spoke of land being sold at low valuation. Was that exclusively to Americans, or was it open to anyone who wanted to purchase?

Mr. WILSON. Oh, it was open to all the world.

Mr. KEARFUL. Under general law?

Mr. WILSON. Yes.

Mr. KEARFUL. What have you observed to be the effect upon the development of Mexico of the operation of American capital there?

Mr. WILSON. Practically all of the material development of Mexico is due to American enterprise, initiative, and capital. I perhaps put that a little strongly. I perhaps should say the preponderating development, because it is always necessary to take into consideration the British, French, and Spanish investments.

Mr. KEARFUL. You think that the development of Mexico up to the time of the downfall of Porfirio Diaz was due to foreign capital and enterprise, of which the American preponderated?

Mr. WILSON. Yes.

Mr. KEARFUL. What do you believe would have been the condition of Mexico without the operation of foreign capital and enterprise?

Mr. WILSON. She would have remained practically an uncivilized State, as she was during the period extending from the revolution against Spain down to the advent of Porfirio Diaz.

Mr. KEARFUL. At the time of the downfall of Porfirio Diaz, how many Americans, if you know, were operating in Mexico?

Mr. WILSON. Seventy-five thousand. This figure I reached by careful estimate by the embassy and after correspondence with all the consulates.

Mr. KEARFUL. In your capacity as ambassador, did you come into close contact with many of these Americans?

Mr. WILSON. Oh, yes; a very considerable number. The American Embassy in Mexico City was really a workshop. The demands for advice and assistance were constant, beginning at 9 o'clock in the morning and extending very frequently if not generally until 1 or 2 o'clock at night. During the troubled period — which describes pretty nearly the entire period of my service in Mexico — we did in the embassy 33 per cent of the correspondence of the Department of State here in Washington. This, added to the circumstance that there were always anywhere from 50 to a half dozen people in the embassy asking for interviews, made the business of the embassy tremendously large.

Mr. KEARFUL. What can you say in reference to the charge that has been circulated industriously in this country that the Americans operating in Mexico were a class of speculators engaged in plundering the Mexican people?

Mr. WILSON. I regard it as a very malicious and wicked falsehood.

Mr. KEARFUL. What was the character of the Americans generally operating there?

Mr. WILSON. Very high. I have had occasion to come in contact with them as much perhaps as anyone, perhaps more than anyone, and I regard the standard of Americanism in Mexico as very high. I have never known, in any part of the world, such conspicuous examples of real Americanism and courage, and the exercise of all those qualities that we call peculiarly American, as I found among the 75,000 people of American origin in Mexico.

Mr. KEARFUL. What class of people were they, in reference to their occupations?

Mr. WILSON. They were in all occupations. There were about 2,000 in the railways; there were probably 5,000 farmers; there were probably 5,000 engaged in mining; and probably as many as 8,000 engaged in educational work and residing in the country for reasons of health, diversion, or investigation.

Mr. KEARFUL. How were the professions represented by Americans?

Mr. WILSON. There were very many American doctors in the country, a great many American teachers, a reasonable number of lawyers —

Mr. KEARFUL. Engineers?

Mr. WILSON. Yes; a very large number of engineers, a great many dentists, some very excellent ministers and pastors.

Mr. KEARFUL. Was there any large number of the class that is found in the large cities of this country belonging to the lower order of society?

Mr. WILSON. None. This element was almost nonexistent.

Mr. KEARFUL. It has also been charged against Americans operating in Mexico that through fraud and bribery they obtained special concessions from the Mexican authorities which enabled them to exploit the country to their own advantage over the Mexican people. Is there any truth in that?

Mr. WILSON. No. No case of that kind ever came under my observation while I was in charge of the embassy.

Mr. KEARFUL. What can you say as to the nature of the concessions, if any, for the development of new enterprises?

Mr. WILSON. All that I am familiar with were granted for fair consideration and obtained honestly. During the entire four years I was in charge of the American Embassy in Mexico City no American representing vested interests in Mexico ever asked any aid from the embassy except in the matter of physical protection. There were instances, of course, where I was called upon to represent some important interests before the Mexican Government, but that was almost without exception under instructions from the Department of State.

Mr. KEARFUL. The concessions that were granted were by a department of the Government under a general law, were they not?

Mr. WILSON. Yes.

Mr. KEARFUL. And the terms of the concession required the concessionaire to expend certain sums of money toward development?

Mr. WILSON. Yes.

Mr. KEARFUL. And for the performance of which he was required to give bond?

Mr. WILSON. Yes.

Mr. KEARFUL. And as an inducement, he was allowed to import the materials necessary for his operations free of duty?

Mr. WILSON. Free of duty; yes.

Mr. KEARFUL. And in some cases for a limited period the products would be exempt from taxation?

Mr. WILSON. Yes; that is a correct statement of the general Mexican policy with reference to concessions. It was a very excellent policy in Mexico. It could not be applied with equal benefit in this country, but in Mexico it worked very admirably.

Mr. KEARFUL. You are acquainted with the policy in this country of municipalities granting street railroad and gas and power franchises?

Mr. WILSON. Yes.

Mr. KEARFUL. And exempting the grantees from taxation and giving them special privileges for the purpose of inducing them to invest their capital?

Mr. WILSON. It is the same thing, only we call them privileges and in Mexico they call them concessions.

Mr. KEARFUL. We call them franchises here. You are also familiar with the policy of the American Congress in making large land grants for the construction of railroads, and guaranteeing the indebtedness of certain of the railroads?

Mr. WILSON. Yes. The difference is that the Mexican concessions are usually granted to foreigners. Our concessions, so called, if you can call them that, are never granted to foreigners.

Mr. KEARFUL. It was necessary to grant them to foreigners in Mexico because they furnished the only available capital?

Mr. WILSON. It was necessary in the case of Mexico, because not only was the foreigner the only source from which the capital could be procured, but the Mexican who had wealth would not invest his money in that way.

Mr. KEARFUL. Can you give an estimate of the amount of American money that was invested in Mexico at the close of the rule of Porfirio Diaz?

Mr. WILSON. My estimate while in charge of the embassy was that there was a billion two hundred million dollars of American capital invested in Mexico.

Mr. KEARFUL. Can you give an estimate of the amount of other foreign capital invested in Mexico?

Mr. WILSON. My estimate of the combined investments of all the other countries amounted to about the same as the American investment. In other words, the American investment was equal to that of all other countries combined.

Mr. KEARFUL. Can you give a statement of the other foreign populations in Mexico? You stated that there were about 75,000 Americans.

Mr. WILSON. The next in order numerically were the Spanish. I believe the Spanish population of Mexico was nearly as large as the American.

Mr. KEARFUL. How about the other nationalities?

Mr. WILSON. The French population was very considerable, the German population was very large, the Italian population was considerable.

Mr. KEARFUL. And the British?

Mr. WILSON. My impression is that there were about 8,000 British in Mexico, nearly all of whom were in Mexico City.

Mr. KEARFUL. What was the American population of Mexico City at that time?

Mr. WILSON. About 10,000.

Mr. KEARFUL. How were the railways of Mexico owned and managed at that time?

Mr. WILSON. I think perhaps it would be better to state the thing in a different way.

Mr. KEARFUL. State it in your own way.

Mr. WILSON. Originally, the railways of Mexico were owned entirely by foreign investors, made up from American and European sources. Under Mr. Limantour, when he was Minister of Finance, the Mexican Government adopted a policy of securing control of these different systems. This policy finally resulted in the union of the Mexican Central with the Mexican National Railways, which union carried with it all the branch lines and dependencies, concentrating practically everything under Government control except the line from Mexico City to Vera Cruz, which remained the property of British investors, and independent. This consolidation of the railway system was brought about by the very simple process of a continuous guarantee of the interest on the bonds of the railways by the Mexican Government. The Mexican Government guaranteed a rate of interest of 4 per cent to the bondholders in return for the privilege of voting their stock, but the Mexican Government put practically no money into the railways of Mexico. The money came from the United States and Europe. I do not know whether I have made that clear or not.

Mr. KEARFUL. I think so. I understand that the Government control of the railways was effected by means of the guarantee by the Government of the railroad bonds at a certain rate of interest, in consideration of which the control of the stock was turned over to the Mexican Government.

Mr. WILSON. Yes. It is a very great mistake to suppose that the Mexican Government ever owned any part of the railways of Mexico.

Mr. KEARFUL. What class of people managed the railways of Mexico?

Mr. WILSON. The general management was in the hands of Americans, and in addition to this general management there were about 2,000 American employees in active railway service. There was considerable hostility against these American railway employees, which usually cropped out in some drastic regulations by the Government which affected American employees only. During the time of Mr. Madero there was a very concerted effort made to dislodge the American employees, and I remonstrated with the president, and he promised that the regulations would not be put into effect; but they were put into effect, and this apparent act of bad faith led to some very unpleasant passages between the president and myself. I made an effort to protect these men, most of whom had lived in Mexico for a great many years and raised their families there. They were finally all driven off the railways and not even furnished railway transportation to the United States. President Taft interested himself in their behalf, and obtained employment for a large number of them on the American railways.

Mr. KEARFUL. Are you prepared to state the causes of the downfall of Porfirio Diaz?

Mr. WILSON. Yes; I think so.

Diaz had two great domestic policies. The first was the development of the material resources of the country. That part of his policy he carried out with marvelous success. He invited foreign capital into Mexico, and along with the investment of capital came large foreign immigration, usually of younger men full of enthusiasm, initiative, and organizing genius. With the aid of these foreign elements which he invited into Mexico, and with the aid of the capital which they represented, Diaz developed Mexico in material ways. He covered the country with a network of railways, developed her agricultural, mining, and commercial resources, and over all of his work of his creation he maintained a system of law and order unsurpassed in any country in the world.

The second branch of his policy was the awakening of the national consciousness and morale. This policy he did not successfully carry out because of the undermining influences of advancing years. He said to me upon one occasion: "I hoped during my time to develop Mexico materially and spiritually. I have developed her materially, but I must leave the task of her spiritual development by evolution to my successors."

During the last 10 years of the Diaz régime the Government was maintained by the legend which Diaz had created, but had fallen off materially in vigor and efficiency. During the last 10 years the cabinet was made up very largely of extremely old men, some of them over 80 and none of them younger than 60. These men naturally had passed their years of active usefulness, and they were, moreover, totally out of touch with such currents of public opinion as existed in Mexico. During these last 10 years Diaz grew infirm and lost some of the quick penetration of public men and watchful care over public interests, and the evils resulting from the President's notable decline especially in the last five years, were accentuated by the circumstance that nearly all of his advisers were in the same class with him. These conditions led to the causes which brought on the revolution.

The actual causes were, first, the government of the country by a close circle of so-called Cientificos, together with the probability that this type of government would be continued under the generally accepted and selected successor of Diaz, Ramon Corral. The Cientificos were really a very excellent body of men in so far as they had any real corporate existence, and if their subordination had exercised equal intelligence and probity in the management of public affairs the consequences which followed might have been avoided. Ramon Corral, Limantour, and Oligario Molino directed the affairs of the country. I believe all of them were honest men, but there were a large number of men serving under them who were not honest.

That is the first cause. Second was the race question. Every Indian in Mexico who is in touch with the traditions of his race believes and hopes that eventually the white race will be expelled from Mexico and a new empire of the Montezumas set up in the palace of Chapultepec. He carries this belief into all his transactions. To it may be attributed in a very large measure the excessive barbarities which have been committed by the Indian races during this revolution.

Mr. KEARFUL. Is that your conception of the present Carranza doctrine of "Mexico for the Mexicans"?

Mr. WILSON. That is what it amounts to, although Carranza himself is a white man. "Mexico for the Mexicans" under the rule of democratic institutions means Mexico for the Indians, because if the majority rules the Indian will rule in Mexico.

Mr. KEARFUL. And "the property of the foreigner for the natives"?

Mr. WILSON. Yes; and, of course, you understand that that means not only an Indian rule in Mexico, but it means the rule of a population 80 per cent of which is unable to read or write.

The third cause was hatred of the foreigner. You must distinguish between the race hatred and hatred of the foreigner, because hatred of the foreigner was shared equally by the whites and the Indians, and the word "foreigner" there applies to the newcomers. From the race standpoint it applies equally to the Spaniards who came in with Hernando Cortez.

The invitation of the Diaz government brought into Mexico a vast army of foreigners, most of them from the United States. These foreigners converted Mexico from a desert into a paradise. They reaped generous profits from the situation. They were a thrifty lot. They accumulated fortunes as a result of industry and perseverance and ingenuity, and they immediately became the objects of envy and suspicion and dislike on the part of the Mexicans who had not availed themselves of the opportunites that lay all about them and were quite content to let the riches of the soil slumber on without interruption. Practically all of the railways belonged to foreigners; practically all the mines. Practically all of the banks and all of the factories were owned by the French. A very considerable part of the soil of Mexico, probably over a third, was in the hands of foreign-born elements, and practically all the public utilities were in the hands of Americans or British. Naturally, this foreign ownership excited hostility, which was not lessened by the circumstance that those interests, or whatever they may have been, had been honestly acquired.

The foregoing constitute the causes of the revolution against Diaz. They would not ordinarily constitute cause for revolution. We have endured much more in this country, for instance; but they did constitute the causes for the revolution in this instance, and no other causes can be shown by anyone competent to discuss the history of the revolution.

Mr. KEARFUL. You are, of course, acquainted with the principal business street of Mexico City, Avenida San Francisco?

Mr. WILSON. Yes.

Mr. KEARFUL. Have you observed the nature of the businesses along that avenue, as to whether they were in the hands of foreigners or Mexicans?

Mr. WILSON. They were almost wholly foreign owned. The merchandizing business of Mexico City is almost wholly foreign. I do not suppose it is necessary to indicate the branches in which they are engaged. It is of no importance, I imagine, here; but the most interesting and best improved part of Mexico City is what they call the Colonias, which have been built very largely by the foreigners.

Mr. KEARFUL. Will you proceed to describe the beginning and the progress of the Madero revolution which resulted in the downfall of Porfirio Diaz?

Mr. WILSON. Yes. When Madero first attracted my attention he was engaged in the business of making incendiary speeches, usually of very little intellectual merit, before audiences in remote parts of Mexico. These meetings were usually interrupted by the soldiers, and generally Madero was put in jail, his release following some days afterwards. He never appealed to popular sympathy in Mexico. He was a practically unknown person in public affairs who appeared at the psychological moment.

He was regarded by those who knew him, and especially by his own family, as a man of unsound mind and of dangerous tendencies. He was insignificant in appearance, halting and spasmodic in physical characteristics, stammering in speech, and unable to state any circumstance or opinion lucidly and clearly.

He was a man of absolute personal honesty, of excellent morals, and I believe of sincere patriotism, but easily misled and easily made the victim of more audacious and clever intelligences.

Madero in no sense overthrew the government of Diaz. The government of Diaz collapsed by reason of the desertion of friends, and a tide of anarchy which broke out and surged all about the capital city. Madero rode into power over the ruins of the Diaz government.

In the month of June Madero entered Mexico City as a private citizen, after Diaz had resigned the presidency and left the country.

I do not know, but I think if you are afforded an opportunity to consult the records which we have here, but which I prefer to not place in the hands of the committee unless they are demanded, you will find that on the very day of his entrance into Mexico City I sent a dispatch to our Department of State predicting the continuance of the revolution and the probable final overthrow of Madero.

My reasons for making this prediction were, first, the natural tendency of the Mexican people to anarchy and revolution, a tendency now given full range; second, the utter inadequacy of the announced Madero platform, policy, and personnel in dealing with the situation thus created.

This prediction was amply fulfilled, because the revolution never ceased. The revolution begun against Diaz continued without any interruption whatever through the time of Madero, and in the midst of all the terrors of this revolution, which swept from all over Mexico right up to the gates of the capital city, Madero was elected to the presidency by a total vote of 19,989 in a population of 15,000,000; Reyes, the only other candidate for the presidency, being prevented by violence from prosecuting his campaign, the violence being organized and directed by Gustavo Madero.

Mr. KEARFUL. The brother of the President?

Mr. WILSON. The brother of the president. The Reyes meetings were interrupted and dispersed. His meetings were interrupted and he was driven from the platform and organized crowds of lower classes assaulted him with rocks, etc. The same methods are being employed in Mexico City today by Carranza against Obregon. This is not relevant to this part of the testimony, but it is a circumstance that it might be well to note.

Madero entered into the government undoubtedly with patriotic resolutions and with good intentions, but his cabinet was composed of radicals on the one hand and conservatives on the other, and the resolution of one day was revoked upon the next. Whatever resolution was taken was hysterical and spasmodic, advancing and retreating in accordance with the preponderance of this or that element in the cabinet.

All of this was due to the character of the president, who was one day the friend of the rich and the next day the friend of the poor, and he vacillated between the rich and the poor until there were neither rich nor poor for him. He was finally left absolutely alone, with no support except the public office holders and his family, 100 of whom were stated to be holding public office.

During this period the anti-Americanism in Mexico first became general. It had existed hitherto under all governments to a certain extent. It was noticeable in the last stages of the Diaz régime, when Rodriguez, a Mexican, was hung, or boiled or something, by a mob in Texas.

Mr. KEARFUL. Lynched.

Mr. WILSON. There are lots of ways of lynching. I think he was boiled. It resulted in a widespread protest in Mexico. In the City of Mexico mobs invaded the streets and burned the American flag, assaulting Americans everywhere, and in a number of cities of the Mexican Republic Americans were obliged to defend themselves in their homes.

Mr. KEARFUL. Were there exaggerated accounts of this treatment of Rodriguez by way of pretext for the outbreak of anti-American expressions?

Mr. WILSON. My opinion was at the time that these anti-American outbreaks had been encouraged secretly by the Diaz people for the purpose of distracting public attention from the revolutionary tendencies which existed at that time in Mexico.

Mr. KEARFUL. There was an effort to unite the Mexican natives through their sentiment against the "Colossus of the North"?

Mr. WILSON. Yes. That was my theory about it, borne out by some evidence which I had, although it must always be remembered that Diaz and his government were not anti-American, but, on the contrary, very pro-American.

A MINING ENGINEER TESTIFIES

TESTIMONY OF NILS OLAF BAGGE.

Mr. KEARFUL. State your full name.

Mr. BAGGE. Nils Olaf Bagge.

Mr. KEARFUL. What is your business?

Mr. BAGGE. Consulting engineer, 38 Park Row, New York.

Mr. KEARFUL. How long have you been in Mexico?

Mr. BAGGE. I went to Mexico in 1898, making examination of mines in Sonora.

Mr. KEARFUL. How many years have you spent in Mexico since that time?

Mr. BAGGE. On and off, 16 years.

Mr. KEARFUL. Are you acquainted with the conditions in Mexico under Porfirio Diaz?

Mr. BAGGE. Yes, sir.

Mr. KEARFUL. What were they as to law and order?

Mr. BAGGE. They were splendid.

Mr. KEARFUL. Was there any difficulty about transacting business or traveling in any part of the Republic of Mexico?

Mr. BAGGE. None at all. I have traveled on mule back from the Atlantic slope to the Pacific slope several times without any gun or protection of any kind.

Mr. KEARFUL. Could you do that now?

Mr. BAGGE. Oh, no.

Mr. KEARFUL. When did the conditions change?

Mr. BAGGE. They changed in 1913 and 1914. That is, as far as if affected anything against the Americans. We, of course, were in more or less difficulties between the two conflicting factions, but not as Americans. But in 1913 or 1914 that feeling against Americans commenced to develop.

Mr. KEARFUL. You say in 1913 or 1914. Can you place the date at the happening of some event?

Mr. BAGGE. Yes; at the time that Orozco began fighting as a red flagger, I think they call them; fighting Villa, who was then fighting under Carranza.

Mr. KEARFUL. That was in 1914, was it not?

Mr. BAGGE. It may possibly have been. I have not the date with me. It seemed to me, though, it was in 1913.

Mr. KEARFUL. The American forces landed at Vera Cruz in April, 1914, and Huerta abdicated in July, 1914.

Mr. BAGGE. Yes; but Huerta disposed of Madero in 1913, was it not?

Mr. KEARFUL. In February, 1913.

Mr. BAGGE. And then Orozco fought under Huerta.

Mr. KEARFUL. Yes.

Mr. BAGGE. At that time a good many outrages had been committed against the Americans, and no retaliation had been attempted, or at least had not been accomplished, and regard for American life had been growing less and less, and that was in 1913.

Mr. KEARFUL. And how have the conditions been since that time? Have they been better or worse?

Mr. BAGGE. They have been particularly bad since Carranza gained control.

Mr. KEARFUL. When was that?

Mr. BAGGE. That was in the early part of 1915.

Mr. KEARFUL. What was the feeling toward the Americans under Diaz and Madero and Huerta?

Mr. BAGGE. The very best, and particularly well in Mexico City; treated as well as we deserved if we acted decently.

Mr. KEARFUL. What have you to say about the statement that has been made often in this country, sometimes emanating from high official sources, that Americans operating in Mexico are not entitled to consideration because they were engaged in exploiting the Mexicans.

Mr. BAGGE. That is mendacity, I think. Most Americans went into Mexico to examine the resources, and they found mines dormant, exhausted, unprofitable. I will give you a few data as to that.

In the years 1872 and 1873, Mexico's gold production was

$976,000; the silver production was $21,441,000. This was the period before the advent of American-built railways.

In the years 1882-83 — that is one decade afterwards — the Mexican gold production was $956,000, and the silver production was $29,565,000.

Ten years after, in the year 1900-1901, at the time when the cyanide method was introduced into Mexico by Americans, the gold production was $8,843,000 and the silver production was $72,368,795.

Now, that shows that when the Americans built the railroads and opened arteries of trade, and also more ores to be moved, that material benefits came to Mexico.

Mr. KEARFUL. What was the condition of mining properties in Mexico generally when the Americans went in there? Did the Americans, when they went in, find rich, profitable mines, which they took away from the Mexicans for the purpose of exploitation?

Mr. BAGGE. They did not. They found, as I said, the industry dormant, the mines virtually exhausted. They brought their organization ability and industry and their application of up-to-date methods and applied them to that industry, and, as I show by the statistics given you, increased the output. They found that the old bonanza, which had, in years covering centuries, produced these hundreds of millions on which Mexico is exploited as a marvelously rich country, were all worked out, the Mexican had taken the cream and the American got the skimmed milk, but he took the skimmed milk and made it profitable by his ability.

But, before that, I want to say that the Mexican asks and receives a better price from the American than the American would receive from one similarly situated. The reason for that is, in my judgment, that Mexico had been the land of promise; it had been very well advertised, and the cheap labor, of course, was an incentive, which enabled the Americans, with their better knowledge of working on a large scale, to work these properties.

Mr. KEARFUL. What effect did the operations of Americans have upon the conditions of labor in the mines?

Mr. BAGGE. Well, the Americans found that the Mexican mine owner, in all cases, practically, kept the store, known as the tienda; that the peon, who got very low wages, would be allowed credit, and eventually was in debt to the store. The result was he never had a chance to either take care of himself or his family, or do anything for them.

Mr. KEARFUL. What effect did the American operations have upon that system?

Mr. BAGGE. Well, Americans raised the wages, not because they wanted to compete with the Mexicans, but because their larger-sized operations required more men. That, of course, gave rise to a feeling against the Americans amongst the well-to-do Mexicans, because they raised the wages of the peons. The Americans never ran stores, unless the property was so far away from the railroad that it would be a help to the Mexicans.

Mr. KEARFUL. What about the actual working conditions in the mine? Were they better?

Mr. BAGGE. The Mexican works his mine different from the way we do. He is an excellent miner, a wonderful prospector, but he knows nothing about sanitation. He has no ventilating system, and he works by manual labor where we will apply machinery to lessen the labor, and we installed ventilating systems, something the Mexican had never before had. We put in hoists and cages, where a Mexican would have to carry his ore to the surface on his back, sweating blood all the way for a few centavos a day; there could not be any more of a beast of burden than an ordinary Mexican in the ordinary Mexican mine.

Mr. KEARFUL. How was that condition under the American operations?

Mr. BAGGE. We have applied the same methods we have applied here; sanitation, ventilation, safer system of stopping, whereby we have less accidents from caves; we do not rob the pillars of the mine, like the Mexican has done. After he has taken his bonanza, he would cave his property. That we would not permit. An American would not go into a Mexican mine to work under those conditions, so, of course, we could not expect the Mexican to work where an American would not go in.

Mr. KEARFUL. You worked the Mexicans under the same conditions that you worked the Americans?

Mr. BAGGE. Yes. I will say this, the Mexicans themselves, the mine owners, have improved their methods very much in that regard since they had the example of the American methods, and, at the same time, their methods are still very crude.

Mr. KEARFUL. So that the operation of the American miners has been to improve not only the conditions in their own mines, but those in the Mexican mines themselves?

Mr. BAGGE. Yes; that is so.

Mr. KEARFUL. And with respect to the payment of wages; did the American continue the payment from the tiendas?

Mr. BAGGE. No. In the first place you can not apply that the same as the Mexican. It is a little way of doing business. An American does not do it in that way. It is too much difficulty.

I will give you an illustration: A Mexican peon is proverbially improvident. He will not buy a week's supply, probably because he has not the money, so he buys it three times a day. His lard or sugar, he would buy his day's supply three times a day; and the result is that it is a little, picayune amount of business that an American could not bother with. If they tried to run a store, they would always run it at a great loss. If they had run a store, it would have been a financial loss to the company. That is something we learned in this country, but a good many Mexican mines in the early days obtained their only profit from the stores, and none from the mines.

Mr. KEARFUL. Are you personally connected with a mining company?

Mr. BAGGE. I am president of the Almoloya Mining Co.

Mr. KEARFUL. Where is that company operating?

Mr. BAGGE. In Chihuahua, between Jiminez and Parral.

Mr. KEARFUL. With what success have your operations been conducted?

Mr. BAGGE. A total loss of about $450,000 to date.

Mr. KEARFUL. What amount of money has been invested in that operation?

Mr. BAGGE. Altogether I have been instrumental in bringing in about $1,500,000 of American money into Mexico. We have taken out possibly $250,000 in profits.

Mr. KEARFUL. Who contributed that money?

Mr. BAGGE. Most of it myself, and investors in smaller and larger sums.

Mr. KEARFUL. You purchased the shares of stock in your company?

Mr. BAGGE. Yes. And I would say this, which is hardly understood here, that most of the mining operations of Mexico, and the people living there, are only employees or hired help. Those are the ones who have suffered; also the stockholders in these different companies. Like all American companies, capital is raised by a few men getting together a syndicate and arranging the preliminaries and then raising the money from a number of investors.

Mr. KEARFUL. When did you begin operations?

Mr. BAGGE. Our company, in 1902.

Mr. KEARFUL. When did your difficulties begin?

Mr. BAGGE. At the start of the Madero revolution, 1909, I think it was.

Mr. KEARFUL. Please describe what happened then with reference to contributions and depredations, etc.

Mr. BAGGE. Well, at that time I was president of a company known as the Compania Minera Rio de Plata, over on the western side of the State of Chihuahua, at the junction with the State of Sonora and Sinaola, 13 miles from the railroad. At that time we had about 300 mules packing in machinery and supplies and bringing out bullion and concentrates, and one of the best packers we had was a man named Orozco.

Mr. KEARFUL. Pascual?

Mr. BAGGE. Pascual Orozco. I brought in six .30-.30 Winchesters for the use of the mine, because it is a pretty rich property, and in that property and all other properties in Mexico we paid full value for every dollar in sight in that mine, which was $350,000 gold. We put in a mill costing about $500,000 gold.

There is one thing about the exploitation claimed against Americans in taking out these millions from Mexico, and that is seldom considered, but it costs from 70 to 85 per cent of what you obtain to produce the silver bullion, and that money is applied to wages and supplies which go to Mexico, so, if you take out $1,000,000 in bullion, about $850,000 of that stays in Mexico. The price of producing an ounce of silver varies, of course, in some cases up to over 50 cents an ounce. It possibly is higher now because other things have gone up, though present silver is higher than it has been since 1873.

Mr. KEARFUL. But you are not able to take advantage of that under present conditions, are you?

Mr. BAGGE. Not at all. We have quite a lot of ore too low grade for us to work at the time the revolution started, and which we could make money on today, but we can not get at it.

Mr. KEARFUL. Do you have any special concessions from the Mexican authorities which gave you advantages over the Mexicans in that locality in operating mines?

Mr. BAGGE. None at all. I could have gotten what they call concessions, which means practically licenses, but the duties and obligations that they bring with them are such that it is not worth while to bother with them.

Mr. KEARFUL. Please proceed to describe the troubles that you encountered at the beginning of the Madero revolution.

Mr. BAGGE. We had no particular difficulty with Orozco, because he was a friend of ours, and respected Americans, I think, considerably.

Villa at that time appeared, and he used to make his headquarters south of Allende.

Mr. KEARFUL. What year was that?

Mr. BAGGE. That was in 1910; but he was not very formidable at that time. That is, we never took him very seriously. Our real trouble started in 1913 and 1914, after the administration ordered us out of Mexico. That forced us to abandon the mine, and fungus grew up on the timbers and quickly rotted them, and we had much difficulty to operate, and we were robbed occasionally; that is, had to give something to the cause, gasoline or dynamite, or corn, beans, and clothes, and occasionally a little money.

Mr. KEARFUL. By whom were these exactions made?

Mr. BAGGE. Well; they were so many I can not remember off-hand, but there were Urbina and Villa —

Mr. KEARFUL. Urbina was under Villa?

Mr. BAGGE. He was under Villa in Durango; Herrera, Hernandez —

Mr. KEARFUL. Who is he?

Mr. BAGGE. He is under Carranza.

Mr. KEARFUL. Who else?

Mr. BAGGE. De la Fuente.

Mr. KEARFUL. Who was he?

Mr. BAGGE. He was not a bandit, but he was an engineer, really, that tried to become president of Mexico for a little time, but I think he was one of the adventurers of Madero against Huerta. He did not last very long. It was Herrera came up and took our superintendent, who was an American, and he took the two superintendents of the adjoining mines, both Mexicans, and very fine Mexicans at that, and he held all three of them for a ransom.

Mr. KEARFUL. Who did this?

Mr. BAGGE. Herrera, under Carranza, and he got a check for 5,000 pesos from one of the superintendents and they let him escape. The other Mexican could not give any check or promises. I think his company was too poor, so they took him down to a pumping station about a mile and had our superintendent look on while they shot him. He was a very fine young fellow.

Then, they took our superintendent to the railroad station, and the train came along and they searched the train and found four Mexicans on there, made them get off the train and told them to run, and the whole bunch then shot at them, and thought it great sport. Then they took our superintendent eventually and marched him about 60 kilometers behind the mounted troops, only one man guarding him, eating their dust, and they had then impressed him as a soldier of the cause, and by promising to pay 750 pesos to Herrera's brother, who was operating at Parral at that time, and which we did eventually pay, he got back in a few days in bad physical condition, and we had no further trouble with Herrera.

Mr. KEARFUL. Your superintendent was an American citizen?

Mr. BAGGE. An American citizen; yes.

Mr. KEARFUL. Did you report this incident as to ransom and payment of 750 pesos to American authorities?

Mr. BAGGE. Oh, no.

Mr. KEARFUL. Why not?

Mr. BAGGE. What was the use? We got over that some time before.

Mr. KEARFUL. What was the reason for your attitude?

Mr. BAGGE. Because other people had tried that and found that they got no satisfaction. The general feeling among the Americans was that the best thing to do was to take their medicine.

Mr. KEARFUL. What was the feeling of the Mexicans toward Americans up to the time of the resignation of Huerta?

Mr. BAGGE. Well, previous to the Madero revolution, I distinctly remember there was quite some agitation in Mexico which claimed "Mexico for Mexicans." That was backed by the middle class of Mexicans, the school teachers and the notaries and the middle-class people. They saw one mine after another that was a failure under the Mexicans become prosperous under the Americans, and I think it raised a little bit of jealousy, and at that time there was a lot of labor agitation in Mexico, and these agitators would go and try to form labor unions, not exactly as we have them here, but on that line. They also agitated at that time to eliminate the American railroadmen from operating the Mexican trains, and, of course, eventually the American railroad men were withdrawn as train conductors and engineers as soon as the Mexicans were capable of running them themselves. I think Madero was partly responsible for that agitation; at least, he never did suppress it, but there was no feeling against individual Americans. There was the very best kind of feeling.

Mr. KEARFUL. Up to what time?

Mr. BAGGE. Up to 1913 and 1914.

Mr. KEARFUL. Up to the time when the Americans were ordered out of Mexico by this Government?

Mr. BAGGE. At that time, when no reprisals were made for raping of American women and children, and we quit. Up to that time I think the Mexicans did respect us.

Mr. KEARFUL. You heard the testimony of Mr. Knox, of the attitude which took the form of denominating Americans as "white Chinamen"?

Mr. BAGGE. Oh, yes.

Mr. KEARFUL. Is that correct?

Mr. BAGGE. That is very common. You will hear Mexicans say, "What kind of people are you, anyhow? We have raped your women; we have spit on your flag, and insulted your Government, and killed your men, and still you will not fight."

That is a common thing in Mexico.

AN OIL PIONEER TESTIFIES

STATEMENT OF EDWARD L. DOHENY.

(The witness was duly sworn by the chairman.)

The CHAIRMAN. Please state your name, residence, and occupation?

Mr. DOHENY. Edward Lawrence Doheny; residence, Los Angeles, Calif.; occupation, at present, oil producer.

The CHAIRMAN. I will ask you a preliminary question or two, Mr. Doheny.

Where are you engaged in the production of oil?

Mr. DOHENY. In California and in Mexico.

The CHAIRMAN. How long have you been engaged in the production of oil in Mexico? I will say, rather, I will qualify that: How long have you been engaged in Mexico in prospecting or producing oil?

Mr. DOHENY. A little over 20 years; in fact, 20 years last May I made my first oil prospecting trip into Mexico. We brought our first well in 19 years ago last May.

The CHAIRMAN. Mr. Doheny, you have been present during the hearings before this committee and you know the general course of the investigation and have heard the testimony. I think it might be well for you just to make a statement of your efforts in Mexico, what you have done, how you commenced, under what laws you were operating, whether you have any concessions or special grants, or what is the source of your titles to your properties, and leading up to what you are doing now. I think if you will do that in your own narrative way we will get along better.

Mr. DOHENY. Commencing with my experience in prospecting for oil or earlier?

The CHAIRMAN. Earlier, if you choose to. You were always prospecting for something, and have been, have you not?

Mr. DOHENY. Well, since 1875.

The CHAIRMAN. When did you go to Mexico?

Mr. DOHENY. I first went to Mexico, into Mexico prospecting, in 1887. I first became acquainted with Mexico and New Mexico in 1873.

The CHAIRMAN. And you speak the Spanish language, do you?

Mr. DOHENY. I have been trying to speak it for something like 46 years, without very much success.

The CHAIRMAN. Suppose I just help you out a little by asking you a question or two. What were you doing in New Mexico?

Mr. DOHENY. I went down to New Mexico from Fort Leavenworth, Kans., with a bunch of shave-tail mules for Lieut. Wheeler, of the United States Geological Survey, to use for pack animals in the survey of the boundary line between Arizona and New Mexico. We arrived at Fort Marcy on the 9th of May, 1873, and Fort Marcy is situated near Silver City. Soon after that I took up the business of prospecting for gold and silver and followed it with varying success until 1892.

The CHAIRMAN. Now, in prospecting, Mr. Doheny, were you prospecting for some one else, in behalf of some one else; in other words, were you representing capitalists or were you doing it personally?

Mr. DOHENY. Well, Mr. Chairman, I have always been prospecting for myself. I was never fortunate enough to get a position to wean me away from the desire to prospect.

The CHAIRMAN. You had plenty of money at that time to live on, did you, Mr. Doheny?

Mr. DOHENY. I did — well, I often lived a whole year through on less than $50. The cost of living did not interfere with a good shot, where game was plentiful, and where salt did not cost very much. I did not always have sugar in my coffee, but I had an appetite which helped to make everything we eat very satisfactory.

The CHAIRMAN. And you continued prospecting for minerals, you say?

Mr. DOHENY. Until 1892. In 1892 I turned my attention to prospecting for oil.

The CHAIRMAN. That was after you left Silver City, N. Mex.?

Mr. DOHENY. That was in Los Angeles, after I left Silver City, N. Mex.; it was in Los Angeles.

The CHAIRMAN. You were in Kingston, N. Mex. —

Mr. DOHENY (interrupting). I discovered Kingston district; was one of the discoverers, with Harry Elliott and Bob Forbes, Tim Corcoran, Sam Miller, Jim Delaney, and Tom Brady. We were the first party that discovered minerals on the head of the Percha Creek in New Mexico.

The CHAIRMAN. That was the North Percha?

Mr. DOHENY. That was the Middle Percha. We made our discoveries on the Saw Pit Gulch branch of the Middle Percha.

The CHAIRMAN. Before you became interested in oils in California?

Mr. DOHENY. Yes, sir; I discovered the Los Angeles oil field in the fall of 1892, and continued in the oil business with the discovery of three different fields in California before I finally went to Mexico in the year 1900. During my prospecting I will say that I became acquainted with a man with whom I was associated until his death, Mr. C. A. Canfield. Together with him and Mr. A. P. McGinnis I made a prospecting trip to Mexico in May, 1900, and saw some good indications of oil in a certain region lying west of Tampico, in the State of San Luis Potosi, and returning to the States we decided upon the acquisition of lands in that section and an endeavor to develop petroleum in Mexico. We were largely induced to do this by the representations of the president of the Mexican Central Railroad, Mr. A. A. Robinson, lately deceased that if we would make a development of petroleum in Mexico they would purchase the oil from us for fuel on the Mexican Central Railroad.

Mr. Robinson became acquainted with the desirability of oil as a fuel through my efforts in introducing fuel oil on the Atchison, Topeka & Santa Fe Railroad in California, of which company he had formerly been a vice president and chief engineer. He, in fact, suggested to me to make a trip to Mexico, saying that Mexico was without any substantial fuel supply, the coal being of indifferent quality, and that his railroad company was obliged to get its coal from Alabama in the United States. He sent to me transportation for a car and party and I had it for several years, each year for several years, before I finally found the time when I took with me the two companions above named. We had letters from Mr. Robinson introducing us to his agricultural agent and the officers of his road, who kindly moved our car to various parts, so that we might examine for oil indications. As a consequence, we found very satisfactory indications about 35 miles west of Tampico in the State of San Luis Potosi, near the boundary of the State of Vera Cruz. In May of 1900, we were importuned at that time by certain Americans in Tampico, of which they were few, who evidently saw a chance to exploit us by endeavoring to act as our representatives in the procuring of oil lands, and to avoid them we returned to the States and came back again in August to interview the owners of these oil lands.

The first property which we purchased was a tract of land known as the Hacienda del Tulillo, meaning the hacienda of the tule. This property contained about 280,000 acres and was owned by a man by the name of Mariano de Arguinzoniz, a Mexican who lived in the Ciudad del Maiz. This gentleman had the property on the market for sale and asked $250,000 for it, or about something like $1 per acre, American money, and he found out what we desired it for and what I could do, and he finally told us that he had taken something of the Chapopote, which is an Indian word and which means tar, and had sent it to England to have it analyzed. He gave us a copy of the analysis which he received. He encouraged us to believe that it contained a large amount of illuminating oil, not, however, at our request, as we knew more about such oil indications than he did. He succeeded in getting us to pay him $325,000 for the property, $75,000 more than his original price.

The CHAIRMAN. Just one moment. You had the title to that property, of course?

Mr. DOHENY. Yes, sir. I will go back and say that before I went to Mexico on this trip, I interested some other gentlemen in addition to the two who accompanied me. Among them were R. C. Kerens, of St. Louis, late ambassador to Vienna; E. D. Kenna, at that time first vice president of the Atchison, Topeka & St. Louis R. R., Chicago; Mr. W. G. Nevin, general manager of the Atchison, Topeka & St. Louis R. R. Co., in Los Angeles, long since deceased; and J. A. Chanslor, of California, the latter an associate of Mr. Canfield. Mr. Kenna, who had visited Mexico, was also well acquainted with Mr. Robinson, the president of the Mexican Central, and he suggested that he (Kenna) give me a letter of introduction to some attorneys whom he knew, and who he thought might be useful to us in case we decided to buy any land in Mexico.

The CHAIRMAN. Mr. Kenna was a lawyer also, was he not?

Mr. DOHENY. Mr. Kenna was a lawyer also, and he was the head of the law department of the Santa Fe. He gave me a letter of introduction to Señor Pablo Martinez del Rio, who, he said, spoke English well, and was the attorney for the Mexican Central

Railroad. Mr. del Rio has long since deceased. He gave me a letter of introduction to Joaquin de Cassasus, also since deceased, who he said was the leading attorney of Mexico. Mr. Cassasus was afterwards the ambassador to the United States from Mexico.

When we arrived at Mexico on our August trip we had already wired to Mr. Arguinzoniz, who owned the property which we desired to buy, and met him at Las Tables, in San Luis Potosi, and closed the bargain verbally, or orally, and we asked him to travel with us to the city of Aguas Calientes to meet one of these attorneys who would act for us in drawing up the minuta or bill of sale. We told Mr. del Rio — he was our choice as attorney, we had wired him telling him who we were and what the nature of our visit would be, and we asked him if he would come to meet us at Aguas Calientes and close the transaction. We received a message in the affirmative, and we made the contract there at Aguas Calientes, and closed the preliminary contract or minuta by the payment of $25,000. Our check on a California bank was given, which Mr. del Rio unhesitatingly indorsed on the strength of the letters which we showed him.

Sr. Arguinzoniz, the owner of the land, agreed to furnish him with all the evidences of title, and the final papers were to be drawn up for us to receive title to the land at a later date, which was accomplished in November of the same year.

I might say here, now, with reference to these particular titles, or to this particular tract of land, rather, that among the title documents which we received from Sr. Arguinzoniz, was a book about 14 inches long by 12 inches wide by about 6 inches thick, which contained very many documents in writing concerning the title to this property. They were of various dates, in the handwriting of various scribes — the most wonderful chirography I have ever seen. The change from one scribe to another was evidenced in the character of the handwriting. They bore the signature and rubricas of the various grantors and grantees. It seemed that the property had been granted by the King of Spain to the Marquis of Guadalcazar in the year 1581, and bore evidence that the title had remained practically in the same family down to the time of the granting to ourselves, merely changing from one set of heirs to another.

Mr. del Rio assured us that if all the lands which we purchased had titles as perfect and clear as the Hacienda del Tulillo, we never need have any concern about our right of ownership.

The incidents connected with the acquisition of this land and our relations with the owners would cover more pages, perhaps, than you desire my testimony to take up, but it might be stated briefly that Mr. Arguinzoniz, when I last saw him alive three or four years ago, after 16 years of the relation of grantee and grantor, he was still my very warm friend and never had expressed any regret that he had parted with the property which afterwards proved to be more valuable than he supposed it was.

Attorney del Rio took the precaution to tell us that under the Mexican code unknown or unsuspected values might represent, if not referred to in the purchase documents, a possible claim on the part of the former owner to an interest in the property, so he secured a release from Mr. Arguinzoniz of all of his rights to what was then called in Mexico the derechos del subsuelo. That means the rights of the subsoil. In all of our dealings, so far as I know, the right of the subsoil was purchased in addition to the right of the superficie or the surface.

Having acquired this piece of ground we immediately proceeded to develop it, with results that are shown from year to year in the annual reports that I have sent out to stockholders, copies of all of which that I have in my possession, together with the first prospectus that we ever issued, I will be glad to furnish to your committee if you desire me to.

The CHAIRMAN. We shall be very glad to have you file them, sir, if you can.

Mr. DOHENY. They contain a statement to our stockholders of the result of our expenditures and efforts from year to year in a way that my memory could not possibly enable me to state at the present moment.

The CHAIRMAN. What dealings, if any, in connection with this first development did you have with the Mexican Government or officials?

Mr. DOHENY. I may say that we acquired, of land adjoining the land above named, about 150,000 acres more in the extinguished hacienda of Chapacao, making, all told, about 448,000 acres of land in one tract.

Our titles were similar to those to the Tulillo, but the lands were divided up among families in very much small tracts.

We were so certain of the absolute honesty and integrity of Señor del Rio that without any further introduction than just our meeting acquaintance and the letter of Mr. Kenna, we met him at our bank in Mexico and placed in his hands $600,000 to be used to make payments on the various properties when and as they became due under the contracts of purchase.

As proof of his appreciation of our confidence in him Mr. del Rio proceeded to inform us that he thought that it was a very unwise thing for us to expend so much money in Mexico without first being certain that we were going to make a valuable discovery. He really felt sorry to see us so anxious and sanguine about the development of something which would mean a great deal to the people of Mexico. He wished to have us meet the president of Mexico and explain our plans to him. Mr. del Rio was not exactly persona grata with President Diaz, as his father, the elder del Rio had been the minister in France of the late Emperor Maxamillian, and as Diaz had been a war opponent of Maxamillian and largely responsible for his overthrow, he naturally did not feel very friendly toward the del Rio family.

The introduction to Gen. Diaz was brought about, however, through the efforts of our own minister in Mexico at that time, Gen. Clayton, and when we explained to Gen. Diaz our hopes and expectations with regard to the development of petroleum, he was very much pleased, and said that he would be glad to facilitate our efforts in every way; that the development of petroleum that could be used for fuel would save the public domain from being denuded of the immense quantities of timber that were being continually cut off for use on railways and for other purposes, and that it would augment the supply of native fuel and save the money which was being sent out of the country for foreign coal.

I suppose that the general was in the habit of making these assuring remarks to everybody, but I am quite certain that he did not think our little enterprise was going to be successful.

Mr. Canfield and myself were really, I think, the only two members of our own party who were very sanguine of the results.

The CHAIRMAN. Pardon me right there, Mr. Doheny. Were there any oil wells at that time in that vicinity or neighborhood?

Mr. DOHENY. I am just coming to that, Mr. Chairman.

Mr. del Rio, our attorney, suggested to us that inasmuch as our undertaking was a very hazardous one, we might as well take advantage of all the opportunities offered by the Mexican Government to those who would undertake to establish a new industry, and he told us about the statute which required the Department of Fomento, upon presentation of the proper kind of evidence that an industry was to be inaugurated not in active operation anywhere in the Republic, the said department was obliged to give a so-called concession for the right to import free of duty, the foreign materials for starting the enterprise, and also freedom from Federal taxation, except the stamp tax, on those materials for a period of years.

We were obliged, in order to get this immunity, to furnish a certificate from the governor of each State of the Republic of Mexico to the effect that the oil-producing business was not being carried on in his State. This was very easy to obtain from the governors of all of the States except Vera Cruz. Gov. Dehesa, of the State of Vera Cruz, hesitated very much in giving it, because an effort had been made to produce petroleum in Vera Cruz and he was not, himself, certain that it had been abandoned. But when we furnished proof that it had been abandoned for several years, the certificate was obtained and our attorney obtained in his own name a concession from the Department of Fomento, at that time presided over by Señor Escontria, whose name has been mentioned here, giving him the right to import, free of duty, for a period of 10 years material and supplies with which to develop petroleum on lands which were described and which were the lands that I have already told you that I purchased, and with which description we had to file a map marking the places upon said lands where we expected to do the developing.

We also had to agree to expend a certain amount of money within a certain number of years. I think the amount was $500,000 in Mexican gold within five years. At any rate, when the concession was presented by Mr. del Rio, to us, with the offer to assign to us or the company which we might organize, Mr. Canfield hesitated about our taking it because he could not see where the word "concession," as we understood it, applied to the sort of a contract we were making.

We were obliging ourselves to spend $500,000 on that property within a certain length of time, but after that we were merely to be relieved from the duties which were not very considerable and the taxes, which were also inconsiderable, unless we made a big development, for a period of years.

We finally accepted that concession, and that is the only concession of that sort ever granted in Mexico to anybody, and has lapsed nearly 10 years ago.

The CHAIRMAN. That was simply to induce you to invest capital in an entirely new enterprise in the Republic of Mexico?

Mr. DOHENY. Yes, sir. Our first effort to find oil was begun in the spring of the following year, in February, in other words, by the establishment of a camp on the Tampico branch of the Mexican Central Railway at a point which was known as Kilometer 613, as a telegraph pole at that point indicated, showing the distance south of Aguascalientes.

Mr. H. R. Nickerson, since deceased, vice president of the Mexican Central Railroad, kindly cut the main line for us and put in a siding 300 or 400 feet long, so that our private car and freight cars could be shunted onto this line siding and we could have delivered to us on the ground the materials needed for establishing the camp.

I mention this fact, though it may seem trivial, because of the associated facts, which are that the Mexican Central Railway for the greater part of the distance between Tampico and the town of Cardenas, about 150 miles distant, ran through a country which, although one of the earliest visited by Europeans and having evidences of civilization existent long before the European visitation, was still what would be known in western parlance as a "wild country." The railroad was cut through a jungle so dense that, except where breaches were cut, only a bird or other small animal could penetrate it. The climate and rainfall were such that in cutting the ties it was soon supplanted by a new growth so that the stumps of the cut trees were hidden within a year or two. The forest on either side of the railroad had furnished ties for more than 20 years, and still the roads through which those ties were hauled to the railroad were so covered that they could scarcely be discovered.

The right of way for a distance of 20 meters on each side of the road was kept clear; except for that, the land which we purchased, so far as could be ascertained for the railroad, was a dense, impenetrable jungle covered with fog in the night and in the morning. Being below the Tropic of Cancer, we had extraordinarily hot weather at the time we first visited it, although the winters were very delightful, and at the time we undertook to establish our camp the weather was especially fine.

I am afraid I am going to get this too long, Senator.

The CHAIRMAN. It is very interesting, indeed.

Mr. DOHENY. Our first effort to develop, because of the distance from supplies, necessitated the building of a home for the superintendent and employees to live in; the building of an ice and cold-storage plant; a water-distillation plant so they could have fresh, cool water; and an electric plant so that they could have fans to make living bearable during the night. We put in the materials for a sawmill, machine shop, boiler and blacksmith shop, and brought our supplies for all these materials from Pittsburgh, Pa., by Ward Line steamer from New York to Tampico; and then by rail, stopping at kilometer 613 in the jungle, which is now known as the town of Ebano.

The camp was started there on the 12th of February. The first rig was up and ready for drilling on the 1st of May. The first well was brought in on the 14th day of May, 1901.

Before buying the land, however, the summer previous I went with Mr. Maginnis to Boston to see Mr. Robinson to get him to make good his promise to contract to purchase oil from us if and when we developed it, and to make good his promise, also to facilitate us in moving men and supplies there by giving us freight and passenger accommodations. We made a satisfactory contract to supply his railroad with oil from Aguascalientes to Tampico, a distance of about 500 miles.

The CHAIRMAN. Was that the first oil ever used in Mexico?

Mr. DOHENY. The first oil ever produced or used in Mexico in substantial quantities.

The CHAIRMAN. The first used on locomotives?

Mr. DOHENY. It was not used at that time on locomotives. The terms of the contract required that we should notify the railroad companies that we had a supply of oil available, and they should then turn over to us a locomotive that should be equipped at our own expense and operated with all the costs for equipment and for reconversion to the coal in case we failed to consume the oil satisfactorily.

On the 15th day of May I notified Mr. Robinson that our company was prepared to supply oil for one locomotive, from a well that we had just brought in the day before that seemed to be good for 50 barrels a day. I notified him by telegraph, using the language of the contract in the notice.

Much to my surprise and great disappointment, about two weeks later I received a letter by mail from Mr. Robinson stating that he had been instructed by the new chairman of his board of directors to notify us that that contract had been abrogated.

To make a long story short, we did not sell any oil to that railroad company for nearly five years. We did not have any market for our oil before we commenced, as we had thought we had provided by a perfectly good contract, but we simply had a good case for a lawsuit. We did not bring the suit, but we organized a paving company in the City of Mexico and put up a little refinery at Ebano, in order to prosecute our development.

As a result of the organization of that paving company, we finally paved about 50 per cent of that part of the City of Mexico that is now paved, and did all of the paving done in the cities of Guadalajara, Morelia, Tampico, Duranzo, Puebla, and Chihuahua. Thus failure to have a railway contract with the Mexican Central Railroad gave Mexico the best pavement on terms cheaper than probably any country in the world, and the cities named soon became among the best paved cities in the world, having an asphaltum pavement, what is called an A-1 asphalt pavement, consisting of a 6-inch concrete base, an inch of binder, with 2½ inches of asphaltic wearing surface.

That company did business until the revolution on the basis of half payment of the contract price when work was completed and the remaining 50 per cent to be paid in equal payments over a period of 10 years.

When the payment became due the engineer of the City of Mexico was to examine the work in question and furnish a certificate that it was in good condition. In other words, the pavement must be just as good at the end of 10 years as it was when it was first accepted by the city engineer. This was under the Diaz administration.

The contracts in every way were patterned after a form suggested by ourselves and approved by them. There was no big profit in that business, but it gave us a reason for being in Mexico and something to show our stockholders as to what we were accomplishing there, until such time as our production would be great enough to enable us to go to the expense of taking it to a distant market.

The Mexican Central Railway Co., whose line ran for 35 miles through our property, had not yet made up its mind that it was a wise thing for it to buy its fuel from us. The wells which were developed during the first four years varied anywhere from 10 barrels a day to 50 barrels a day. They were shallow wells, and while we had felt that greater production was to be obtained at greater depth, the entire lack of a market kept us from drilling to the greater depths, which afterwards proved to be most productive.

In 1904 we determined to put one well down, and it was the No. 1 well, to what we believed to be a lower producing formation.

The doubts in the minds of the drillers and even of the superintendent, and, I may confess, of the president himself, made this work necessarily very interesting, and it was watched closely. At a depth of 1,450 feet we developed a flowing well, which produced the first day about a thousand barrels of oil. The second day it increased, and it eventually was producing, when I arrived there from Los Angeles, about 1,700 barrels a day, of about 10 gravity, the heaviest oil I had ever seen produced from an oil well in such quantities.

That well, by the way, is still capable of producing about 800 barrels a day after 15 years of continuous flowing.

When we again called the attention of the railroad company to the supply of fuel which was available for their use, they claimed the oil could not be used, it being, as they said, too heavy. At our own expense we equipped an engine for them and proved that the oil could be used, and I later on made a contract with Henry Clay Pierce, the chairman of the executive committee of the road, to furnish his company with oil for a period of 15 years. That contract will expire next year; and as long as Mr. Pierce had control of the road the contract was lived up to by him and by us, and since he lost control of the road to the national railways of Mexico it was lived up to by the national railways.

After the national railways lost possession of the road to the constitutionalist government, we furnished oil to them at a very much reduced price, and are doing so at the present time at that price.

The original price for which this oil was sold was 55 cents a barrel, graduated down to 45 cents a barrel, averaging 49 1/6 cents a barrel delivered on board cars. Three barrels and a half of the oil were equal to a ton of coal. The vice president of the railroad, Mr. Hudson, who is now president of a railroad in Cuba, told me at the end of a year that their saving had been greater than their total cost of oil; in other words, the oil had cut their fuel bill down to less than one-half of what it had originally cost.

During this period the Government of Mexico took little notice of the oil business. There seemed to be a hostility toward us on the part of the minister, Mr. Limantour. That hostility, however, did not appear to be shared by any of the heads of the other departments, with whom I may say we became very well acquainted during the first years of developing in Mexico.

The International Geological Congress met in Mexico in the year 1905, I think — I will not be certain about the date — and the president of the Geological Institute in Mexico City at that time was Prof. Aguilera. Prof. Aguilera had made up his mind that there was no oil to be discovered in Mexico, and was very much aggrieved to think that his predictions had been disproved by the work of a couple of American prospectors; so that during the years when we were selling as much as 1,000 barrels a day the public records in Mexico City did not show any production whatever of oil. Those records to that extent are incorrect today.

I might say here that shortly after we began, at the suggestion of President Diaz, the minister of Hacienda sent two experts to our property to investigate the oil possibilities and make a report, so that the Government would have some knowledge of the progress of our work and its possiblities. The two men sent were both well-known young geologists, one being Ezequiel Ordoñez, the other being Mr. Virreyes. Those two men made very different reports. Mr. Ordoñez made a report to the Government almost in line with our own report to our prospective stockholders made the year previously. Mr. Virreyes in his report confirmed the opinion of Mr. Aguilera that oil could not be discovered in any quantities in Mexico.

Because of his difference with the president of the Geological Institute, Ordoñez was discredited and had to leave the institution.

The moment our first big well was brought in, Mr. Aguilera and others, who seemed to be imbued with socialistic instincts, endeavored to bring about nationalization of petroleum, and in that year President Diaz was prevailed upon to appoint a committee made up of attorneys, members of the supreme court, and one or two scientists to investigate the question as to whether or not petroleum could be nationalized or included among the minerals that the Government could reserve even under the surface of privately owned lands.

Our attorney, Mr. del Rio, notified Mr. Canfield and me by wire about this, and we went down to the City of Mexico and were there during the period of the investigation, which we followed, of course, with great interest, because our right to operate these lands under the statutes depended largely upon the report made by this committee.

As the records show, when the matter had finally been argued, after several weeks of discussion and study, all of the members of the academy of jurisprudence except one voted in favor of the resolution which was made to the President that the Government had no claim whatever to the oil beneath the surface of private lands.

This report, of course, relieved us of a doubt, but only a doubt, which we had that they were not justified in obstructing our efforts to develop petroleum, and we continued with renewed energy. The condition of affairs in the United States, however, especially after the steel depression of 1903, together with the failure of the railroad company to live up to its contract with us, discouraged so many of our stockholders that they sold out. As will be observed from the prospectus which I expect to place on file, our stockholders at that time included 54 names of men who were widely known throughout the Nation as serious and successful business men.

The uses of petroleum in the United States had not at that time developed to such a great extent as they have since. The gasoline engine was not known as a very successful piece of machinery; gasoline, though not exactly as it had theretofore been, a waste product, did not command the price that it does at the present time. Fuel oil was being used on a few railroads in California and in Texas. The development of the Beaumont, Sour Lake, Saratoga, Batson Prairie, and Humble fields in Texas furnished an oversupply for that region, and the jungles of Mexico did not seem attractive to our own stockholders, much less to other oil developers, to start new companies in Mexico, so that we were practically the only company for a period of five years. I think I will increase that and say for a period of six years, except for a desultory effort made by Sir Weetman Pearson to develop a field many hundreds of miles to the south. Nevertheless, Mr. Canfield and I had such faith in the productiveness of this territory — and that fact since then has been developed that we had not found the richest spots — that we prospected north and south of Tampico, on horseback, on foot, or with railroad train, and even bought a yacht in the city of New York and took it down to Tampico on the Matanzas, a Ward Line steamer, and penetrated the numerous rivers as far as the draft of the yacht would permit.

We saw enormous oil exudes, which to us were absolutely certain indications of the existence of profitable pools of oil to be developed. We found those exudes in every instance a source of danger, not only to animals, but to human beings. They were a death trap, in which birds, reptiles, and animals had been captured from time immemorial, like the Brea beds west of Los Angeles; their victims reach back into the dim ages of the past.

Here I may say, for purposes of illumination, that west of Los Angeles, on a property of which I was a party to the development, bones were found near the surface and are still to be seen, some of them within 2 feet of the surface, which had been exhumed and assembled in the museum of Los Angeles, which showed that the tar exudes had been coming to the surface there for a period of not less than one-quarter of a million years — the complete bones of the giant sloth, the imperial elephant, the saber-tooth tiger, the camel, and many other animals, such as the original California horse, the giant bear, the giant wolf. Numbers of these animals' bones have been gathered, to the extent of not less than five or six hundred of each class, except, perhaps, the hairy elephant and the camel, of which there were less than 50 of each found.

These exudes are typical exudes in an asphalt-bearing country where geological disturbances have permitted or compelled the oil to find vent on the surface. This is true in Mexico as it was in California; and the Mexicans, like the early Californians, found these exudes, which they did not understand, a great source of danger to their stock and to their children.

They surrounded them with fences made of thorny brush or of barbed wire, if it were convenient, so as to prevent them from destroying their live stock and persons. This condition exists all through the Huasteca region of Mexico, as it does in many places in California.

The exudes have always been known to the inhabitants, even to the primitive inhabitants of ancient times, as shown by the buildings, the roofs of which have been tarred to keep out the tropical rains.

Into this country we went, talking to the inhabitants, through an interpreter, telling them of our desire to buy these places that they themselves avoided and neglected; and where we could not buy the surface we would offer sometimes to buy the subsoil rights, and in no instance did we hide from the owners the fact that we wanted to buy the subsoil rights, even though we had to buy the surface to acquire such rights. In no instance was there any deception practiced upon these people. In every instance the deeds were recorded in the public registry whenever the amount involved in the transaction was of sufficient volume to justify registration. I believe there is a sum below which they will not register a document.

Every trip we made to Mexico — and I made 65 trips during a period of 15 years, my wife accompanying me on 28 of these trips — I sought out the officials of the Government with whom we had to deal in the City of Mexico and kept them informed constantly of our progress. I was engaged very busily in denying rumors published in Mexican periodicals to the effect that we were an agent of the Standard Oil Co. or a subsidiary of that organization.

At that time the Diaz Government was very much opposed to monopolies, and Gen. Diaz asked me point blank if we were in any way connected with the Standard Oil Co. When I told him no, he asked me to promise that I would never sell out to them without first letting him know, so that the Mexican Government could have the opportunity of buying the property before allowing it to pass into the hands of a very strong foreign organization.

I have kept my promise to him and to his successors up to the present time.

The character of the country I have described in many of my reports, but I will say briefly here it was one which was enormously attractive to Mr. Canfield and myself, after we lost fear of the malaria and yellow fever which seemed so prevalent when we first went there.

Tampico at that time was a miserable little seaport, where disease of many sorts, filth and poverty, and pestilence seemed to prevail. Men that we met one day we would see carried off to a cemetery the next, having died of yellow fever. We buried 45 men from one of our own camps who died of "vomito." The dangers of the country there seemed to be more to the health of the person than in any other way.

A familiarity with the climate and the fact that we could live there without being victims of the climate and diseases that were prevalent, finally gave us a feeling of security and we ignored the climate entirely and have since found that there is no objection to the climate of the jungle country; that by proper hygienic conditions being established and careful living, life is just as comfortable there and just as secure as it is in more salubrious climates.

The people of the country, I may say, were almost as strange to us as was the climate when we first went there; and I want to say that there really ought to be a chapter recorded here on the nature of our experience with the people of that country.

Our then superintendent was a man named A. P. Maginnis, who had been a contractor and later on was the tax commissioner of the Atchison, Topeka & Santa Fe Railway Co. in California. He was a very genial, pleasant man who knew nothing at all about the technology or development of oil, but had a great heart and was a man of great fortitude. When we dropped him in the jungle at Kilometer 613, and our train pulled out for the United States and we sat on the observation end of the private car looking at him and his family whom we had left there, I think I felt almost as sorry for him as if we were marooning him in the middle of the Gulf of Mexico without any way of getting to the shore.

He showed, however, his great ability for withstanding the hardships of a pioneer life, even in that jungle country; and when we returned some weeks later he had a very comfortable house built, with cots covered with mosquito bars, so that we were protected from mosquitoes, and everything to make the place a very desirable and delightful place in which to live.

He commenced in February, and we returned again in May, just before the first well came in. We guessed about the time the first well ought to be finished, and as we have frequently done since, we hit it within two days' time.

On the trip which we made in May I had people from Pittsburgh, St. Louis, and some friends from Los Angeles, with my wife and myself; we had a large party and a very fine trip. We traveled through the jungle. We met the people that Maginnis was employing, the Mexicans being largely machete men, called peons. They used the long-bladed knife in their work, whether it was cutting brush or digging up the soil to plant, or anything else; the machete seemed to be their principal tool to work with. They had to be broken in to use a pick and shovel for excavations and railroad cuts, etc., but they were tractable, and while very awkward at doing any kind of physical labor, they soon learned and became like other laborers, very satisfactory.

When we first took this territory we found that our vendor had employed 45 or 50 men as ranch hands, principally looking after cattle. The wages were 36 cents a day, Mexican currency. The Mexican dollar at that time was worth 38 to 40 cents in American money, so that their wages varied from 12 to 15 cents a day, American currency.

On the railroads a little higher wage was paid the section hands; they got 50 cents a day, Mexican currency. We started our employees off at 60 cents a day. Mr. Maginnis, being a railroad man, was opposed to breaking the custom of paying wages; but, without any intimation from Canfield and myself, he increased the wages 10 cents a day, and when Mr. Canfield and myself arrived on the scene, I suggested to him that he pay 75 cents a day, which he did; and then a little later on we increased it to a dollar a day.

This was not done, however, without a good deal of protest on the part of the railroad company and the other employers of labor in the country, principally the haciendos (the farmers), who found that our greater rate of wage was demoralizing the labor element.

By the way, the laborers of this section were not natives of the Tierra Caliente, or jungle country, but were brought from the higher altitudes, in the Tierra Templada, or Tierra Frio, most of them coming from a town called Cerritos, on the Tampico Branch of the Mexican Central. When we first started in there, our first work was to clear away the jungle and make room for the camps. As soon as it was possible to employ skilled American men to do carpentry work, drilling, etc., they were brought from the States.

The problem which we realized we had to solve was how to accommodate the Mexican laborers to contact with the more highly skilled, high-tempered, and highly paid American laborers, and how to keep harmony between them at all times, and not make ourselves disliked in the country of the people where we had come to establish this new industry.

The CHAIRMAN. Will you please suspend a moment? This is a very interesting chapter in the history, this labor proposition. Would it inconvenience you for us to take a recess now before going any further? You are opening this labor chapter, which is very interesting and instructive.

Mr. DOHENY. I am here at your command, Mr. Chairman.

The CHAIRMAN. The committee will be in recess, then, until tomorrow morning at 11 o'clock.

Mr. DOHENY. If I am making too long and rambling a story of

this I wish you would suggest it, so I can cut it down in some way.

The CHAIRMAN. We have made up our minds in going into this to try to get for the American people a true picture of Mexico and the conditions there, and what Americans have done in Mexico, and I do not know anyone who is more capable of giving at least the latter part of it, at any rate, than yourself.

Mr. DOHENY. I thank you.

Recess

The CHAIRMAN. If you are prepared to continue your very interesting relation, we will be glad to hear you.

Mr. DOHENY. If I remember rightly, Mr. Chairman, I was relating the result of our operations down there in Mexico upon the labor conditions in that part of Mexico.

I have brought with me today some copies of the annual reports which I made to our company, the Mexican Petroleum Co. (Ltd.), for the years 1912 down to 1918, inclusive, during which years I thought it advisable to comment upon the labor conditions as well as the other conditions, so as to keep our stockholders informed as to the effect of the varying conditions there and elsewhere upon the business in which they were interested.

With your permission, a little later on I will undertake to read specific portions of those reports so that you can catch the idea that was in our minds then and now as to what our duty was and is toward the Mexican people and the Mexican Government. I will also offer, for you to place in your records if you desire, a copy of each one of those reports.

In the meantime, and as a prelude to this placing in the record of these reports made from year to year, I think it would be throwing some light upon the situation here if you knew that from the very beginning of our industry there we were deeply interested in the question of our relations to the laboring classes of Mexico.

It is needless to say that I myself was quite familiar with the fact that a great many of the people of Mexico, who worked for wages, had for a great many centuries been employed under conditions which are entirely foreign to those of our own country; and without desiring to criticise the laws and customs of Mexico, I am compelled, however, to admit that the system which obtained there was not altogether to the disadvantage of the laborer or peon; that there were many features of it which were to his advantage, and many others, again, which were abused so as to operate greatly to his disadvantage, but never, except in very rare instances, to the extent detailed by the letters of John Kenneth Turner, published in the *American Magazine,* and in which Mr. Turner picked out the very sorest spot in Mexico to describe as a sample of the conditions there. Mr. Turner's description of the conditions in Mexico, relating what he saw in the Valle Nacional, are much more exaggerated and, consequently, much more unfair, than many of the statements made in the famous book which was published before the Civil War and which had so much to do with inflaming the minds of the people of the North against the people of the South in our own country. I refer to the book of Mrs. Harriet Beecher Stowe, which has been dramatized and presented to all the people of the United States so many times under the name of "Uncle Tom's Cabin."

The people of the Southern States never had one-hundredth part as much cause to complain of the exaggerations stated in that book as have the fair-minded and well-meaning and humane haciendados of Mexico to complain of the publication to the world of the conditions in one of the sorest spots in that country as being typical of the entire conditions there.

In 1903 or 1902 — I am not certain now which year — there was held in the City of Mexico a Pan American conference at which there were in attendance a great many men from the United States and from several Central and South American States.

I happened to be in the City of Mexico at that time with friends from Pittsburgh, St. Louis, and Los Angeles, and, not wishing to intrude upon the President of Mexico at a time when there were so many other strangers there demanding his attention, I merely sent word of my presence and desire to pay my respects, through the medium of a messenger, so that I could make a record which I have kept up ever since of always having called upon the chief executive of the nation whenever I visited the capital.

Gen. Diaz, however, sent for me and the party who were with me, and when I apologized for trespassing on his time when he was so busy he said he was very pleased indeed to talk to men who came to talk about practical affairs; that he was not as much in sympathy as people might think with the discussion of affairs in a general way which led to no practical solution. He endeavored to get us to develop iron in his own State of Oaxaca, told us about the prospects he had seen in the mountains in his boyhood; told us that he desired our company to have success, for three reasons: First, because he thought that any foreigners who left their own country and went into a distant land to make investments were entitled to reward for their energy and daring; next, he was quite sure that the development of petroleum, such as we were hoping to find, would result in the saving of the forests on the mountains and cheapening the fuel to the industries, thus enabling the industries of Mexico to profit and expand because of the new supply of fuel. But, more than all else, he hoped we would be successful, he said, because he knew that in undertaking to develop a new industry of this sort we would necessarily be obliged to bring into the country skilled workmen from America, and that his acquaintance with the working conditions in the United States was such that it was his ambition to have as many of those methods translated to Mexico as possible.

He told us of his early hopes with regard to the bettering of conditions of his own people, and in the midst of his conversation about the futility of his endeavor to alleviate the working conditions of his own people he stopped, choked up with emotion, and the tears rolled down his cheeks. He begged our forbearance, and later proceeded to apologize for his emotion by saying that he never contemplated the failure of his design in bringing good conditions to the working people of Mexico without being overcome as we had seen him.

The men who were with me were hard-headed men, coal producers of Pittsburgh, iron men from Pittsburgh and St. Louis, a farmer from Nebraska, and prospectors from California. Every one of us believed, and every one of them who were with me and who are still alive, believes that Gen. Diaz's heart was as close to that of the laboring man of Mexico as any other Mexican who has ever lived there before or since.

He told us that the way to treat the Mexican peon was to treat him as a friend, not as a mercenary; that he should be made to believe that the place where he worked was his home. If a small piece of land and a house to live in could be assigned to him as his own he would be contented, but as a mercenary he did not make a good laborer.

He told us that we must be patient with the ignorance and the lack of initiative in the Mexican workman. He called our attention to the fact that they could not learn by instruction, that they must be taught by precept, by example; that they were very imitative, that anything they saw others do they could learn to do, and do well; that they would be faithful to those whom they worked for if they were treated well. He told us that his greatest desire for our prosperity in Mexico was the example which our workmen would present to the Mexican workmen of how to work, how to live, and how to progress.

We left that meeting feeling that as long as we treated the Mexican laborers well in Mexico we would have the friendship of the chief executive. This afterwards proved to be true.

At that time, as I related yesterday, our superintendent was a railroad man who was little experienced in the oil business. We had developed oil and found that our market had disappeared at the command of the chairman of the executive committee of the company with whom we had the contract. Being a prospector, and having led many a forlorn hope, I was not as discouraged as it was thought I would be, and did not desist from the endeavor to develop oil in Mexico because of the failure of a market with the natural customer with whom we had an agreement — a railroad company crossing our own property. Many of our stockholders became discouraged, however, and sold out. From being a one-eighth owner of the property in the beginning, I soon became the owner of over 40 per cent by purchasing the holdings of all those who wished to sell, and always at cost or a profit to such investors.

My associate, Mr. Canfield, was at that time not easy in a financial way, so that he could not partake to the same extent that I did in this accumulation of the stock of deceased stockholders.

Senator BRANDEGEE. What was your capital at that time?

Mr. DOHENY. At that time we had no bonds outstanding. All of our expenses were paid for in the first instance by loans which I made to the company and which at one time amounted to the sum of $652,000. These loans were repaid to me later on by assessments levied upon the stock. All of our stockholders were well-to-do or rich men; consequently, we thought it was only fair and just to ask them to contribute to the expansion of the company by practical contribution in the form of assessments. It may be that that tax upon them was the cause of many of them losing their faith in the company and being desirous of selling out.

Senator BRANDEGEE. Was your corporation organized under the laws of Mexico?

Mr. DOHENY. Our corporation was organized under the laws of the State of California.

By the way, I might interject here, if it is to the interest of the committee, that later on in my testimony, in the proper place, I would be glad to explain the system of inside financing which enabled us to develop this wonderful territory in Mexico without going to the people with either a stock issue or a bond issue that would be sold to the public.

Senator BRANDEGEE. Was your company always of the same name as it has now?

Mr. DOHENY. The Mexican Petroleum Co.: yes, sir.

Senator BRANDEGEE. What is the capital of it now?

Mr. DOHENY. The capital of the company remains the same, but we organized a new company with the same name, except that we added the word "Limited." under the laws of the State of Delaware — The Mexican Petroleum Co. (Ltd.) of Delaware. That company acquired about 99 per cent of the stock of the original company — The Mexican Petroleum Co. of California — and also all of the stock of three other companies which were organized to take over lands which we had purchased subsequently and which the stockholders of the original company did not desire to participate in.

The capitalization of the Mexican Petroleum Co. (Ltd.) of Delaware, which holds all of the stock practically of the Mexican subsidiary companies, as well as of our Mexican Petroleum Corporation, which has large distributing stations and refineries in the United States and South America, is $60,000,000.

Senator BRANDEGEE. Is that the company whose securities are listed on the exchanges?

Mr. DOHENY. That is one of the companies whose securities are listed on the exchanges.

Senator BRANDEGEE. That is the holding company?

Mr. DOHENY. Yes, sir.

Senator BRANDEGEE. The reason I ask these questions at this point is that you were saying how you acquired the stock of the others who wanted to sell out.

Mr. DOHENY. That was the stock of the first original company.

Senator BRANDEGEE. I will not pursue this inquiry now because, I assume, that later on you will probably file some statement giving a financial explanation of the affairs of the company.

Mr. DOHENY. Yes, sir; I will be glad to do so.

I might as well say, while we are dealing with that phase of the subject, that we have still another company called the Pan American Petroleum Transportation Co., which has furnished all of the ships for carrying the oil away from Mexico to distant markets, the capital of which is also quite large and whose investment indirectly in the Mexican business has been as essential to the development of the Mexican business as the investments of the Mexican Petroleum Co., which were made within the Territory of Mexico.

Senator BRANDEGEE. I think, perhaps, inasmuch as you have this all in mind in your own way, I had better let you proceed in your own way and make your general statement first and then later on, if anything occurs to me, I will ask you about it. It tends to throw you off in the continuity of your thought —

Mr. DOHENY. Just as you please, Senator. My first thought was to explain the labor situation and, probably, I have done so in a very verbose way; but I want to say that because of the discouragement of the development of oil in Mexico — oil sold as low as 3 cents a barrel at Beaumont, Tex. There was small consumption of oil, and not the many uses to which it is now put and for which it is being used in a very large way. The panic of 1893, or the depression which followed the flotation of the great United States Steel Corporation, the opposition on the part of Americans interested in selling imported oil to Mexico, the failure to be able to make earnings in substantial amount because of the abrogation of our contract, all caused the discouragement of most of our stockholders and the consolidation of the stock in the hands of a very few.

I am telling this because it is a part of the essential history of the company and shows the difficulties under which we labored.

I had a very valuable property in California, which I sold to one of the large railroad companies for a very substantial sum of money, over a million and a quarter dollars. I made up my mind that I would devote my entire time and capital to the successful development of Mexican properties, notwithstanding the discouragements. I bought for that purpose three lots in an addition to the City of Mexico and calculated on duplicating my present residence at Los Angeles in the City of Mexico, and, if necessary, making Mexico my home and becoming a resident there without, however, giving up my American citizenship.

I was so convinced of the enormous production that it was possible to develop in the Mexican fields that I felt justified in giving the personal attention which the business would require from somebody deeply interested, in order to prevent its abandonment by the stockholders.

As a first step in this campaign of development which I determined upon, I acquired the services, or at least retained the services, of the gentleman who had managed my property in California which I sold to the railroad company.

I wonder if it will be considered lengthening this testimony too much if I make a little comment upon his character and upon what his association with me really means?

The CHAIRMAN. The committee are inclined to let you just follow your own course. We think that the story that you are telling is one which is not only very interesting, but that it is necessary in order that the American people themselves should understand what Americans have done in Mexico.

Mr. DOHENY. The gentleman I referred to is Mr. Herbert G.

Wylie, who was the general manager of the Petroleum Development Co. and who had been known to me for seven or eight years and associated with me for nearly four years. I realized that to develop this property economically, advantageously and in every way successfully I must have a man with the greatest possible constructive genius, energy, and fortitude to endure all of the hardships and privations and difficulties and obstacles that were to be encountered in this far away and little frequented country. Mr. Wylie was born in Dublin, Ireland, raised in Belfast of a family of four brothers, clergymen; an uncle who was chief justice on the supreme bench of Ireland. His family was divided between Home Rule and Orangeism. His own father was a very strong opponent of Home Rule, and he himself had been the president of the Christian Endeavor Society of California, and was a very devout Presbyterian, as he still is. I was and am of Irish-Catholic origin, south of Ireland parentage, born of two rebellions; and the association between the north and south of Ireland in the Mexican Petroleum Co. has, in my opinion, produced the greatest staple producing organization in the world today.

I selected Mr. Wylie because of his known religious convictions, his great energy, his constructive genius that I had already become acquainted with through his four years of association with me and the four years of knowledge of him that I had had prior to employing him. My only fear was that because of his restless energy and dynamic force he would be too impatient and intolerant of the easygoing, awkward and, I might say without reflection, ignorant ways of the Mexican laborer. But I talked with Mr. Wylie and told him what my idea was about how these people ought to be handled, quoting as largely as I could from the language of Gen. Diaz. Without much comment he suggested to me that he thought he could handle the situation.

He went to Ebano and took charge, in October, 1902. We were employing at that time two or three thousand Mexican laborers to clear away the jungle, make roadways, build a refinery, and carry on the general operations of the field, but we increased the number largely, built fairly good houses for them to live in, gave instructions throughout the camp that any white man or any American who found that it was impossible for him to work with the Mexicans must come to the office and get his time; that we were in a country where the labor must necessarily be that of the citizens of the country; that we could not expect or hope to change their customs except as they might change them themselves, voluntarily, by the example we had set them. We must be patient with them. To my own knowledge, he rebuked and dispensed with the services of one of our most valuable foremen because he found him impatient with the Mexican labor.

I think this phase of the history of our company might probably be better described by reading clauses out of the various reports.

I have with me here the annual report of the Mexican Petroleum Co., Limited, of Delaware, and its subsidiary, the Huasteca Petroleum Co., for 1912.

Perhaps before I read from this report I ought to tell about the organization of the Huasteca company. I have not referred to that.

After Mr. Wylie had been at Ebano in charge of operations there for four or five years and had developed a large supply of very heavy oil which was proving to be a satisfactory locomotive fuel, Mr. Canfield and I made up our minds that it was worthwhile to undertake to find oil of a different character which could be devoted to more diverse uses.

With that end in view we explored the regions to the north and south of Tampico and acquired some extensive properties there, shown on the maps which are attached to these annual reports which will be submitted later on.

Some of those properties were obtained in fee simple, as were the properties of the Mexican Petroleum Co. of California. Some were obtained by cash rental. We did not succeed in getting any of them on a royalty basis. The natives who wished to dispose of the land usually wanted to sell outright for cash or else receive a specific sum in cash annually for the right to the subsoil values. When we talked about a royalty, they did not have any faith in the discovery of oil, because none had ever been discovered. The material which promised a supply of oil was always considered a nuisance and a danger, and they would rather get some certain value for it than to run the risk of getting a profit as the result of the exploitation.

We therefore organized three companies, one, the Huasteca Petroleum Co., in which we put the largest tracts which we acquired in fee simple; the Tamiahua and Tuxpam Petroleum Cos. we organized with lands which we carried under lease, some of which we have since acquired the fee simple title to.

In order to acquire this property it was necessary to have roadways and other means of transportation from the city of Tampico through the jungles to our first scene of development. It was also necessary to be able to move this production to such market as we might find after production commenced. We adopted a plan of preparedness which did not commend itself to very many of our associates. That plan was to prepare for the thing which we hoped and expected to develop — prepare for the production of oil; so that when we commenced the development in 1909 of the Huasteca properties we also commenced the building of a pipe line 70 miles long, with 10 pumping stations and facilities for the storing of oil, all at a cost of about $1,700,000. At the same time we commenced to drill the wells. The facilities were ready even before the wells came in, and many of the people who knew about the efforts which were made to be prepared for a big production were rather sarcastic in their comments that they made upon our forehandedness. Nevertheless, within a few weeks after the first well came in the pipe line was completed in time for the second well.

The first well, by the way, Casiano No. 6, we succeeded in shutting in as soon as it filled all of the storage tanks in this vicinity. The second well, Casiano No. 7, we brought in unexpectedly. The pipe not being cemented, the oil could escape from behind the pipe, and did escape through crevices in the ground, so that when the well was shut in a great spring of 3,000 barrels of oil flowed daily from the ground 200 yards away from the derrick, with the result that we had to leave the well open, with quite a flow into a reservoir and thence into a creek, and had to burn up several hundred thousand barrels in order to keep it from creating a greater devastation by flowing undirected.

This well started off with a production of about 70,000 barrels a day unrestrained and 25,000 barrels a day partially shut in, with a pressure of 285 pounds to the square inch. It came in on the 10th of September, 1910. It was 9 years old yesterday, and is flowing at the same rate that it did when it first came in. It has produced over 100,000,000 barrels of oil, all of which has been marketed and saved, except the first loss, which was occasioned by our not having the entire pipe line quite completed when it came in.

As to the other companies, we have never made much development on their properties, and they have remained as they originally were, the properties of the subsidiaries that I have named.

This report, therefore, of 1912 refers to the operations of the Huasteca Petroleum Co., which I have just described, and of the Mexican Petroleum Co. (Ltd.). I will rapidly read these parts that I have marked here for reading and then submit the report to the stenographer. This is dated April 8, 1913, and is the report for 1912:

HISTORICAL.

The companies owe their origin to the hope and belief of a very eminent railway manager and president (Mr. A. A. Robinson, of Topeka, Kans.) that, inasmuch as the discovery of fuel petroleum in substantial commerical quantities had been made by two of the organizers of your companies in the State of

California, and that successful appliances and processes had been developed for the satisfactory use of the same as railway-locomotive fuel, that there might be found somewhere adjacent to the railway lines of the Mexican Central Railway, in the Republic of Mexico, deposits of similar fuel that could be likewise used profitably by said railway company in lieu of the high-priced coal fuel then and theretofore being imported into Mexico from the United States.

Encouraged by the liberal offers of assistance from Mr. Robinson, the president and first vice president of your company journeyed to Mexico early in 1900, for the purpose of prospecting for possible petroleum-bearing lands. Being pioneer prospectors of very many years' experience, they were not long in discovering the existence of plentiful surface indications, in the form of extensive oil exudes, which identified what is now the most productive (in proportion to the developments) and famous of all the oil regions of the world.

Their first trip was made in May, A. D. 1900. On a return trip, in August of the same year, they purchased two large haciendas, which now comprise the holdings (about 450,000 acres) of the Mexican Petroleum Co., of California. Upon their return to the United States they immediately proceeded to organize said company for the purpose of developing the lands so acquired.

Immediately after the organization of the company steps were taken to have it protocolized in Mexico, so that it would be authorized to do business in that Republic. The Department of Fomento of the Republic of Mexico at that time, as ever since, was earnestly endeavoring, under the laws of Mexico, to promote the investment of domestic and foreign capital in the building up of new industries. This department is authorized and empowered by law to grant certain privileges to companies and individuals creating new industries. Under the provisions of said law your subsidiary acquired the right to import free of duty, for a period of 10 years, the materials necessary to develop the petroleum industry; also the right to immunity from all Federal taxes (except the stamp taxes) for a like period. The granting of this concession establishes the fact that the industry of producing petroleum was not then being carried on anywhere within the Republic of Mexico. Your company is, therefore, the pioneer in its line of work in that Republic.

The Mexican Petroleum Co. never asked for or obtained any other concession of any kind from the Government of Mexico. At the time that the Huasteca Petroleum Co. was organized, its lands being situated many miles south of Tampico and remote from any railway transportation, it was known to its organizers that pipe lines would be necessary for the transportation of any petroleum which might be developed, to Tampico, the natural delivery point of that region. A concession was, therefore, solicited and obtained from the Department of Fomento for the free importation of materials for the construction of such pipe lines and freedom from taxation for the customary period. Except for the concessions herein named, no concessions, special privileges, or aid have ever been solicited or received from the Government of Mexico, or any State thereof. All of the lands belonging to and controlled by your companies are either owned in fee simple, having been purchased from individual owners, or are held under lease at cash rental, under contracts with individual owners. Your companies acquired no public lands in Mexico, by concession or otherwise.

The reason for putting that in the report is the reason for now giving it to the committee, because we did not want to fall into the category of those who caused the Bolshevik tendencies today in

Mexico, notably through the writings of people who are today largely responsible for the Bolshevik conditions in Russia.

I really should not comment very much on that, because when I go into the subject I get to expressing an opinion; and if I were to express my opinion of some of those who are responsible for the bloodshed in Mexico and the bloodshed in Russia, I might possibly be subject to a charge of libel.

The CHAIRMAN. If it would not interrupt your train of thought, and if you can recur to it, you used an expression with reference to your company's preparing to do business in Mexico that is not generally understood. Of course, you and I understand it. You referred to the protocolization of your company. Americans generally do not understand what "protocolization" means. You were dealing with an American company in Mexico?

Mr. DOHENY. Yes, sir.

The CHAIRMAN. What procedure did you have to follow?

Mr. DOHENY. No foreign company can have any standing in the courts of Mexico to defend itself or to initiate litigation for the purpose of acquiring any legal protection unless it is known in the courts of Mexico; and it becomes known through a law which provides for the protocolization or the registering of foreign companies. When a company is protocolized there, as I understand it, they can protocolize themselves either as a foreign company holding all of their rights as a foreign company, or they may protocolize themselves abandoning their right to appeal to their own Government, making themselves purely a Mexican company. This was stated to us by our attorney, and we asked him to have our company protocolized as a foreign company which retained all of its rights as such to appeal to its own Government for the settlement of any dispute which was properly subject of diplomatic appeal. So that our company is registered in Mexico in such manner that it may bring suits or be sued in the courts of Mexico in the ordinary way.

The CHAIRMAN. The method used is to have the Mexican Ambassador here certify that the company is legally organized under the laws of some State of this Union. With that certificate attached to the articles of incorporation they are taken before a court of competent jurisdiction in Mexico, which court appoints as interpreter. The interpreter, after regular court proceedings, makes a translation of all the documents and the court authorizes the company to do business and issues a testimonial or a copy of the articles of incorporation in Spanish. Under the Mexican law you then become authorized to do business and have all the protection of the courts.

Mr. DOHENY. Many of the legal acts which we had to perform down there were, of course, better known to our attorneys, and I did not give much attention to it.

The CHAIRMAN. Certainly. For that reason I call attention here now to it, because the majority of the American people do not know about it.

Mr. DOHENY. But it constitutes a notice that such an organization is there. It can not do anything surreptitiously, because its purposes, its own charter, are as well known to the authorities of that country as they are to the authorities of our own country.

The CHAIRMAN. And it legalizes you absolutely to the same effect, as a matter of fact, as if you have been organized under the Mexican law.

Mr. DOHENY. The next document which I wish to submit, and from which I will read a short passage, is the annual report of the Mexican Petroleum Co. (Ltd.) of Delaware and its subsidiaries, the Huasteca Petroleum Co. and the Mexican Petroleum Co. of California, for the year 1913. Most of these reports contain a historical statement of the company for the benefit of new stockholders each year, so that much of it reads very much like that of the former year, but it also refers to developments made and contains whatever there is new that will be of interest to the older stockholders.

What I am about to read now may be of interest, because it refers to the preparations which our company made to take care of the employees in Mexico. This is on the fourth page of the report for 1913, the last paragraph, beginning:

The company began its work in a country foreign to its stockholders. The place of beginning was more than 2,500 miles from the nearest oil-well supply establishment at that time. There was not sufficient population in the immediate vicinity of its property to supply the requirements of the company, and all classes of labor, skilled and otherwise, both foreign and native, had to be brought from distant places. The first development was begun in the midst of a tropical jungle, the effect of the climate of which had to be met by the immediate installation of proper sanitary facilities for the workers. The native laborers, while working for a very low wage (36 centavos per diem), were not accustomed to the continuous application which was necessary in the opening up of an oil field. The American imported workingmen found it difficult to perform their customary duties in the much warmer climate of that region. The railroad companies had to be persuaded and educated to use the oil as fuel. The same was true of all the other Mexican industries, which have since come to depend for fuel upon the production of the oil fields. The competition of a wealthy and well-established paving corporation in the City of Mexico had to be met before a market could be found for any of the asphalt product of the company's refinery. The very limited and slowly increasing market did not seem to justify carrying on development at a very extensive rate. Nevertheless, the stockholders of the Mexican Petroleum Co. showed their faith by authorizing the immediate installment of an ice and cold-storage plant, a sawmill, a machine shop, a boiler and blacksmith shop, an electric plant, an asphaltum refinery, a cooperage plant, a large warehouse, the building of 15 kilometers of standard-gauge railway, the purchase of 2 locomotives, of 25 tank cars, the building of one-half a million barrels of steel oil storage, the building of proper housing for employees, the employment of a competent doctor, the provision of a fully equipped modern hospital, and the construction of a 6-inch water line from the Tamesi River, 14 miles distant, with necessary pumping station.

Before any other company commenced to produce oil in Mexico the Mexican Petroleum Co. had been in operation for four years, had produced and sold several million barrels of oil, had contracted to supply for a period of 15 years the Mexican Central Railway Co. with 6,000 barrels of fuel oil daily, which contract it still continues to fill, and to which it has added contracts with the National Railways of Mexico, the Interoceanic Railway, the Vera Cruz & Pacific Railway, and the Mexican Southern Railway, thus supplying with fuel oil nearly 85 per cent of the railway mileage of Mexico until May 10, 1920. The total production of the Mexican Petroleum Co. up to March 5, 1914, was 15,020,927 barrels of oil. The company now owns 450,000 acres of land in fee; its (pioneer) concession having expired four years ago, it has no concession of any kind. The titles to this land, which were purchased from individual owners, are traceable back through said owners by documents in the possession of the company to the year 1583.

Owing to the unsettled condition of the country during the year 1913 a limited amount of drilling was done on the property of this company, one well having been completed in the company's 'Chijol district' having a capacity of 1,500 barrels daily. The producing capacity of the older wells has remained unchanged during the year. However, they have not been permitted to flow to their full capacity because of the interrupted and uncertain deliveries of oil to the company's customers. As no change can be discovered in the character and quantity of the production, we feel warranted in holding the belief that the present rate of production can be continued for many years to come and can be greatly increased by drilling whenever conditions justify.

In this same report I have devoted a chapter to the disturbed governmental conditions in Mexico; and I want to say here that attached to this report is a map of that portion of Mexico on which our properties are situated, which was copied from the very best Federal map of Mexico and which contains marks indicating just what property we acquired.

This chapter begins:

It is not possible to analyze the indirect effect upon general business in Mexico – the business of foreigners in that country – the business of Americans – the Mexican oil business in general – and the business of your particular companies, without dissertating upon the vexed questions of that Republic in a manner entirely at variance with the policy of the management of your companies. Your company officials have always endeavored to hold the company in an absolutely neutral position with reference to political affairs in Mexico, discouraging all expression of opinion on the part of its employees, and at all times meeting all of its legal obligations to the de facto Government in control of the vicinity in which its business is being done.

Much has been printed, by many newspapers and other periodicals in the United States, on the one hand about the unfair exploitation of the people of Mexico by wealthy and so-called grasping corporations, owned and controlled by foreign capitalists, and on the other hand about the unjust and flagrant violation of their rights and violent interference with their liberties on the part of the different Mexican authorities toward foreign corporations and their employees. It is not our desire to animadvert upon the correctness or fairness of such publications. It is deemed advisable, however, owing to the immense amount of information and misinformation that has been given publicity with regard to Mexicans and their attitude toward foreigners, and especially Americans, to enlighten you as to the real situation anent your companies.

From our first advent into the jungle regions of the Huasteca, 30 miles west of Tampico, then a commercially unknown, though favorably situated, port on the Gulf of Mexico, your management was under the necessity of dealing with Mexican people of every degree of poverty, wealth, education, social and political standing. Your lands were purchased from landowners and prices paid therefor higher than had ever before obtained in that region. In fact, your agents found the hacendado a keen, shrewd trader, not easily hurried into concluding a bargain, who formed his conclusions as to the price he should put upon his property as much from the eagerness displayed by the would-be purchaser as from its value to himself, or the ordinary prevailing prices. Every landowner who sold us land during the early years of our operations was the envy of his neighbors, and was convinced that he had made a good bargain. Our Mexican attorneys, who were among the most prominent in the Republic, were convinced that we were paying altogether too high prices for these lands and often advised us against our seeming waste of money, because our desire to accomplish as much as possible in a short space of time frequently resulted in the price of desired lands being increased greatly by the owner, who, like our attorneys, had little faith in the ultimate success of our efforts to develop petroleum, and regarded the opportunity that offered of selling their land as being an especially fortunate epoch in their lives.

The commencement of development gave us our first introduction to the Mexican laborer, generally known as the "peon," and let me say here, in contradiction of all that has been heretofore said or may be said hereafter, that the Mexican "peon" is, and has been from the beginning, for us a most satisfactory employee. He performs his task whether in the cold, drizzly weather of the "norther" season or under the full glare of the tropical noonday sun with as much fortitude and much more good humor than the average laborer of any class known to the American employer. He prefers "piecework," called "tarea" work, to day's work, because with the former arrangement he can work at will, beginning his task before sunrise, resting during the midday heat, and completing as much as he desires to do during the cooler hours of the evening. He will work, however, at day's work, and work well, according to his knowledge and experience in the work he has to do.

Your companies have constantly employed for more than 13 years from 2,000 to 5,000 peons, provided them with food and housing for themselves and their families, thus bringing your officials into direct contact with and maintaining upon your properties from ten to fifteen thousand people. All of the centers of employment were established at places that had heretofore not been occupied. In other words, at the scene of your oil developments new towns have sprung up, five of which are now established centers of population where are to be found every convenience of the most modern farming or mining town in the United States.

At this point I would like to submit a photograph of the schools down there, and of the children coming from them. I do this in defense of our company against the possible inferences from the creditable work being done by other institutions that the oil companies are neglecting the children in their part of the country. This is a picture of the school children, and this is a picture of the schoolhouse on the Huasteca Petroleum Co.'s property. Those school children were taught by teachers who were nonsectarian, and the buildings are open to any representative of any church who may desire to come there and use it for religious purposes.

The CHAIRMAN. At whose expense was that schoolhouse built?

Mr. DOHENY. All the work done on all our properties, including that house, was done at the expense of the Huasteca Petroleum Co. and the Mexican Petroleum Co.

The CHAIRMAN. How are the schools maintained?

Mr. DOHENY. They are maintained at the expense of our company's treasury. If you desire, I would like to leave those pictures as part of my testimony.

The CHAIRMAN. They are so interesting that we will make an effort to have them put in the printed record.

Mr. DOHENY (reading):

These five places are Terminal, Ebano, Tres Hermanos, Casiano, and Cerro Azul. Telephones and electric lines, automobile roads, good brick, stone, and lumber houses for offices and dwellings, store to accommodate the needs of the population, good bathing facilities, absolute absence of any liquor-vending establishment, a schoolhouse for children, an officer to maintain peace and order, these are the things which distinguish the oil camps established by your companies in these hitherto primitive regions.

The "peons" have collected in these camps from every direction, largely from the table-lands of Mexico, although a great many of the laborers belong to the native Indian population of the Huasteca.

I want to call your attention to what I am going to read now, Mr. Chairman, because you are familiar with the western towns of the United States.

It is quite noteworthy that although the Ebano, now more than 13 years old, has had a population varying from five to ten thousand people –

In 1913 the population was from two to seven thousand people. (Continues reading:)

All of the adult males of which were constantly employed at good wages, it has never been distinguished by that first and most familiar addition to the western prairie or mountain town in the United States, a graveyard occupied by men who "died with their boots on." No Mexican, nor, for that matter, American, has ever been killed in a quarrel among our employees.

The "peon" first came to your company to take employment at 50 cents Mexican currency per day, at a time when the Mexican peso was worth 40 cents in American money. The 50 cents paid by us was a large increase over the 36 cents per day which was the going wages in that country before our advent. The labor supply not being plentiful, inducements were offered to men to come from more distant parts of the country, and the rate of wages was increased to 60 cents, then to 75, and within two years to $1 per day. The more apt laborers were, as necessity suggested, given employment that required more skill and their wages were correspondingly increased. At the present writing we are paying from $1.50 to $9 per day, Mexican currency, to Mexican workingmen of various degrees of skill and intelligence.

I may add that at the present time, in 1919, the lowest wages we pay is $2.50 per day, and we pay as high as $16 per day to Mexican workingmen. Most of the skilled workingmen have developed their skill on our own properties. (Continues reading:)

At your companies' stores, all of the employees have even been enabled to purchase such goods as are sold, at prices which did not contemplate any profit to the company.

Any profit that might be shown on the books was always credited to the stores and the prices lowered accordingly, so that our stores have been maintained at a risk of loss, and at no profit. (Continues reading:)

They are furnished with pure drinking water, plenty of ice, the care of a doctor when required, and their houses are, at the company's expense, inspected and kept in good sanitary condition.

I wish to say that we did not go any further, because we did not want to make ourselves competitors of the merchants in the country. We only wanted to supply our people with such things as they must have from day to day and could not get in the town. (Continues reading:)

To the merchants of Tampico and the surrounding country, the establishment of our industry has been a great boom. The company stores were merely supplied with such goods as it was absolutely necessary for the inhabitants of your camps to have at hand for daily consumption. The system elsewhere in vogue, of supplying practically all the needs of employees from company stores, has not been adopted by your companies. Consequently, the bimonthly payments of large sums in wages to the thousands of workingmen in your employ have necessarily increased the business of all producers, merchants, and vendors of goods and food, of whatever character, thus adding very materially to the general prosperity of that section, the industrious population of which had been and is being, as hereinbefore stated, greatly increased by the importation of Mexican and foreign employees, to carry on the business of oil development.

I might interject this statement, in proof of the last paragraph I have read, that the town of Tampico had a population estimated at about 8,000 in 1900, when we first went there. Its streets were paved with rough stones, lower in the center than at the curb, which made the center of the street the natural drainage and, I might say, sewerage of the city. The city now has a population of fifty to sixty thousand people. It has many new business blocks built by the American people. Its streets were paved by our companies with arched centers.

Before we paved the streets an American contractor took the contract and put in a good sewerage and drainage system, and a good supply of healthy water has been brought in, so that Tampico today, with fifty or sixty thousand population, is not only one of the most sanitary but is one of the busiest and has one of the happiest communities of any city in the world, not excepting the United States. And it is the only city in Mexico which today can lay claim to all the advantages that I have named, and which are directly traceable to the advent of Americans into Mexico, in a business which had never before been carried on in that Republic. (Continues reading:)

At the time that your company made its first contract with the Mexican Central Railway Co., in August, 1900, that railway company was paying $4 a ton United States currency for coal fuel delivered to it at Tampico. Later, when deliveries of fuel oil were actually begun to the railway company at 75 cents American currency per barrel, the cost of the coal which the railway company was buying, delivered at Tampico, had been reduced to $3.45 United States currency per ton, 3 1/2 barrels of oil being fully the equivalent of 1 ton of coal. All economies considered, it is easily understood how it was possible, as stated by the vice president of the Mexican Central Railway, for said company to save 50 per cent of its former fuel cost on such locomotives as were converted to use oil fuel. The labor of handling the fuel on the locomotives was also changed from the man-killing process of shoveling coal in the hot, tropical weather to merely giving proper attention to the automatic oil-burning appliances substituted therefor.

I want to say, in connection with what I have just read, that from this paragraph this conclusion is inevitable: That is, that the railway which at that time — the time of this report — was largely owned and controlled by the Mexican Government, was saving in fuel cost a larger amount of money than was actually being paid for the fuel to the oil producers. So that the profits which, as had been said, might be shown in the oil business, was at that time shared to a certain extent by the Mexican people, in better wages to the employees, a better price for goods, more profit on goods because of greater quantities sold, taxes upon the oil produced, stamp taxes upon all the books used to keep account of oil operations, and, last but not least, an amount of profit which was equal to the entire price received for their efforts by the oil companies, in the way of a saving on fuel used by a railway which was one-half owned by the

Mexican Government. It seems to me, therefore, Mr. Chairman, that the charge that the only people who derived any profit from the production of oil in Mexico must have been made by people who were not informed as to the Mexican oil situation. (Continues reading:)

You can thus realize that the pioneering begun by your company and afterwards supplemented by many other oil developers resulted in the increase of wages from 36 centavos per day to an average of more than 200 centavos per day and the establishment of better living conditions and increased opportunities for employment to all the laboring people in that part of Mexico.

It increased the market value of his land to every landowner of the Huasteca region to whose property even a suspicion of oil value attached from the nominal price of 1 peso per hectara for unimproved, and 10 to 15 pesos per hectara for improved farming land, to the extravagant prices which are now being obtained by many landowners for lands that it is deemed advisable to exploit for oil production or oil-stock selling.

It reduced the cost of fuel in the railways and all industries that were so situated that they could take advantage of the substitution of oil for coal fuel, an amount greater than the total amount received by the oil producers for the oil thus consumed in Mexico.

In brief, your company discovered the basis for, and pioneered the development of, a hitherto unsuspected resource in the Republic of Mexico, which increased wages and brought about better conditions of living for all the poor people, which increased the land values for all the landowners, which gave increased business to all the farmers, merchants, bankers and artisans, which reduced the cost of operation to the railways and other industries, all without taking away from any individual, municipality or political division of Mexico, anything the existence of which had theretofore been known or even suspected. We, therefore, claim that those who, even in their minds, include the petroleum companies among the corporations that have exploited the people of Mexico or their country disadvantageously, are misinformed, or have not given proper consideration to the true history of petroleum developments in Mexico.

Your company, and so far as your officers know, all petroleum companies in Mexico have been a blessing to the communities in which they have operated. They deserve the respect and protection of the Government of Mexico and of the United States. They deserve the good feeling and friendship of all the people of Mexico, and particularly of those residing at and near Tampico, who have been more directly benefited as before related. They deserve commendation of all people everywhere, because of their confidence in nature's resources which gave them courage to undertake developments in a new region of hitherto unsuspected wealth, the first step in the carrying out of which necessitated the establishment of modern villages, and the bringing of opportunity for honest employment at good wages, and the necessary education and enlightenment which accompanies such employment, to a multitude of human beings not formerly so fortunate.

Notwithstanding much that has been reported which might suggest the contrary, we believe that the feelings of the Mexican people of our vicinity toward our companies have largely been influenced by the above-mentioned considerations. As to their attitude, we have this to record: That during more than three years of internecine strife, carried on in a country rough and wild in its character, sparsely populated, with few railroads and few wagon roads, where none were anxious openly to declare allegiance to either contending party, where more or less disorganized bodies of armed men roamed at will, privileged to commit depredations upon those who were suspected of opposing the party to whom they professed allegiance, no attack was ever made upon your employees or your companies' oil camps.

Frequently armed bodies of men invaded your camps, demanding food and money, and taking such arms as they could find, and live stock as they required. Their demeanor toward the camp superintendents was invariably courteous, and no malicious destruction of property was ever indulged in. Even at the time in the latter part of April and during the first half of the month of May of the present year, when the feeling against Americans ran very high in all parts of Mexico, and especially near Tampico and in the State of Vera Cruz, when it was deemed necessary that all Americans should withdraw from that part of Mexico, which they did, and left the property of oil companies of great value scattered throughout a wide region entirely at the mercy of a people with whom it seemed probable our people might soon be at war, the natural fidelity of the Mexican employee and his friendliness toward your company, which had been a friend to him, was amply demonstrated by the care with which he conserved the property left in his charge. Except for the appropriation of horses, mules, automobiles, auto trucks, cattle, etc., as necessary war measures by both armies, no damage was done or permitted to be done to any of your company's properties. The provisions of every sort — store supplies, small hardware supplies, and many other valuable and easily removable articles — were entirely unmolested.

No act of vandalism was perpetrated against the oil reservoirs, pipe lines, pumping machinery, or refineries. The product of your continuously flowing wells was so faithfully conserved by the Mexican employees in charge that your general manager was able to report that not more than 5,000 barrels of oil were lost during the 30 days' absence of your American employees from the properties.

Upon their return to the property, they were welcomed by the Mexicans in charge as returning friends, not as whilom enemies. The business of the company was resumed as before the hegira of the Americans, and your company's officers recognize that the company and its stockholders owe a debt of gratitude to these particular individual employees, and that the Mexican working people are entitled to more respect and confidence than had theretofore been positively known.

This rather unusual accompaniment to the annual report of a corporation is submitted to you for the purpose of convincing you that the basis of your company's business in Mexico is not such as to class it among the so-called predatory corporations that exploit a people and a country and derive sustenance and profit by sapping the life blood of the country and unjustly withholding the profits due to labor. Neither is it so regarded by the great mass of the people of its acquaintance in Mexico.

It thrives on no special concessions; its lands were all purchased outright, at higher than going prices; the labor and material it uses are paid for with honest money; the result of its development have been beneficial to all affected; the profits which it made were more largely shared by the Government-owned railways of Mexico than by ourselves, the stockholders; the millions of dollars expended for all purposes have by no means all been recovered in the form of dividends. The principal part of your great investment is represented by the lands honestly acquired, which have great value, and by the developments judiciously made, which have produced gratifying results.

I want to submit this for your files, if you care to use it, Mr. Chairman.

The CHAIRMAN. It will be filed.

Mr. DOHENY. Each of these reports contains something worthwhile reading, it seems to me, to throw some light on the subject, but this one, I assure you, is the longest one, and you will not be tired by the sound of my voice in connection with the other reports, as in connection with the one just submitted. These others contain more pictures and fewer words, and probably will be more interesting and instructive.

I want to read from page 41 of the annual report for 1914 of the Mexican Petroleum Co. (Ltd.), of Delaware. I copied in this report a part of the last report, because I thought there were so many new stockholders of the company that they might be interested in knowing what we had to say the year before, which still applied to the present situation for the current year. So what I first read will be with reference to this excerpt from the last report.

The above excerpt is quoted from the report of last year, because the facts and opinions therein expressed have not in any way changed.

During the past 12 months of continual struggle between warring parties in Mexico, each endeavoring to obtain ascendancy over the other and establish a Government with officials of its own choosing, large bodies of armed men have moved back and forth over great areas of the country foraging upon the towns and farms, bringing about much destruction of property and causing a state of fear and unrest to pervade communities everywhere, with the result that business of nearly every kind has largely stagnated, but more especially the business of producing foodstuffs.

The region where your properties are situated is the latest to become the scene of struggle for possession on the part of the warring parties. Immediately after the taking of Tampico from the Huertistas by the Constitutionalists, in May, 1914, an era of peace and progress began in the Huasteca region. Your companies, and many other oil companies, resumed work of development, which gave employment at good pay to all who desired work. The schism in the ranks of the Constitutionalists later on did not immediately affect conditions in the Huasteca oil region.

I might say the schism I referred to is that resulting from the disagreement between Villa and Carranza. (Continues reading:)

Toward the latter part of 1914, however, the railroads of Mexico having largely fallen into the hands of the particular division not in possession of the oil regions, an effort was made by them to drive their adversaries away from the only available native sources of supply of locomotive fuel. This caused the coal fields north of Monterey and your oil district at Ebano to become the scenes of many sanguinary conflicts. The party that held the town of Ebano nearly all of last year is still in possession of that place, but besieged by a large army of the opposing force.

I want to say that the town of Ebano and the oil camp were besieged for four months by Tomas Urbino, with about 14,000 Villa troops, and it was held in opposition to him by Jacinto Treviño, a Carranza general with about 6,000 troops. As a result of the siege of Ebano hundreds of cannon shots penetrated our different steel reservoirs, making holes from 4 inches to 8 inches in diameter, through which the oil escaped. Our pipe lines were broken, the smokestacks shot away from all our refineries, our office buildings partially destroyed with cannon shots, hundreds of thousands, probably millions of pockmarks on the steel tanks where rifle bullets struck them without penetrating, and about 800,000 barrels of oil destroyed, showing that the siege was not merely an attempt to starve out, but an actual attempt to capture the town, which was favorably situated for defense, and which was surrounded with trenches in every direction occupied by the attacking force, at a time, I think, prior to the making of any trenches of the European war; at any rate, contemporaneous with that time. (Continues reading:)

As a result of the war in the neighborhood of Tampico, food supplies have been cut off and the quantity on hand either commandeered for military uses or almost entirely consumed. There was little or none for sale in the market places. A large number of the poorer people in Tampico were facing starvation. Upon being notified by your terminal superintendent of these conditions, your management immediately authorized the purchase in Texas of quantities of rice, corn, beans, and flour, their transportation to Tampico and distribution among the people, thus relieving the situation. At the present writing there is no actual want in that city, although conditions farther south in some of the interior towns are pitiable and fast becoming alarming, ordinary articles of food, such as flour, rice, corn, beans, etc., being entirely exhausted.

This account of the conditions, and the action taken by your officials, is given here so that you may appreciate the fact that the Mexican Petroleum Co. and its subsidiaries are known in Mexico as the friends of the people and the supporters of no faction.

In conclusion we feel rather grateful to say that, notwithstanding the four years of changing governmental conditions in Mexico, no great direct loss or injury has been suffered by your companies because of the struggle for supremacy between the opposing parties in that Republic. The indirect loss, because of the interruption to business, was necessarily very great. The direct losses, while considerable, were entirely incident to war conditions and were not the result of malice or desire on the part of any of the warring parties to injure your properties. The interruption to your business, due to the great and deplorable conflict in Europe, have also caused substantial indirect losses.

I would like to submit this copy of this report of 1914.

The CHAIRMAN. It will be filed.

Mr. DOHENY. This accumulation of evidence is offered just for the purpose of showing the attitude of foreign corporations, and I think I am justified in saying that every other company down there has assumed the same attitude; that there has been no effort made to favor any faction, and while the individual employees, both Mexican and American, may have had their own likes or dislikes, or their own opinion as to who ought to succeed, it has never been allowed to influence our companies or, I am quite sure, any other company operating in the Huasteca region.

I am going to read an extract from our annual report for 1915, on page 11. This is going to carry you back to a time which precedes the organization of our companies. I quote in this report a letter which I tried to find, and telegraphed to New York yesterday for it and was unable to get it, that I wrote to Mr. R. C. Kerens, of St. Louis, who has since deceased, but was formerly United States ambassador to Austria. This letter shows what we thought about the country in 1900, when few people knew anything about it, and fewer had any faith in the success of our enterprise down there. I quote from my letter to Mr. Kerens:

The geological construction of the country we found to be somewhat similar to the eastern portion of the Joaquin Valley in California – the sedimentary rocks being still practically horizontal – the disturbances, therefore, being very few and not very extensive.

In that particular I want to acknowledge that I was wrong.

The oil exudes of that region are to be found in the locality of these disturbances and are of the most promising character. The place visited in June, near Chijol, about 3 1/2 miles from the Mexican Central Railway, was such as to enthuse us very much as to the prospect of developing oil there in large quantities and suitable for fuel purposes. A visit to a point called Cerro de la Pez, about 3 miles from the Mexican Central Railway, on the south side of said railway, not only confirmed the opinion which we formed at our first visit but satisfied us beyond all doubt of the existence of a very extensive region which is underlaid with a rich deposit of oil-bearing sand, the oil from which makes its appearance on the surface at such points as the disturbances in the overlying rocks will admit of.

At the particular point above referred to we found a conical-shaped hill, the apex of which was composed of a dark, crystalline rock of igneous origin, which had undoubtedly been forced up through the sedimentary strata. From the rocks so disrupted the oil had exuded and flowed down the hillside into the valley, forming great beds of asphaltum by passing off of the volatile parts thereof. At various points around the base of the hill the gas and oil could still be seen issuing from the ground; and at one point a great pool of oil had accumulated in a depression immediately overlying the point of exude, and the gas rising through the oil kept it in a constantly boiling condition, the bubbles and froth formed by the escaping gas covering the surface of the oil. Mr. Canfield ran a pole down into it to a depth of 10 feet or more and "swished" it around, demonstrating that there was quite a pool of oil of excellent quality for fuel purposes. The nature of this exude would indicate that the quantity of oil was not only considerable, but that the gas pressure would be great enough to insure wells of large daily production, and probably sufficiently light in quality to be more valuable for other purposes than for fuel.

We visited other oil exudes on the same rancho, and examined in many places the rock exposures, and satisfied ourselves fully that the existence of these asphaltum deposits at such points as the oil prospector would naturally expect to find them, taking into consideration the stratigraphy of the country rocks, their frequent occurrence over such a large area, and their similarity in every respect to the very best and richest exudes to be found in California, justifies the belief that we have obtained possession of a vast field of liquid fuel, which may possibly prove to be more valuable as a refining oil.

Without wishing to make it appear that we are extravagant in our ideas, we do not feel at all timid in saying that the Mexican lands which we have acquired have all the earmarks of containing within their limits oil territory equal in oil value per acre and many times greater in extent than the Bakersfield district in California.

This letter was written in September, 1900, and before the organization of the Mexican Petroleum Co.

In February of the following year — 1901 — the Mexican Petroleum Co. (California) having been organized, the first work of development was undertaken at a point on that company's property, now known as "Ebano," then merely a kilometer post on the Tampico branch of the Mexican Central Railway, 35 miles west of Tampico, in the midst of a tropical jungle, and likewise well within the boundaries of a 400,000-acre tract belonging to the Mexcian Petroleum Co. in fee and fully paid for.

With supreme faith in the accuracy of their judgment, the managers of the Mexican Petroleum Co. procured the building of a railway siding and the establishment of a station, which they named "Ebano."

Ebano has the distinction of being the first oil camp established in the Republic of Mexico. Its founders were ardent believers in "preparedness." Not without misgivings on the part of some stockholders and directors who invested in this enterprise because of their faith in its originators, the camp at Ebano was early provided with facilities which are usually considered as justifiable only where a permanent industry is to be established. An ice and cold-storage plant to provide pure distilled water and proper refrigeration for meats, etc.; an electric-light plant to furnish light which would not menace the safety of the camp from possible gas development; a sawmill and carpenter shop to facilitate the construction of proper housing for men and supplies; an up-to-date machine shop, blacksmith shop, and oil-supply warehouse all followed each other in quick succession as important adjuncts of the new camp.

I might read more from that on that same subject of preparedness, and if it suits the chairman I can do so.

The CHAIRMAN. Just suit yourself.

Mr. DOHENY (reading):

Within a month after the first drilling rig was completed the prophecy of satisfactory oil development was fulfilled by the bringing in, at a depth of 525 feet, of a well which yielded 50 barrels of oil daily.

Disappointed in finding a market with an expected customer – located in a country where oil as a fuel substitute for coal was entirely unknown – with a product so heavy that it offered little inducement to refine it for illuminating or lubricating oils, the prospects of profiting by the discovery thus made seemed so remote that the holders of a large proportion of the stock of your oldest company withdrew their support and disposed of their interests.

The certainty, however, of eventually developing a sufficient market to justify the enterprise was so great in the minds of a few of the stockholders that the work of development was continued and an efficient operating organization provided.

For five years the annual reports to the stockholders were most monotonously similar in their recital of substantial sums expended with encouraging results, so far as production was concerned, but with practically no sales and no net earnings.

I might say that continued for nearly five years more, so that those who think the American oil developers who went into Mexico found a bonanza at hand by means of which they immediately became rich need to study the history of the first 10 years of occupation of the oil territory by Americans.

Eventually a contract was made with the Mexican Central Railway Co. to supply its locomotives with fuel oil for a period of 15 years. Eleven years of that contract have expired and neither the railway company nor the Mexican Petroleum Co. have defaulted in their compliance with its terms, except as prevented by "Fuerza mayor." Sixteen million barrels of oil have been delivered and consumed in its fulfillment. Its operation furnished nearly the whole basis for many very satisfactory annual reports.

Six years after the establishment of Ebano, and still before the advent of any other oil companies in that part of Mexico, the wonderfully rich lands – now owned and controlled by the Huasteca Petroleum Co. and its subsidiaries, the Tuxpam Petroleum Co. and the Tamiahua Petroleum Co. – were acquired by the founders of the Mexican Petroleum Co. (California).

Six years of experience in Mexico in developing and supplying a market for petroleum and its products had forewarned your associates against the errors which many others have later committed. Having visited the scene of the abandoned efforts of the late Cecil Rhodes and other British financiers to discover petroleum under the guidance of the most prominent and widely known English "oil geologists," and having purchased, or acquired under terms of cash rentals, these supposed "oil lands" from native owners, who were skeptical of their oil value and unwilling to lease them on a royalty basis, but willing and anxious to sell for cash, your associates then determined to carry out their policy of "preparedness," which was to be rewarded so satisfactorily after the five years of persistent application, without return, on your Ebano property.

I might say here, to throw a little light on the history of oil development in Mexico, that many years before we undertook to prospect Cecil Rhodes, the great explorer of South Africa, had his attention called to the possibilities of Mexico. A company was organized, called the London Oil Trust, through the efforts of a man named Burke, who was an associate of Rhodes, and operated under the direction of the late Sir Boverton Redwood, who died last year, a most eminent oil geologist. They expended over 90,000 pounds without any results, and abandoned their efforts.

We now have on one of the properties which they acquired, but a short distance remote from their attempted development, developed the greatest oil well the world has ever known and probably ever will know — Cerro Azul No. 4 — which yields the measured production of 261,000 barrels per day.

In 1909 the machinery for drilling several wells, the pipe for building 70 miles of 8-inch pipe line, 10 mammoth oil pumps for the establishment of five pumping stations, 70 miles of right of way, and hundreds of acres of land for storage tanks, and twelve 55,000-barrel steel tanks to complete the first unit of development were all planned for, purchased, acquired, and constructed in anticipation of the oil development which followed.

These acts of "preparedness," at a cost of nearly $2,000,000 (American gold), were not fully completed when the first great gusher at Casiano was "brought in." The second gusher followed close upon the first, being completed on the 11th day of September, 1910.

I see I was mistaken, Mr. Chairman, in my statement a while ago. It is nine years old today.

The storage tanks at Casiano had been filled by the first gusher. The pipeline to Tampico, 70 miles distant, was not yet quite completed. A delay in acquiring a right of way left a gap of 12 kilometers in the line, when Casiano No. 7 commenced to belch forth oil at the rate of over 60,000 barrels per day. The unexpected bringing in of this gusher made it impossible to complete control of the well. When shut in to about 285 pounds pressure per square inch it yielded oil at about 25,000 barrels per day. When completely shut in the oil flowed to waste through numerous crevices and around the outside of the casing. As a result the right of way was quickly obtained and the 12 kilometers (about 7 miles) of the gap in the pipe line were completed in less than a week.

It required nearly 18 months' time to purchase the right of way, acquire and lay the pipe line, and construct the pumping stations. If preparation to store and transport the oil had not been begun until after Casiano No. 7 was brought in, your company would have lost oil at the rate of 750,000 barrels per month during all of the time that was required to build sufficient storage and a pipe line to care for it.

The annual report for that year should have brought much satisfaction and consolation to the stockholders of the Mexican Petroleum Co. (Ltd.), which had already been organized two years. It contained so much of mere promise, however, and such a long recital of expenditures and debts incurred, and so little in the way of net earnings, except such as consisted of oil placed in storage, for which there seemed, to them, no adequate market, that one of your oldest officers and directors (whose faith in the enterprise, by the way, is evidenced by the fact that he has increased his holdings of stock and securities every year during the 16 years of its existence), stated in a semijocular tone, "If our prosperity were much greater, it would bankrupt us."

That was after we had been 10 years in Mexico. We had made such immense sums of money by robbing the Mexican people that one of our stockholders, a man 80 years of age, said if we had a little more prosperity we would go bankrupt.

As in the years from 1901 to 1905 with the Mexican Petroleum Co. (California) when its wells were capable of producing many thousands of barrels of oil daily and no market was available, and the company was financially unable to build adequate storage, so the Huasteca Petroleum Co. seemed to be confronted with a similar situation, except that it was financially able to and did provide standard steel and concrete storage to the amount of over 10,000,000 barrels capacity.

Nevertheless, the advantage of a substantial and adequate market appealed to your management, with the result that two substantial contracts were quickly entered into, which extended over a period of five years each. The earlier contract has already been completely filled. The second and larger contract for 10,000,000 barrels will be completed in August of this year. It is obvious that these deliveries were necessarily made at the end of the company's pipe line in Tampico Harbor.

A campaign was immediately entered into for the sale of larger quantities of oil for fuel and other uses locally in Mexico. The possibilities of such a market were soon largely exploited with satisfactory, though necessarily limited results. The great need of your company at that time was an unlimited market, which could only be reached with marine transportation facilities. Unremitting and unsuccessful efforts were made to acquire tank vessels by charter. Without depending, however, solely upon the chartering of vessels from strangers, your associates formed a company to contract for the building of necessary tank steamers for the purpose of placing the same at the service of the Huasteca Petroleum Co. A fleet of six steamers was contracted to be built in England. The first of the fleet, *S.S. Herbert G. Wylie*, was received in February, 1913, and the remaining five by due course of contract.

I think, Mr. Chairman, that unless you desire me to read further I will submit this annual report for 1915 for such purpose as you desire.

The CHAIRMAN. It will be filed.

Mr. DOHENY. I merely desire to comment on this by saying that not only had no American oil company, except our own, paid a dividend on its stock, but that all of the investments made in Mexico which resulted in the discovery of oil would have been absolutely useless except for the enormous investments made outside of Mexico. So that brings me to the point of calling your attention to one of the great errors made by Mexicans and Americans as to the value of Mexican oil. It is not exactly a parallel illustration, but I am going to use it, nevertheless, by saying that the value of oil underground, that is not known or demonstrated to exist, is measured by the oval circle. When it is brought to the surface it then bears the same relation to its value at a market that any other substance does.

And I want to state that there are oil wells in Mexico today that, if their valves were opened, would produce a large amount of oil, but the owners have no pipe lines, no harbor facilities, no tank steamers with which to carry it to market, and consequently the oil has very much the same value, so far as the present time is concerned, as ice has in the continent of Greenland. If it could be transported to New York or Washington these warm days it would undoubtedly find a ready market and be very valuable, but nobody would pay a very high price for it in its present location. That is true of the oil underground in Mexico, even where wells have tapped it and it is available. So that the taxes, such as Mexico has placed today upon oil, should be compared with its value at the derrick, not at New York City, where American capital has expended millions upon millions of dollars in building refineries and storage facilities and tank steamers for transporting it. The taxation today levied by Mexico on oil products runs from a minimum of 20 per cent to over 50 per cent of the value at the well. That can easily be demonstrated by figures, and if your committee is interested in that phase of the dispute between the oil companies and the United States Government on the one hand and the Mexican Government on the other, we will be glad to submit a table illustrating our ideas of what the values are in Mexico, and what percentage of that value we are paying in the way of taxes to the Mexican Government.

The CHAIRMAN. We will be glad to have the table submitted. The Treasury Department of the United States has requested the committee to furnish it with eight copies of the hearings of this committee, as the hearings proceed.

Mr. DOHENY. I read briefly from the Annual Report of 1916, a marked paragraph, on an unnumbered page, but it is the next page to the last:

During the month of November, 1916, the president of your company, accompanied by several of the officers and some stockholders, with their wives, visited Tampico by sea and went to the various parts of your properties, including Ebano, 38 miles west of Tampico, and Casiano and Cerro Azul, 90 miles to the south. The traveling to the interior was done without arms, without a guard, wholly unprotected, and with no expectation of other than the very best of treatment from the people who might be encountered, in which we were not disappointed. Another trip of inspection was made during the month of March, 1917, covering the same ground. The party, 15 in number, included the president, two vice presidents, and several large stockholders of your company, also representatives of several influential New York financial houses and journals and some California oil men not interested in your stock. As to the physical condition of the property, the "esprit" and optimism of the local management, the demeanor and attitude of the people of the country, and the prosperous and active appearance of the vicinity and business generally, and especially that of your companies, all the visitors expressed themselves in the most enthusiastic language.

There is a particular reason for reading that one paragraph. The report has much in it that may be of interest, and if you desire I will file it. The reason I have read the one paragraph is because I wanted to call attention to something which most people up here in the United States, and even most Mexicans, do not seem to understand, and that is that there is an immense amount of risk attached in going to any part of Mexico by rail. Consequently my voyage with my wife and friends and their wives was made by water from Galveston to Tampico. After we reached Tampico and were in the vicinity of the oil camps we thought it was safe to go through the oil region with our people. That was a little over two years ago. So that the security with which Americans prospected and traveled, both for pleasure and for business, all over Mexico 20 or 30 years ago and up to 10 years ago was narrowed down to a much smaller region as soon as political troubles commenced, and that, of course, in my opinion, was very natural. The district in which it was safe to go has since narrowed, until today it is deemed unsafe to even go in the places where we thought it was safe two years ago.

So that security for travelers in Mexico has not increased with the quietness that is said to prevail down there.

The best evidence of that is that people wishing to go to those regions are afraid to go by rail, and no trains are running from Monterey to Tampico. At least so I am informed by Mexican gentlemen who arrived in New York from Mexico a few days ago. One of those gentlemen said that if I wished to send somebody to Tampico the route by way of Victoria would be unsafe; it would be necessary to go from Monterey to Saltillo and San Luis Potosi, and then back to Tampico, a detour of some 300 miles. That is in the State of which Gov. Osuna is at the present time governor. It is a border State, adjoining the Rio Grande and the Gulf of Mexico, and has for its largest city and southern terminus the port at Tampico, where all of the oil companies, or nearly all of the oil companies, have their offices, receive their supplies, and ship much of their oil; but, nevertheless, the road through that State, governed by the appointee of Gen. Carranza, is considered unsafe — in fact one of the most unsafe in Mexico.

I am merely calling attention to the facts in reference to this, just as they exist today.

I will read a little from a report of 1917, the annual report for 1917. I wish you would bear in mind, Mr. Chairman, that these reports were all issued fairly late in the year following that which they bear date of. (Reading from Annual Report of 1917:)

As with all other large business concerns of this country, the past year has been an epochal one with your companies. It was expected, and logically so, in the early part of 1917 that the gross business and earnings of your companies would be greatly increased during the current year. Preparation had been made to increase largely, in fact to more than double the amount of tonnage which would be used to move oil from your company's terminals at Tampico to the market. In no spirit of criticism nor complaint, it is necessary to inform you that in this respect you were doomed to meet with disappointment. The menace of war, which made itself known in the spring of 1917, brought with it, to your management, a realization of the necessity of a greatly increased supply of petroleum to meet the coming war needs. They realized also that it is the patriotic obligation of every American citizen and business concern to do the utmost to strengthen the hands of the Government whenever the need might arise. With a desire to do our part, your management wired to the President of the United States an offer of all of the facilities of your companies, to be used for such purposes as he might deem necessary.

In the month of June, when your company had nine steamships of 60,450 tons, one having already been commandeered by the British Government, six of the remainder were volunteered at the request of the Navy Department, and were placed in the service of the United States Government to carry petroleum products transatlantic. As new steamships which had already been ordered built for your company's service were completed, additional takings were made by the Government, with the result that 65,000 tons of shipping provided for moving oil for your company from Mexico, to its customers, were used to carry petroleum products of other companies from north United States Atlantic ports to the war zone, for the use of the various allied armies.

You were told on page 27 of the report of 1915 that "anticipating the delivery of these steamers, your management made contracts for the sale of crude and fuel oil to responsible customers . . . equal to the total deliveries possible with the tank steamers on hand and to be received from builders."

The volunteering of a large part of your fleet, the requisitioning of others of your tank steamers, and the delays which occurred in the construction of the remainder, limited your company to supplying only the customers to whom they were bound on time contracts at former prevailing prices, and of foregoing the sale of any oil at the better prices which the greatly increased demand stimulated. A calculation was carefully made of the loss of earnings to your company, by reason of the diversion of some steamships and the failure to get others. That amount, conservatively determined, is in excess of $6,000,000 for the last six months of last year.

We figure it out for the period of the war at a little over $17,000,000. (Reading further from the report:)

You may have the consolation of knowing that in so far as your investment in this company is concerned, you have made the supreme investment sacrifice of risking the very existence of the ships, without which your business could not be carried on, and of sacrificing all of the earnings and profits which it was planned the ships should produce for your company during the remainder of last year, after they went into the Government trans-Atlantic service, and for such period in this year as they will continue in such service. Inasmuch as the average price of the contracts which we are legally and morally bound to fulfill with the use of the steamships that remain in your possession, is very much below the price which now obtains for like products in similar markets, your sacrifice is much more than what might be calculated by considering the percentage of your ships which has been employed exclusively in war service, moving none of your products.

In this great emergency, when the struggle, not only for national existence but for civilization itself, is being carried on against a most ruthless and powerful foe, no citizen or business concern does its full duty unless it does all that it is possible for it to do. The consciousness that your companies have not been backward in this respect should bring to you great satisfaction.

I think that brought many a peculiar smile on the faces of our stockholders, who looked to the profits of this company to meet the higher cost of living brought on by the war. (Reading further:)

The production and the sales of oil from your properties in the past year were nearly identical, the increase of oil in storage during the year being limited by the storage capacity, which was already nearly full at the end of 1916.

It is desired to call your attention to the following: That the total number of barrels disposed of during the year was 17,587,128; that the price received therefor was $17,457,292.49, an average price of 99 1/4 cents per barrel. In former years the average price received per barrel was much less than shown for this year, being 85 cents in 1916, 67 cents in 1915, 64 cents in 1914, and 58 cents in 1913.

The greater price received this year was not due, however, to any increased price for the oil at the point of production in Mexico. There were very many more productive wells in existence in Mexico during 1917 than during any prior period, and the proportion which the potential capacity of the wells bore to the transportation facilities was much greater than formerly, and consequently, although no regular market price exists for oil at the well in Mexico, it is a fact, nevertheless, that purchases could have been made at as low a price per barrel as during former years. The increased average price received by us was due largely to an increase in the proportion which was refined and which was delivered at distant points, the selling price of which was increased by the cost of refining and transportation. Six million eight hundred six thousand and forty-seven barrels of crude and fuel oil were sold f.o.b. Tampico at an average of 53 1/3 cents per barrel, while 46,134,430 gallons of crude gasoline, produced at the Topping plant at Tampico, sold at approximately 11 cents per gallon, and 9,682,174 barrels of crude oil were sold and delivered at various foreign ports at 91 cents per barrel.

From the above it will be seen that the average selling price of oil at Tampico, whether fuel or crude, has not varied greatly over the last three years, the variation being due entirely to the fluctuating cost of transportation.

During the past year, your affairs having reached stage where the expenditure of funds for betterments justified it, your directors declared dividends on your common stock for the last two quarters, which amounted to $1,180,263, the rate being $1.50 per share, the equivalent of 6 per cent per annum. The above dividend, added to the preferred-stock dividend of $960,000, makes the sum of $2,140,263 disbursed for 1917.

And I want to say that that is the first dividend paid on our common stock for six years — that dividend for the first half of the year 1917. With your permission, I will submit this also to be filed.

The CHAIRMAN. You may file that.

Mr. DOHENY. Just a few words from this report of 1918, which will bring another phase of the whole Mexican situation before your committee, and it comes in the form of comments upon the exhibits which are connected with the report.

The CHAIRMAN. Suppose we take a short recess here, if you are going to another phase of the subject. The committee will be in recess until 2:15 o'clock.

(Thereupon, at 1 o'clock, the committee took a recess until 2:15 p.m.)

AFTERNOON SESSION.

The committee met at 2:15 o'clock p.m., pursuant to the taking of recess, Senator Fall presiding.

The CHAIRMAN. Mr. Doheny, whenever you are ready we will proceed.

STATEMENT OF EDWARD L. DOHENY — Continued.

Mr. DOHENY. Mr. Chairman, I have still one annual report that I have not filed, and I will say a few words in explanation of it and submit it, as I have the others, as a part of the evidence which we have to offer as to what the conditions are in Mexico.

It seems to me that there can be no better evidence of the dual nature of the oil business, or of any other business carried on by Americans in Mexico, than an explanation of the relative contribution of foreign and of Mexican labor and capital to the production of the materials produced and sold and the proportion of which goes to the benefit of Mexico and the proportion which goes to the benefit of foreigners, and the percentage which each proportion bears to the contribution from each source. This is the annual report of the Mexican Petroleum Co. (Ltd.) for the year 1918, just sent out to the stockholders of that company. It reads as follows:

The consolidated statement and report submitted herewith includes the seventeenth annual statement of the Mexican Petroleum Co. (California), the eleventh annual report of the Huasteca Petroleum Co., the fourth annual report of the Mexican Petroleum Corporation, the first annual report of the Mexican Petroleum Corporation of Louisiana (Inc.), and is the eleventh annual report of your company, which owns 90 per cent of the stock of the Mexican Petroleum Co. (California), and all of the stock of each of the other subsidiaries.

During the year 1917, for reasons set forth in the last annual report, the volume of your company's business was far below normal expectations. The causes which prevented the natural expansion of the business during 1917 obtained to a large extent during 1918. The putting in commission last year of a part of the new fleet of steamers which had been provided, resulted, however, in a noticeable increase in the volume of business over that of the previous year.

Attached hereto will be found a consolidated balance sheet and a consolidated profit and loss account for the year 1918. A study of the exhibits and comparison with 1917 will show that:

Oil inventories are valued at cost instead of at average contract selling values as heretofore.

Mexican taxes paid in 1918 are more than double the amount paid in 1917.

We make no complaint about this increase in taxation, but we want to call your attention to the fact that we shipped 16,700,000 barrels in 1917 and 18,500,000 barrels in 1918, or an increase of 11 per cent. But the taxes were more than doubled.

The amount set aside for income and war taxes increased nearly 800 per cent over 1917.

Taxes paid, plus the amount set aside for completion of tax payments, amount to 60 per cent of the net profits and over 26 per cent of the gross income.

Profits, before deducting war taxes, are more than double the profits for 1917.

Dividends paid during 1918 were $4,128,008, as compared with $2,140,263 paid in 1917.

That is not on account of any increase in the value of the oil at the well in Mexico, because the value of the oil at the well in Mexico had not increased during that period, but it is because a larger percentage of the oil was refined, and all of it was carried a much greater average distance from Mexico, adding the cost of transportation and refining to cost of production, which made a much larger investment for a given quantity and consequently a larger profit for a given quantity of oil.

As I have said, the dividends paid during 1918 were $4,128,008, as compared with $2,140,263 in 1917. That was because we commenced paying dividends for the first time in six years on the stock of the Mexican Petroleum Co. (Ltd.) during the last half of 1917, and we paid them during the whole of 1918.

(Reading further from report:)

Taxes paid to both Governments were nearly $3,000,000 greater than the amount paid in dividends.

That is a matter that I want to call attention to, and I wish it could be put in double-leaded type in this report, because it is something that concerns every industry that is carried on abroad by Americans or abroad by any foreigners in any country; with their costs at home, with their investments in foreign countries, at the risk of confiscation or unjust treatment by foreign governments, they still continue to pay, if they make a profit, their taxes to support their own Government. Therefore, as a matter of right, they should have protection, even if it was not guaranteed to them by the constitution and by the laws of the country from the time of the adoption of the constitution up to the present time.

(Reading further from report:)

Taxes paid to both Governments were nearly $3,000,000 greater than the amount paid in dividends.

We paid nearly — or, in fact a little over — $7,000,000 in taxes and something over $4,000,000 in dividends.

(Reading further from report:)

Oil sales for 1918 were 18,500,000 barrels as compared with 16,736,000 barrels sold in 1917, an increase of 11 per cent. The selling price in 1918 was $26,320,545, as compared with $17,007,209 for the preceding year. This difference is accounted for by the fact that a large proportion of oil sold in 1917 was disposed of in crude form, while nearly all of the oil sold in 1918 was either refined at the company's plant at Destrehan or partially refined at the company's plant at Tampico, Mexico. Still another cause for the increased return from oil sales is the fact that a much larger proportion of the oil sold in 1918 was carried to distant markets, thus using a larger amount of tonnage per barrel of oil moved and adding to the selling price the added cost for transportation.

The selling price of the crude and fuel oil in Mexico has not varied as greatly as the selling price at North Atlantic United States ports. The price at the latter ports was and is affected by the high charter rates for tanker tonnage.

Well, as I am going to file this report, I do not know whether it is necessary to read much more of it, but there is an article here on the market which, while it does not touch directly, does indirectly have some effect on the consideration of this entire subject, and I think I will presume on your good nature to read this article for you.

(Reading further from report:)

The necessities of the great war required the use of all tanker tonnage for the delivery and storage of as large an amount of petroleum products as possible to points where it would be available for various war uses. The signing of the armistice immediately discontinued a very large percentage of the consumption of fuel oil for Navy uses, and of motor spirits and gasoline used by launches, lorries, tanks, autos, and aeroplanes. So successful was the work of the petroleum industry in keeping an adequate supply of all the needed petroleum products at the war bases, that the cessation of fighting found all of the Allied storage on the Continent filled with oil, many loaded tank steamers on route to Europe, and the United States Atlantic storage stations also fairly well filled.

And inasmuch as the oil industry is involved in this Mexican dispute, and may be the subject of contumely not only for its work in Mexico as well as in the United States, I would like to say, without claiming to hold any brief for any other oil company than our own — but I want to include in this statement all the oil companies of the United States — that during the war every American, as well as every English, French, and Italian industry, contributed their utmost to supply the needs of the war, whatever they might be, and wherever they might be required; and it has been stated by those connected with the war supplies in the United States — it was first volunteered by the French, and then by the English war-supply agents — that the only industry connected with the war supplies which was 100 per cent efficient was the petroleum industry. It supplied every need of the Navy, the transport service, the armies, including the airplane service, without any failure and without there being at any time any shortage, although there were two or three times in the history of the war, especially in the midsummer of 1918, when there was a threatened shortage of airplane gasoline, but it never occurred, and the service was so good, carried on entirely under the management of the oil companies themselves, that the close of the war, the signing of the armistice, found every storage tank in western Europe filled with oil, all the tank steamers en route to Europe filled with oil; and many of them had to remain months before they could be unloaded, because the consumption of oil from the reservoirs did not make room for them as at early periods.

(Reading further from report:)

This condition immediately demoralized the movement of oil. A period of transition ensued. New uses for oil are being developed so rapidly that there is likelihood of a shortage both of the supply and of the means of transporting it from the wells to the consumer. The great merchant marine of the United States, which it is said will amount to more than 20,000,000 tons when completed; the substitution of oil for coal because of its greater economy at many industrial plants in the United States as well as Europe; its demonstrated superiority as a naval fuel, which results in its being substituted for coal in all the navies of the world as rapidly as convenience and economy will permit, all tend to develop a demand for fuel oils and motor spirits that will fully tax the future supply. Your management with a view of early benefiting your companies by the new adjustment has been instrumental in organizing a supply company with associates largely interested in the industries of Great Britain, whose efforts will be devoted to marketing the petroleum products of your properties.

The remainder is of little interest not being connected with the subject that I am testifying on, so that with your permission I will submit the report as it is.

While talking on the subject of oil fuel, I was asked by the Fuel

Administration oil branch to submit to them a letter with my opinion on the value to the United States, especially during the war
time, of the American-owned oil fields in Mexico. In answer to
that request, I hurriedly wrote a letter on the 15th of March, 1918.
I was asked by many people, who read it, to have it published,
which I never did. But, much to my satisfaction, I have seen it
quoted in a great many articles since given to the public through the
medium of newspapers and other periodicals. This is not a very
long letter, but it sheds a new light upon the interest which the
United States ought to take in the oil fields in Mexico, as well as
elsewhere in the world, and if it will not be considered too remote
in connection with this matter, I will attempt to read it to you.

The CHAIRMAN. Proceed, sir.

Mr. DOHENY. This is dated March 15, 1918.

It is addressed to Hon. Mark L. Requa, Fuel Oil Administrator,
Washington, D.C.

The future welfare and prosperity of the United States, both during and
after the present great World War, may be said to be largely dependent upon or
at least affected by the uninterrupted operation and control of the oil fields
in Mexico now owned by American companies.

I wish to say for the purpose of showing the importance of this
letter at the time it was written, that it was at the time of the great
German concentration and drive in the spring of 1918, when there
was certainly some doubt as to what the outcome of the war might
be, and this was asked for because of its importance at that time.

(Reading further from letter:)

About 20 years ago Americans discovered, and have developed by the expenditure of scores of millions of dollars and made available, the great oil
production which is now finding its way into the markets which supply the
United States and its Allies, both for industrial and war uses.

Statistics show that approximately 300,000,000 barrels of oil per annum are
being produced in continental United States, from 200,000 oil wells.

Prior to the great development and use of motor engines for many purposes,
notably, automobiles, trucks and tractors, aeroplanes, launches, etc., there was
being produced in the United States more oil than was being used to supply
both the home and foreign markets, and consequently the amount of oil in
storage increased to over 150,000,000 barrels.

This surplus resulted from the discovery of phenomenal oil fields in the mid-
continent region and on the Pacific coast. The gradual falling off in the yield
of the great bonanza oil districts, and the rapid increase in the use of various
grades of petroleum both for the operation of the motor engine and as steam
fuel, have brought about a change to the relation between supply and demand,
so that during the year of 1917 the use of petroleum to supply the United
States markets has been many millions of barrels in excess of the United States
production.

The excess of use over production on the Pacific coast in 1917 amounted to more than 12,000,000 barrels, notwithstanding the fact that western South America, formerly supplied with oil from California, had drawn on Mexico for more than four and one-quarter million barrels of crude and fuel oil.

In the oil field east of the Rocky Mountains an equal amount was withdrawn from storage to supply the demands of the market. This reduction of surplus was unavoidable, notwithstanding that some very rich new oil territory was discovered and developed in the State of Kansas and fortunately made a substantial contribution to the production of 1917; and likewise notwithstanding the fact that more than 30,000,000 barrels of Mexican oil, in addition to that sent to the west coast of South America, were imported to supply the United States and its allies.

The present and coming years will doubtless witness the discovery and development of additional oil fields within the borders of the United States, whose production may largely make up the present deficit of petroleum.

The ensuing year will certainly be one of extraordinary increase in the use of petroleum in its various forms. The new United States aero fleets, whose service is so greatly relied upon, the great numbers of motors and trucks needed to facilitate the movement of American troops, supplies, and munitions in the war area, the fleet of destroyers and submarine chasers that is being created for use in the war zone, the plan for extensive tonnage of petroleum-driven cargo vessels and transports, all lead to the conviction that increasing quantities of petroleum will be constantly required; and that all its sources may need to be utilized to their utmost to provide a sufficient supply.

To rely upon the uncertainty of the discovery of new fields in the United States would be to invite disaster to our arms in the great impending struggle.

Where is relief from this danger to be found? The reply is, by continuing the present and increasing the future movement of petroleum from the oil fields of Mexico to the United States and its allies.

I am going to ask your indulgence while I relate some incidents that suggest the Mexican oil fields as a logical and natural source of supply for petroleum for the United States.

A large part of the lands which are recognized today as the richest part of the oil fields in Mexico were discovered and purchased by Americans in the year 1900. Their active development was begun a year before Beaumont, Tex., was known to the history of petroleum. The difficulties of the climate, the primitive character of the region and people where developments were first begun, its inaccessibility for supplies, the unbelief in its value as petroleum lands, were all fully appraised by its developers. They were encouraged by the Government of Mexico, which understood all of the difficulties heretofore mentioned, to undertake and persevere in the task of proving the truth of the ideas which they formed regarding the quantity and character of the oil deposits of that unfrequented and little-known region, the Huasteca Veracruzana.

Millions of dollars of American money, furnished principally by the original prospectors, were poured into the jungle in payment for pipe lines, railroads, drilling machines, houses, water supply, ice plant, electric plant, machine shops, American labor, and Mexican labor, everything necessary to initiate a petroleum development in a new country. For nearly 10 years the efforts of these Americans, while crowned with success in the matter of the development of oil, from the very beginning of their efforts — their first substantial well being brought in within two weeks after drilling commenced in 1901 — were productive of comparatively meager earnings and no profits. The bringing in, in 1910, of the most productive oil well the world has known, precipitated a situation which threatened financial bankruptcy to the original discoverers of this prolific field. The unrestrainable flow of this well, amounting to three-quarters of a million barrels per month, necessitated the rapid building of reservoirs of steel and cement so that the flow of petroleum would not go into the streams and devastate by flood and fire the region of its location.

Over 10,000,000 barrels of storage was built before plans could be developed for the movement of the petroleum produced by this well to places of consumption.

The original discoverers of this wonderful oil region were Americans. They had been successful oil prospectors in the United States before turning their attention to the neighboring Republic. Their proposed efforts in Mexico were welcomed by the Government of that Republic, which desired to stimulate new industries therein; by the railroad company near whose line the first development was undertaken and which hoped to and did benefit by the development of a superior locomotive fuel supply at 50 per cent of the cost of that which theretofore had been imported for its use; by the merchants of Tampico and vicinity whose business promised to be enhanced by activities thus initiated; by landowners of the region about Tampico who anticipated a wider market for their products and better prices for lands which might be supposed to contain petroleum. Even the laborers, known as peons, who could not then realize the advantage which might accrue to them, have since shown their appreciation and gratitude, by kindly feelings and helpful actions, for the treatment which these Americans accorded to them and which became possible only through the successful carrying on of the plans of these prospectors.

Millions of acres of supposed oil lands in the Tampico region have since been acquired by American, English, Dutch, French, and Mexican companies. The city of Tampico has grown from a comparatively unknown, squalid, pestilential, semi-tropic seaport of about 12,000 inhabitants, to a modern, well-drained, well-paved, metropolitan center of approximately 50,000 inhabitants. Lands that were purchaseable at from 1 peso to 10 pesos per hectare (2.47 acres) have increased in price to a maximum of thousands of dollars per hectare and to an average increased market value of several thousand per cent. The daily wages of laborers have increased from 36 centavos (about 14 cents) in 1900 to 3 pesos per day in 1917, or over 800 per cent.

That three pesos per day is taken as the average of all the wages paid, high and low, by all the American companies to the Mexican workingmen.

(Reading further from letter:)

Many millions of dollars' worth of oil-well machinery, supplies, engines, boilers, and pipe have been brought into this region from the United States to be used in the development of these oil-containing lands. Other millions have been paid out in wages to American and Mexican employees, mostly Mexican. Still other millions have been paid in taxes on petroleum and increased valuations of property to the various governments of Mexico. Wells have been drilled that, conservatively estimated, may be said to have a potential capacity of more than a million barrels per day (which is greater than that of the United States). All of this change has been brought about through the enterprise and energy of Americans who were stimulated by the American pioneer spirit of development and encouraged by the kindly feeling evinced and promises of help and protection made by the Mexican Government under President Diaz and renewed by the late lamented President Madero. During 17 years American and other foreign money has poured into this region in Mexico for the purchase of lands, establishment of camps, and carrying on of oil-well development and production, with no objection from any governmental authority or suggestion of interference until 1917.

In my opinion, 80 per cent of the known valuable oil land holdings of the Tampico region belong to Americans or American companies.

I think I am understating the percentage that is owned by Americans and American companies; that they really own more than 85 per cent of the demonstrated oil territory.

(Reading further:)

The existing wells of these American companies can now, in my opinion, furnish an amount of oil annually much in excess of the difference between the United States production and the amount required to supply America's needs. The present pipe-line and barge facilities are sufficient to deliver at the port of Tampico more than 100,000 barrels per day. There is in the Mexican storage of these companies more than 10,000,000 barrels of oil. The tank-steamer capacity of their fleets is fully sufficient to carry the above-mentioned daily quantity to the average United States Atlantic port. The American owners, as a whole, belong to the class of patriotic citizens who would be greatly gratified if their properties can and will be made to perform a national service in this time of need of their country.

It seems to me, therefore, that these American holdings in the sister Republic are a logical and presently available source of supply for the indispensable petroleum needs of the war.

This letter was written at the request of the Fuel Administration by a man who was known to have had experience in the oil business and judgement as to what our sources of supply of oil were for the immediate needs of the United States and its allies in the war. It was not written as an argument against the spoliation of Mexico.

(Reading further:)

The very latest movements of the German Government, as recorded in the morning papers —

And this I want to call especial attention to, although it does not relate directly to the Mexican question. It does, however, relate indirectly to the situation, because it details the enterprising movements of our British neighbors, commenced during the war.

(Reading further:)

The very latest movements of the German Government, as recorded in this morning's papers, point not only to the intention of that Government to extend its political and commercial influence over vast regions heretofore subject to the influence of and commercially tributary to other nations, but indicate that in so doing the fact has not been overlooked that one of the sources from which naval and commercial strength may be derived is by the acquisition of the great petroleum fields of the Black Sea region and of the regions to the south.

Great Britain's military campaign in Mesopotamia has been said to be largely due to its desire to protect its holdings in some extensive oil regions and to acquire rights in other still undeveloped lands having similar values.

There was published in the papers of the United States many months ago a statement attributed to Walter Runciman, president of the British Board of Trade, to the effect "that it is the policy of Great Britain to acquire as large a control as possible of the world supply of petroleum." This statement is said to have been made openly before the House of Commons at the time the British Government acquired an interest in the Anglo-Persian oil fields.

Three years ago this month I spent several weeks in London in consultation with men who are largely interested in England's maritime commerce. The subject of our negotiations was a supply of petroleum for several steamship lines. During the course of the negotiations it developed that one of the gentlemen had made extensive and expensive experiments to determine the relative value of petroleum and coal as a marine fuel. He told us the result of his experiments, which is to the effect that, used for steam-producing purposes, one ton of oil was the equivalent in power value of two tons of coal. Also, that used with an internal combustion engine, one ton of oil developed a power equivalent to that of six tons of coal, or of three tons of oil consumed to produce steam power. These experiments, made three years ago, were made public a few days ago through one of the scientific journals of America.

I make use of the above information for the purpose of illustrating and emphasizing what I am about to declare with regard to the importance of the Mexican oil fields to the United States.

The experiments above referred to, made by Lord Pirrie —

I would like to interject right here a remark or a few words which, again, I want to say, do not bear directly upon it, and they are to this effect: That I have just lately returned from Great Britain, having spent nearly seven months there and on the continent, and the things which I told the Fuel Administrator a year ago last spring were being worked out have since been worked out. The British Government owns 65 per cent of the stock of the Anglo-Persian Oil Co., which has a concession from the Persian Government on 55,000 square miles of oil territory in Persia, and quite recently, it appears from the newspapers, the British Government has assumed closer relations to the Persian Government, of some port, and it is expected that a mandatory on Mesopotamia will be given to Great Britain, and that the great expenditure of life and money for the purpose of acquiring and holding that territory and preventing the Germans from occupying it, may be partly made up to them by the enormous oil values that are known to exist in Mesopotamia.

It is also known that the British troops occupied the Baku region, which is known to be one of the richest oil fields in the world.

So that by considering the present in connection with the quite recent past, the past when this letter was written, it is easy to be seen that my warning to the United States Government in this letter, which I understand was handed to President Wilson, was not unworthy of some study.

As Cardinal Mercier so kindly acknowledged yesterday — a rather rare acknowledgment from anybody living in Europe — in 1918 the American troops at the supreme moment turned the balance of the war in favor of the Allies. The British Government was in the great drive in March, 1918, when Sir Douglas Haig's "back was to the wall," might be compared to a lion with his tongue stretched out about 18 inches, the German Kaiser with his foot on the lion's throat, but that lion shiftily scratching with the toe of his right hind leg, a location claim to the section around Mesopotamia, while his front half lay prostrate across northern France and Belgium.

The British Government then saw the necessity of holding for its citizens and for the "glory of the Empire," the great oil resources, even though it had to obtain and hold them by what might be considered questionable means, and I say today that the United States ought to hold for its industries and for its people — the people who use the flivver, as well as the people who ride in the limousine — the oil lands that are owned and have been acquired by Americans anywhere in the world, and they should not be allowed to be confiscated by any Government, whether it be British, Mexican, or any other. They ought to be maintained.

I make use of the above information for the purpose of illustrating and emphasizing what I am about to declare with regard to the importance of the Mexican oil fields to the United States.

The experiments above referred to, made by Lord Pirrie —

I may say that Lord Pirrie is my associate in the oil business, and he is one of the greatest business men in Great Britian, and is successful in every respect, and is a thoroughly liberal-minded man and understands fully what oil is to this country as well as to other countries.

The experiments above referred to, made by Lord Pirrie, demonstrate that the people or nation using the internal-combustion engine for power purposes on freight ships can successfully compete with the nation which is confined to the use of coal as a marine fuel and even with the nation whose freighters are equipped with steam engines whose power is derived from the use of oil as fuel.

As between the use of oil and coal the coal user can not successfully compete with the oil user, and hence the fleets, of whatever nation, that depend upon coal as a fuel will, in competition with oil-using fleets, be as surely driven from the sea as the sailing vessel was in competition with the steam freighter. The use of coal for maritime purposes requires coaling stations at many places over the globe, often at places where the nation whose flag the steamer flies has no territory of jurisdiction. The necessity for coaling stations has been one of the many causes of friction between the great Governments of the world. The fewer of these stations that are required the less danger from such friction. The radius of an oil-using steamer is more than twice as great as that of a coal-using vessel. Hence, only half as many fuel-oil stations would be required as coaling stations. The possession of an adequate oil supply suggests the probability of a very large use of the marine internal-combustion engine. With such a freighter fuel stations are almost unnecessary. At any rate, their use would be reduced to a minimum.

As to the advantages in the use of oil instead of coal on naval vessels nothing need be said by me, as the subject has been so thoroughly studied and is so well understood by the Navy Department. It is an acknowledged fact that other conditions being equal, the oil-using navy can vanquish the coal-using navy.

Inasmuch as both Germany and Great Britain are seeking and acquiring sources of supply for large quantities of petroleum, it seems to me that there can be no question but that the United States must avail itself of the enterprise and ability and pioneer spirit of its citizens to acquire and to have and to hold a reasonable portion of the world's petroleum supplies. If it does not it will find that the supplies of petroleum not within the boundaries of United States territory will be rapidly acquired by citizens and Governments of other nations and that our dream of maritime greatness and commercial equality with other nations of the earth will prove indeed a dream and that we have slept while other nations have taken advantage of the opportunities which a bountiful nature has offered to all.

Is such a needed supply of petroleum available to the United States now from within her boundaries? The answer is no.

The rate of increase in the use of petroleum and its products for interior purposes has been so great that it must be expected that within a few years the United States' production will barely suffice for its own consumption. This statement is not intended to, nor should it, be a cause for alarm as to the internal supply of petroleum and its products.

That time has already arrived. At the time this was written we were credited with having less than 4,000,000 motor engines in use on all kinds of vehicles. Today we have over 6,000,000 and Mr. Durand is credited with the statement that in less than 10 years we will have 15,000,000 motor vehicles. Now it requires some 350,000,000 barrels of oil to supply the motor machines in use for every purpose. In 10 years it will require two and a half times that amount unless we use the heavier petroleum products and the heavier gasolines, but even admitting that, there is no question but that we will use at any rate within a year or two more oil than we can produce in the United States. We are up against the necessity for importing oil today in order to supply the demand of every family in the United States that can afford a flivver.

To the uninitiated, the average rate of decrease in the production of oil wells might well be a source of great anxiety. The oil producer, however, is fully aware that the initial production of the first few wells in a new field can not be sustained, even by the continuous drilling of a large number of new wells, and is cognizant of the long-lived character of the decreasing production of existing wells, and also the unceasing efforts which are being made to develop the use of a larger percentage of the crude petroleum.

The oldest fields in the United States, those of the Appalachian region, nearly 100,000 in number, yield an average of less than two-thirds of a barrel per day.

They yield sixty-two and one-half hundredths of a barrel of oil per day.

In the newest oil region of importance, the Rocky Mountains while not a large producer, the 400 wells average over 40 barrels per day. The great mid-Continent field, of comparatively recent development, with nearly 50,000 wells, averages approximately 9 barrels per day. And California, some of whose wells are nearly as old as those of the Appalachian region, and some of its oil districts less than a year old, yields over 90,000,000 barrels per annum at an average of over 30 barrels per day. Twenty wells in Mexico, unrestrained, will yield over 600,000 barrels daily, or an average of 30,000 barrels per day per well.

Perhaps it is not a safe thing to admit that, because that might be one of the reasons why the cupidity of certain elements of Mexico have been excited to the extent to forget all international laws for the purpose of getting possession of the wells and keeping possession of them from those who are really entitled to them.

To keep up the American production of 300,000,000 barrels annually from 200,000 wells, whose yield perceptibly decreases from month to month, is a herculean task, requiring rare courage on the part of the prospectors for new regions, and strong faith and large capital investments for close drilling and extension of developed fields.

Where, then, is the United States to look for the 100,000,000 barrels per annum additional oil now needed for war and industrial purposes, and hereafter needed in increasing quantities in peace times to carry on the pursuits of commerce and industry?

Will we pursue the policy of a hermit state and endeavor to live within ourselves, or will we continue as heretofore to pay tribute to the nations that provide the means for ocean transportation?

As never before in the history of the human race, the need of adequate transportation facilities has recently been brought home to the civilized peoples of the world. For nearly half a century our country has been building at an unprecedented rate great inland railways for the transportation of the people and supplies from centers of production to centers of development and consumption. During this period of rapid interior development and growth, which occupied a large proportion of the time and energies of our people, we have apparently lost our interest or been weaned away from the consideration of one of our former great sources of wealth and power as a nation. For 50 years the American merchant marine has been undeservedly neglected. The necessities of the present struggle have undoubtedly at last awakened all of us to a realization of a fact, heretofore ignored by most of us, which is that adequate transportation facilities are just as necessary for the growth and prosperity of a nation as is great productive capacity. The genius and enterprise of Americans, stimulated by a forward-seeing governmental personnel, will undoubtedly give the proper encouragement and aid to the development of the ocean trade of the United States.

Some difficulties we have, however, to overcome, the principal one being the handicap resulting from the higher paid labor in our country. This handi-cap must not be overcome by a reduction in wages of labor. To some extent, it can and will be offset by the greater efficiency of American labor and its man-agement. Cost of production of sea-going vessels and cost of operation have heretofore interfered with the building up of our merchant marine. Cost of operation suggests not only the labor problem but the fuel problem as well.

Not many decades ago the windjammers gave place to the steam freighters using coal as fuel. The era is beginning in which the coal steamer will be forced to give way to the more economical, more efficient oil-using steamer, which will have a greater radius and greater cargo space per ton capacity.

It has been difficult, except in some few favored localities, to establish any basis for computing the oil value of oil-containing land; that is, the amount of oil which is contained under a given area per acre and the percentage of that amount which is likely to be yielded to the efforts of the producer. Various methods of calculation have been used both by oil geologists and oil-stock sellers. Most if not all of the methods so adopted have been plausible and wor-thy of some credence. In 1893 the writer made an estimate of the amount of oil producable from a given area within the city of Los Angeles, where the thickness of the oil measures had been determined by drilling and its porosity arrived at by experimentation. The boundary of the oil field being also fairly well established, it was estimated that the district should produce approximate-ly 120,000,000 barrels of oil, or about 40,000 barrels to the acre. Statistics now show that approximately that amount has been pumped from the Los Angeles oil field.

In the Bakersfield oil territory calculations made on a similar basis gave ex-pression to the opinion that 400,000 barrels per acre would be produced from certain areas therein. While that field is not yet entirely exhausted, the ap-proximate correctness of the estimate has been sustained. From less than 200 acres at Spindle Top, it is said that over 60,000,000 barrels of oil have been produced without exhaustion. A small area developed by the writer in Cali-fornia has yielded nearly 300,000 barrels per acre. The Casino Basin, owned by the Mexican Petroleum Co., in the State of Vera Cruz, Mexico, with an area of less than 1,000 acres, confined within a perimeter of baisatic non oil-bearing rock, has yielded (through one well whose production has been re-stricted to a little over 20,000 barrels per day by closing the valve until it shows a pressure of 320 pounds to the square inch) over 65,000,000 barrels of oil, and is still yielding at the rate of approximately 700,000 barrels per month. The limits of the Casiano pool are remarkably well defined and the production has already reached the enormous quantity of approximately 75,000 barrels per acre.

All of the foregoing is stated for the purpose of arriving at a basis for belief in the following estimate.

This is the point that I want to lead up to and that explains Mexico.

There are somewhere between 50 and 100 American companies, large and small, that have holdings of supposed oil lands in Mexico, acquired either by purchase or lease.

I think that the latest record shows 152.

The aggregate amount of land so held is not less than 2,000,000 acres —

probably nearer double that amount. The writer, who is familiar with that entire region through journeyings made for nearly 18 years for the purpose of prospecting it for oil indications, estimates that perhaps 10 per c(.t of the supposed oil lands may really contain oil beneath the surface.

There are other vast regions in Mexico where there are indications of commercially valuable oil pools existent beneath the surface. The American-owned area in the State of Vera Cruz, however, is the part whose approximate oil value I desire to call attention to.

Extraction of oil already made in California and the middle continent fields proves that 100,000 barrels per acre is not an excessive amount to expect from favorably constructed oil horizons.

Without going into an explanation of the nature of the oil horizons or oil pools of Mexico, I desire to state that the 90,000,000 barrels of oil already produced by the companies with which I am associated in Mexico seem to justify expectation that the oil pools of that region will yield an amount equal to at least 100,000 barrels per acre. If so, the 10 per cent of the American holdings, which I estimate at about 200,000 acres, will contain 20,000,000,000 barrels of oil.

I do not fix this sum as a calculation; hardly as an estimate, but I mention it as a reasonable amount that may be expected to be yielded by the American holdings of oil lands in the Huasteca Veracruzana lying between the Tamesi River on the north and the Tecolutha River on the south.

This oil field, discovered by Americans, acquired lawfully under the then existing laws of Mexico, through purchase or lease, developed not only without protest but with the approval of the Mexican Government, at the cost of scores of millions of dollars, having a potential daily productive capacity nearly, if not quite, equal to that of the United States, having a reasonable oil valuation of some billions of barrels, is the source of which the United States must look for the supply of petroleum which will justify the building of a commercial fleet that can compete for cost of operation with any other fleet which the great nations of the world may have or construct.

Without this legitimately acquired supply, and with the certainty that the other great oil pools of the world are or will be placed at the service of the other great commercial powers, the hope for an American ocean-transportation system which will serve the purposes of this country in its extension of trade and influence over the seven seas can not be realized.

Mexico is not the only source for petroleum in large quantities, but it has the greatest developed and demonstrated supply, and all other probable sources of great supply are politically, nationally, and geographically less favorably situated than are the American oil holdings in Mexico.

If you consider that letter worth going into the record as part of the history of the oil developments of Mexico, brought out by the request of the Government, I will submit it.

The CHAIRMAN. It is already in the record.

Mr. DOHENY. Now, there are some other phases of the Mexican situation that are not covered by the documentary testimony or the remarks that I have made in reading it that I am sure ought to be known to this committee, if you want to know what has most agitated the minds of people who have been trying to justify the carrying out of article 27 of the recent constitution. It has been said that the right to tax is the right to confiscate. I do not believe, though, that that character of confiscation is one which is reprehensible without examination, but where the confiscation strikes at the title of the property which is being attacked, it is one which, it seems to me, is indefensible, and for the purpose of showing that the oil men are today the subject of more or less confiscatory action, which, in my opinion, is entitled to the intervention of our Government in a diplomatic way, I want to call attention to the fact that crude oil from Penueo district can be purchased at Tampico for 25 cents per barrel. I think it has been offered for something less. It costs about 8 to 10 cents per barrel to carry it down to the Tampico, so that its value to the owner is the selling price less that cost, or maybe 15 to 18 cents per barrel.

The Mexican tax on that oil is 5 cents per barrel, so that I do not think it requires much of a mathematician to figure out that the tax at the well is 33 1/3 per cent, although the Mexican statue says that the tax must be 10 per cent.

Fuel oil, which is the product of the refineries in Mexico, and which is the residuum of the latter oil, has recently been offered to the United States Government to the extent of 8,000,000 barrels at 35 cents per barrel in Tampico. The cost of transporting that oil to the place where it was to be delivered to the United States Government in Mexico is 10 cents per barrel, so that the value of that oil to its owners must be admitted to be about 35 cents per barrel. The tax that is paid on that oil, on millions of barrels of it, no matter what it sells for or where it goes to, every month, to the Mexican Government is 10 cents per barrel, or nearly 40 per cent of its value at the well. The law also provides for a 10 per cent tax on this oil.

Crude oil is being sold by the millions of barrels per month to various American concerns and transported from Mexico at the price of 45 cents per barrel f.o.b. steamers at the pipe-line terminus. Admitting a cost of 10 cents per barrel as a fair charge for piping this oil, its value at the well would be about 35 cents per barrel. The export tax on this oil is 11½ cents per barrel. I will not undertake to figure out what percentage that is, but it is much more than 10 per cent.

Senator BRANDEGEE. Are all these taxes that you have been referring to export taxes?

Mr. DOHENY. Yes, sir; all export.

The CHAIRMAN. In addition to that, are there other taxes paid — stamp tax on the books?

Mr. DOHENY. Yes, sir; there are stamp taxes on the books, and land taxes on the land, and we pay port charges for going in and out of the harbor with our vessels at so much per ton, but the direct tax on the oil is not only greater than the statutes of Mexico provide for, and to that extent are illegal, but they are the only national or Federal tax placed on any oil produced in any country. There is no other nation that places a Federal tax upon the production. The United States Government never raised one cent of revenue from taxes for oil produced in Pennsylvania or any other State. It is an innovation in Mexico, which nobody complains of because of the needs of the country, but it is a new thing and not the custom of any other civilized country. In order to increase the revenues, they openly and obviously violate the law; the petroleum commissioner has chosen to value this oil, not at the well in Mexico, where it has its Mexican value, but at the port in New York, where it has been increased in value by the cost of transportation, which is often from two to three times the value of the oil at the well.

There is another form of confiscation which is not quite as direct as the confiscation provided for in article 27 of the constitution, but it is nevertheless a confiscation and more reprehensible than the confiscation which results from taxation, and that is the confiscation of the rights of the lessee or lessor to take from lands, which he is entitled to take oil from, that which he depends upon for his profits from the land — by preventing him from drilling wells thereon.

The constitution of 1917, with its confiscatory clause 27, was adopted early in that year. Early in the following year President Carranza issued a decree, the legality of which we will not discuss, but it has been attacked not only by the amparos of the oil men, but by the Mexican legal lights in the City of Mexico.

I will submit for your information a copy of the decree of February 19, 1918.

The CHAIRMAN. It may be received in the record.

(The decree above referred to is here printed in the record in full as follows:)

PROVISIONS REGULATING ARTICLE 14 OF THE DECREE OF FEBRUARY 19, 1918, WITH AMENDMENTS DATED AUGUST 8, 1918.

(Translated from Diaro Oficial, Aug. 12, 1918.)

ARTICLE 1. From and after August 16 next entries on petroleum properties may be filed on free lands.

ART. 2. A "petroleum claim" shall be understood to be a solid of indefinite depth, limited laterally by vertical planes passing through the boundaries of a continuous area of not less than 4 hectares and devoted to petroleum development.

ART. 3. By "petroleum development" shall be understood the extraction, reduction to possession or enjoyment of the following substances:

1. Petroleum to be found in ore bodies, beds, and natural deposits.

2. Gaseous hydrocarbons to be found in the subsoil or those seeping through the ground to the surface.

3. Natural deposits of ozokerite and asphalt.

4. All mixtures of hydrocarbons of the several kinds having their origin in natural phenomena.

ART. 4. No land shall be deemed free which shall have received a patent (titulo) for the development of petroleum, or on which there shall be a patent pending.

ART. 5. No land whose owner shall have filed with the Department of Industry, Commerce, and Labor the statement required in pursuance of articles 14 and 17, and transitory article 1 of the decree of July 31, 1918, shall be deemed free; but land shall be deemed free if, though the above-mentioned statement shall have been filed, no claim thereon shall have been made by the person filing the statement or by transferee of this preferential right, within the three months next following the 15th of the present month.

ART. 6. No land shall be deemed free which shall have been leased for petroleum development and the statement relating thereto filed with the department of industry, commerce, and labor in pursuance of articles 14 and 17, and transitory article 1 of the decree of July 31 of the present year; but land shall be deemed free if, although the statement shall have been submitted, no entry thereon shall have been filed by the person making the statement or the transferee of this preferential right within the two months next following the 15th of the present month.

ART. 7. Nor shall land be deemed free which shall have been leased for petroleum development and the statement relating thereto filed with the department of industry, commerce, and labor in pursuance of articles 15 and 17 of the decree of July 31, 1918; but land shall be deemed free if, although the statement shall have been submitted, no entry thereon shall have been filed by the person obtaining the preference referred to in article 15 of the decree hereinabove cited, or by the transferee of this preferential right, within the two months next following the declaration of preference mentioned in the article of the decree above cited.

Transfers of the preferential right mentioned in this article and in the two foregoing articles shall be recorded by public deed.

ART. 8. Nor shall land be deemed free, for the purposes of this decree and without prejudice to article 27 of the constitution, which shall be covered by any franchise (contracto de concesion) granted by the federal government to any individual or corporation for petroleum development.

ART. 9. Lands of common use, waste and national lands, town sites (fundos legales), and commons (ejidos) not subdivided shall not be open to entry.

ART. 10. Each entry shall refer to a single petroleum claim.

ART. 11. Each applicant for a petroleum property shall file his entry in duplicate, with the proper agent of the department of industry, commerce, and labor; such entry shall contain the name, age, profession, domicile, and nationality of the applicant, as well as the location, area, boundaries, and other pertinent data necessary to identify the property in question.

ART. 12. If the applicant be an alien individual, he shall attach to his application a certificate of the department for foreign affairs, establishing that he has complied with the requisites prescribed by article 27 of the federal constitution.

ART. 13. If the applicant be an alien corporation which shall have previously filed the necessary statement regarding the lands which it may own or the rights of the development of which it may be the assignee, the entry shall be admitted and the regular procedure followed, but patent thereto shall be issued only to an individual or a Mexican corporation organized under the laws of Mexico, to whom or to which the applicant corporation shall transfer its rights.

ART. 14. The applicant shall file with his entry a certificate from the stamp office, setting forth that he has deposited the value of the stamps to be affixed to his patent, according to the area of the property on which entry has been filed.

ART. 15. The agent of the petroleum bureau (Ramo de Petroleo) shall receive the entry, shall enter it in his register, and shall record thereon, as well on the original as on the copies, the date and hour of presentation. The applicant may demand that these annotations be made in his presence. If, in the judgment of the agent, the claim be lacking clearness, he shall request such explanations as may be necessary, and shall record them in the original, in the copies, and in the register book. The absence of explanations shall not be ground for a refusal to register the entry. The duplicate shall be returned with the corresponding annotations to the applicant.

ART. 16. Within the three days following the presentation of an entry, and in view of the explanation submitted, the agent shall decide whether it is or is not to be admitted. In the former event he shall dispatch it in accordance with the regular procedure; in the latter event, he shall set down in writing the ground for his decision, which shall be subject to review by the department of industry, commerce and labor, on request submitted by the applicant to the same agent, so soon as the latter shall notify him of his decision not to admit the entry, or within the ensuing three days.

ART. 17. Whenever two or more entries presented simultaneously and referring to the same tract of land shall be declared admitted, the choice between them shall be determined by lot, unless the preference as to the particular entry to be admitted shall be agreed upon between the interested parties.

ART. 18. Whenever several entries on different claims are filed, but having a portion common to all, a drawing covering all entries shall be held. Should the entry favored by lot embrace all entries filed, all remaining entries which shall have been included in the drawing shall, by virtue of this fact alone, be definitely rejected; but should the entry favored by lot comprise only a portion of the land on which entry has been filed, the remainder shall be included in a new drawing to be held as among all applicants, excepting only the applicant favored in the first drawing; and should there remain any portion of the land in dispute after the second drawing, one or more successive drawings as may be necessary shall be held, at which the procedure detailed above shall be observed. Drawings shall be held at intervals of three working days, so that applicants may be present at each of them with their claims duly prepared. Applicants failing to attend any drawing to which they have been summoned shall thereby forfeit the preferential rights acquired under the first drawing.

ART. 19. So soon as an agent admits a claim he shall post it on his bulletin board (tabla de avisos) for a month and shall furthermore cause it to be published three times within this period in the Official Gazette (Diaro Oficial) and in two other journals chosen from among those having the largest circulation in the particular locality. The interested party shall take steps on his own account to see that the insertions are made.

ART. 20. The following shall constitute grounds for adverse claims (oposicion), which shall suspend action upon the claim:

1. The total or partial encroachment upon a petroleum claim on which patent has been granted and which has not been declared forfeited.

2. The claim of the whole or a part of a property on which entry has already been filed, legally submitted, and a ruling on which is still pending.

3. The nonexpiration of the term within which under these regulations preference is granted to any individual or corporation with regard to the whole of a claim or a part thereof.

ART. 21. An adverse claim based on any of the grounds set forth in the preceding article shall be submitted to the agent of the petroleum bureau within 60 days, reckoned from the date on which the entry shall have been posted on the bulletin board of the agency.

ART. 22. The adverse claimant shall submit with his adverse claim a certificate of the chief stamp office setting forth that he has deposited the amount of the rental for one year corresponding to the property in question in accordance with articles 47 and 48 of this law; no adverse claim shall be admitted without the presentation of such certificate.

ART. 23. On the presentation of the adverse claim the interested parties shall be summoned to a meeting at which every effort shall be made to reach an agreement. In this action the procedure set forth in the regulations of the mining law at present in force shall be observed. If it be impossible to reach an agreement, the interested parties shall forthwith be notified that the merits of the adverse claim may be settled either by administrative or judicial procedure.

ART. 24. If the interested parties fail to choose immediately the administrative procedure, action shall be suspended and the records transmitted within 48 hours to the judicial authorities for the institution of judicial proceedings. The adverse claimant may only allege the grounds on which he based his original adverse claim and which expressly appear in the record transmitted by the administrative authorities to the judicial authorities.

ART. 25. If the interested parties choose the administrative procedure for the settlement of their differences, the record of the case shall continue the usual course, in order that the department of industry, commerce and labor, after hearing both parties, may render its final decision in the case.

ART. 26. When once the interested parties have chosen the administrative procedure, they shall not be permitted to resort to judicial proceedings; but if they have chosen the latter, they may, pending the rendering of the final judicial decree, submit the case to the ruling of the department of industry, commerce and labor.

ART. 27. Any ground for adverse claim differing from those laid down in article 20 hereof shall be submitted to the agent, who shall not, however, suspend the regular procedure of the record. The department of industry, commerce and labor, so soon as it receives the case for review, shall decide whether the ground alleged shall or shall not be taken into account. In the former event the case shall be heard and a ruling handed down in accordance with the provisions of articles 23 to 26 hereof. Should the department refuse to admit the adverse claim, the case shall proceed as if no such adverse claim had been submitted, but the rights of the adverse claimant shall subsist.

ART. 28. The department of industry, commerce and labor may take into account during the review of the case any adverse claim submitted, provided the adverse claimant prove that he failed to submit his adverse claim to the petroleum bureau agent through no negligence of his own.

ART. 29. Applicants failing to make the insertions required under article 19 hereof within the terms set by the said article, those failing to give the explanation requested in order that the entry may be admitted within the term set, and those failing to attend the meetings for the purpose of effecting an agreement shall be declared in default (morosos). Every defaulting applicant shall forfeit the deposit referred to in article 14 hereof.

ART. 30. The adverse claimant who shall fail to attend any of the meetings for the purpose of effecting an agreement shall be deemed to have desisted from his adverse claim, except in the case of vis major.

ART. 31. Every adverse claimant who shall desist from his claim or whose adverse claim shall prove to be not well grounded shall forfeit the deposit prescribed by article 22 hereof, which deposit shall be applied to the payment of the rental for one year on the property, reckoned from the date of the claim.

ART. 32. Should no final ruling on the claim be handed down within a year, the applicant and the adverse claimant shall each deposit the amount of rental for one year in the chief stamp office; the same procedure shall be observed each year until a final ruling is given.

The deposit or deposits of the party in whose favor the final ruling is rendered shall be applied to the payment of the rental on the property, and the deposit or deposits of the party against whom the decision is rendered shall be applied to the federal budget in the form of diverse profits (aprovechamientos), but the right of the former to bring suit against the latter for damages in cases where such action is permissible shall subsist.

ART. 33. The department of industry, commerce, and labor may excuse the absences of the delinquent applicant whenever he shall prove, during the regular procedure of the record or its review, that such absences were due to vis major or fortuitous circumstances.

ART. 34. If no adverse claim causing the suspension of the regular administrative procedure in the case shall be presented within the period of 60 days allowed, the petroleum bureau agent shall transmit to the department of industry, commerce, and labor a copy of the record of the case as of that date.

ART. 35. Patents covering petroleum claims shall be issued through the department of industry, commerce, and labor after the petroleum bureau shall have reviewed the record submitted by the agent. These patents grant legal possession of the respective claims without the necessity of any further formality.

ART. 36. Patents shall be issued in favor of the applicant, without prejudice to the rights of third parties excepting in the cases prescribed in article 13 hereof. They may be issued in favor of a person other than the applicant only on proof of the transfer of the rights of the applicant in favor of the said person in a public deed. The interested party shall prove that he has paid the rental corresponding to his property before receiving his patent.

ART. 37. In the case of lands held in common the petroleum development of which shall not have been legally granted, only co-owners may make entry on petroleum claims, and all action under such claim shall be suspended until all the co-owners or their representatives shall meet under the chairmanship of the secretary of industry, commerce, and labor and make an express declaration, duly verified, of their individual rights; upon agreement a patent covering the ownership in common shall be issued to the petroleum claim comprising the subsoil of the land "pro indiviso." The share of each co-owner shall be stated in such patent. The call for the meeting of the co-owners shall be posted on the bulletin board of the respective petroleum agency within a term of 60 days; it shall likewise be published three times within the same term in the Official Gazette and in the two newspapers of largest circulation in the locality.

The department of industry, commerce, and labor is hereby authorized to appoint a committee charged with negotiating before the proper authorities the issue of patents of ownership in favor of such co-owners.

ART. 38. If on the expiration of a period of 90 days reckoned from the date of the call to which reference is made in the foregoing article, all the co-owners of the property in question fail to present themselves, such thereof as fail to present themselves shall be deemed to have forfeited their rights and patents to the property shall then be issued, subject to the compliance with the provisions of this law, to such co-owners as do appear. Whenever those present do not seek to obtain patent covering the petroleum claim to all the land held in common, patent shall be issued for such portion as they wish, and the balance shall be declared free land.

ART. 39. The grantee of a petroleum property may at any time solicit a reduction in area. The petition to this effect shall be submitted to the proper petroleum agent together with the plat of the reduced claim and the original patent.

The new patent shall cancel the former patent, and no stamp tax by way of patent shall be assessed; but the grantee shall be bound to fix the boundary marks of the reduced property within the period set by the department of industry, commerce, and labor. So soon as the reduction shall have been agreed upon, the excess land shall be declared free.

ART. 40. The grantee of a property may extract therefrom all substances mentioned in article 3 hereof, without any other limitation than that of not trespassing by means of his extraction work on adjoining properties and that of complying with the provisions of this law and of such regulations as may later be enacted on petroleum department.

ART. 41. Operators of a petroleum property may occupy within the boundaries of a claim, subject to authorization of the department of industry, commerce, and labor, the surface area necessary for the work of extraction and for the immediate storage of the oil extracted, paying in such event the corresponding compensation to whomsoever may be thereto entitled; any judicial action instituted hereunder shall not delay the prosecution of the work.

ART. 42. Operators of a petroleum claim shall acquire easements of passage and of pipe lines on obtaining permission from the department of industry, commerce, and labor; they may likewise build such pipe lines and pumping stations as the development of the property requires on payment of proper compensation to whomsoever may be thereto entitled; any judicial action instituted thereunder shall not retard the carrying out of the work.

ART. 43. Operators of a petroleum property shall have the right to establish storage tanks and refineries, subject to the approval of the department of industry, commerce, and labor, and to the assent of the owners of lands it is sought to occupy. In the event of failure to obtain such assent, condemnation proceedings of the area necessary for such work shall be instituted.

ART. 44. Operators of petroleum properties shall have the right to build wharves, loading stations, and submarine pipe lines, subject to the approval of the department of industry, commerce, and labor, and in conformity with the provisions enacted on the subject by the department of finance and public credit and of communications and public works.

ART. 45. Only the respective grantees shall have the right to build storage tanks or refineries on petroleum claims.

ART. 46. The grantee of a petroleum claim may enjoy the surface waters for the needs of his operations, in pursuance of the general law on the subject. He may use the subsoil waters for the same purpose, subject to the approval of the department of industry, commerce, and labor, and on payment of the corresponding compensation to whomsoever may be thereto entitled.

ART. 47. The grantee of a petroleum claim on leased land shall pay the tax fixed by articles 2, 3, and 5 of the decree of July 31, 1918, making such distribution as is established in article 12 of the same law.

ART. 48. The grantee of a petroleum property on land not leased shall pay an annual rental of five pesos per hectare and a royalty of 5 per cent of the output.

ART. 49. Taxes shall be due and payable from the date of the entry and shall be paid in two monthly periods in advance; payment shall be made during the first fortnight of each period of two months.

ART. 50. Within a period of one year from the date of the issue of a patent the interested party shall build boundary marks at the vertices and other clearly defined points and such other intermediary marks as are necessary to make each boundary mark readily visible from the one before; he shall be bound also to present in duplicate to the petroleum bureau the plat of the land thus marked out. This plat shall fulfill the requirements of the department of industry, commerce, and labor, and the ratification or rectification of the patent shall be in conformity with such plat.

If the grantee shall fail to comply with this obligation, the department of industry, commerce, and labor shall impose upon him a fine varying between 50 and 1,000 pesos, according to the size of the property and the recurrence of the offenses; it may likewise cause this work to be done at the expense of the grantee.

ART. 51. The interested party shall, within two years reckoned from the issue of the patent submit in duplicate to the petroleum department the plans and descriptive data relating to the proposed work for the development of the petroleum property. These plans and data shall follow the requirements fixed by the department of industry, commerce, and labor.

If the grantor fails to submit the documents provided for in this article, the department of industry, commerce, and labor shall assess him a fine of 50 to 1,000 pesos, according to the size of the property, granting him another term within which to submit the said documents; no development work shall be begun until compliance shall be had with this requirement.

ART. 52. Within three years, reckoned from the issue of a patent, the grantee of a petroleum property shall be bound to prove to the satisfaction of the petroleum bureau that work on the development of this property has been begun.

ART. 53. The ratification or rectification mentioned in article 50 hereof may be made at the request of the owner of the property, of interested adjoining owners, or as a matter of course by a ruling of the department of industry, commerce, and labor. In this last event the final decision of the department of industry, commerce, and labor shall not affect the rights of the owner of the claim nor those of the adjoining owners who believe their interests are prejudiced.

ART. 54. Grantees of petroleum properties shall be bound to furnish the department of industry, commerce, and labor such technical and economic data as it may demand through the petroleum bureau; they shall likewise be bound to admit on their properties pupils from public schools who may be sent for practical study of the petroleum industry and to afford them every facility in their task. These obligations shall likewise be imposed upon the grantees of pipe lines, refineries, storage tanks, and loading stations.

ART. 55. Patents to petroleum properties shall be forfeited for the following reasons: Through failure to pay the tax referred to in articles 47 and 48 hereof; through failure to comply with the conditions laid down in articles 52 and 54; through suspending work for a period of six consecutive months without cause, after the work of development shall have begun; or through any grave infraction of the regulations of development (reglamento de explotacion).

ART. 56. Forfeiture shall be declared by the administrative authorities through the department of industry, commerce, and labor, after opportunity shall have been given to the interested party to be heard in his own defense, provided he can not prove that his failure was due to "force majeure."

ART. 57. In the event of forfeiture through failure to pay the rental prescribed, the corresponding declaration shall be made within four months following the period of two months within which the failure to make such payment occurred.

In the case of forfeiture through failure to pay the royalty prescribed, the declaration shall be made within the period of two months following that in which the ground for forfeiture occurred.

ART. 58. In the case of the declaration of forfeiture of any petroleum claim, patent to which shall have been issued to any assignees, such claim shall only be open to entry during the three months following the declaration of forfeiture by the prior assignees and by the owner of the surface of the property, who, to this end, shall make a declaration in the form prescribed in articles 15 and 17 of this law in order that the petroleum bureau of the department of industry, commerce, and labor may admit the entry of the last assignee of the right of development.

If the property whose patent shall have been declared forfeited be operated by a third party through a contract still in force, the contract of development shall subsist, the new assignee taking the place of the former assignee for the purposes of the said contract.

ART. 59. The actual operator of a property, officially recognized as such, whose patent shall have been declared forfeited, but who is not the grantee of the property, shall enjoy a preferential right of entry, valid within the 30 days following the term granted in the foregoing article to the several assignees of the right of development and to the owner of the surface of the property, provided none of them have made use of these rights.

He shall likewise enjoy this preference in the cases of forfeiture not included in the foregoing article, within the 30 days following the date on which the declaration of forfeiture shall have been posted on the bulletin board of the respective agency.

ART. 60. Every property comprising leased lands, patent to which shall have been declared forfeited, shall be deemed to be "free land" on the expiration of the terms fixed in the two foregoing articles and of the 30-day period from the date on which the declaration that the land is subject to claim shall have been posted on the bulletin board of the respective agency.

ART. 61. Every property comprising lands not leased, and title to which shall have been declared forfeited, shall be deemed to be free land 30 days after the declaration of forfeiture shall have been affixed to the bulletin board of the respective agency.

TRANSITORY ARTICLES.

1. Entries may be made only on land, statement regarding which shall have been duly submitted and whose area exceeds 4 hectares, provided there exist at present on them wells either in a state of production or which are being drilled, and provided further, that they are corrected by permits previously granted, and provided still further, that statements relating thereto shall have been filed in accordance with the decree of July 31, 1918.

2. The decree of July 8, 1918, and all laws, regulations, and provisions are hereby repealed in so far as they conflict with the present decree.

V. CARRANZA.

MEXICO CITY, *August 8, 1918.*

Mr. DOHENY. This decree provides that article 27 should be put into execution by the recognition of the Government as the owner of all the oil beneath the land which for years has been operated by the various oil companies, and that in carrying out such recognition they shall file manifestos or documents showing the basis of their titles, etc., and that they shall pay rental for those lands at a certain rate per given area, and also royalties at a certain percentage upon the production; that any company refusing to do so would have its titles confiscated or, at least, the right to operate the land would revert to the land government by May 27 of the same year, 1918.

This decree brought forth from the State Department a letter, dated April 2, 1918, which established the policy of this Government with regard to such a decree.

I would like to submit a copy of the letter of April 2, 1918, as showing the attitude assumed by our Government, and which attitude has been attacked within the last few days by witnesses, who find fault with the sense of justice of our State Department, by attempting to prove — although they were not qualified to do so — that the Mexican Government has not attempted to confiscate American property.

The CHAIRMAN. We shall be glad to have that letter go into the record.

(The letter above referred to is here printed in full in the record as follows:)

MEXICO, *April 2, 1918.*

EXCELLENCY: The decree of the 19th of February, 1918, which was published in the Diaro Oficial on the 27th of February last, establishing a tax on oil lands and oil contracts executed prior to the 1st of May, 1917, etc., has been brought to the attention of my Government, and I am under instruction to state to your excellency that my Government has given careful consideration to the effect which this decree, if carried into operation, will have upon American interests and property rights in Mexico.

PROVISIONS OF THE DECREE.

The said decree provides for the imposition of certain taxes on the surface of oil lands, as well as on the rents, royalties, and production derived from the exploitation thereof. It is noted also that among the provisions for the collection of such taxes is one requiring that payment in kind shall be delivered to the Mexican Government at the storage stations of the operators. Articles IV, XIII, and XIV of the said decree seem to indicate an intention to separate the ownership of the surface from that of the mineral deposits of the subsurface and to allow the owners of the surface a mere preference in so far as concerns the right to work the subsoil deposits upon compliance with certain conditions which are specified.

While the United States Government is not disposed to request for its citizens exemption from the payment of their ordinary and just share of the burdens of taxation, so long as the tax is uniform and not discriminatory in its operation, and can fairly be considered a tax and not a confiscation or unfair imposition, and while the United States Government is not inclined to interpose in behalf of its citizens in case of expropriation of private property for sound reasons of public welfare, and upon just compensation and by legal proceedings before tribunals allowing fair and equal opportunity to be heard and given the consideration to American rights, nevertheless the United States can not acquiesce in any procedure ostensibly or nominally in the form of taxation or the exercise of eminent domain but really resulting in the confiscation of private property and arbitrary deprivation of vested rights.

NOT A NEW PRINCIPLE.

Your excellency will understand that this is not an assertion of any new principle of international law, but merely a reiteration of those recognized principles which my Government is convinced form the basis of international respect and good neighborhood. The seizure or spoliation of property at the mere will of the sovereign and without the legal process fairly and equitably administered, has always been regarded as a denial of justice and as affording internationally a basis of interposition.

My Government is not in a position to state definitely that the operation of the aforementioned decree will, in effect, amount to confiscation of American interests. Nevertheless, it is deemed important that the Government of the

United States should state at this time the real apprehension which it entertains as to the possible effect of this decree upon the vested rights of American citizens in oil properties in Mexico. The amount of taxes to be levied by this decree are in themselves a very great burden on the oil industry, and if they are not confiscatory in effect — and as to this my Government reserves opinion — they at least indicate a trend in that direction. It is represented to the State Department that the taxation borne by the oil fields of Mexico very greatly exceeds that imposed on the industry anywhere else in the world. Moreover, it would be possible under the terms of the decree, in view of the fact that the Mexican Government has not storage facilities for the taxes or royalties required to be paid in kind, by storing the same in the tanks of the operators, to monopolize such storage facilities to the point of practical confiscation thereof until emptied by order of the Mexican Government or by the forced sale of the stored petroleum to the operators at extravagant rates.

SURFACE AND SUBSURFACE RIGHTS.

It is, however, to the principle involved in the apparent attempt at separation of surface and subsurface rights under this decree that my Government desires to direct special attention. It would appear that the decree in question is an effort to put into effect as to petroleum lands, paragraph 4 of article 27 of the constitution of May 1, 1917, by severing at one stroke the ownership of the petroleum deposits from the ownership of the surface, notwithstanding that the constitution provides that "private property shall not be expropriated except by reason of public utility and by means of indemnification." So far as my Government is aware no provision has been made by your excellency's Government for just compensation for such arbitrary divestment of rights nor for the establishment of any tribunal invested with the functions of determining justly and fairly what indemnification is due to American interests. Moreover, there appears not the slightest indication that the separation of mineral rights from surface rights in a matter of public utility upon which the right of expropriation depends, according to the terms of the constitution itself. In the absence of the establishment of any procedure looking to the prevention of spoliation of American citizens, and in the absence of any assurance were such procedure established, that it would not uphold in defiance of international law and justice the arbitrary confiscations of Mexican authorities, it becomes the function of the Government of the United States most earnestly and respectfully to call the attention of the Mexican Government to the necessity which may arise to impel it to protect the property of its citizens in Mexico divested or injuriously affected by the decree above cited.

The investments of American citizens in the oil properties of Mexico have been made in reliance upon the good faith and justice of the Mexican Government and Mexican laws, and my Government can not believe that the enlightened Government of a neighboring Republic at peace and at a stage in its progress when the development of its resources so greatly depends on its maintaining good faith with investors and operators, whom it has virtually invited to spend their wealth and energy within its borders, will disregard its clear and just obligations toward them.

Acting under instructions, I have the honor to request your excellency to be good enough to lay before his excellency, the President of Mexico, this formal and solemn protest of the Government of the United States against the violation or infringement of legitimately acquired American private property rights involved in the enforcement of the said decree.

Accept, excellency, the renewed assurance of my highest consideration.

HENRY P. FLETCHER.

Mr. DOHENY. I did not intend, when I started in on this line of talk, to make an argument, but I merely intended to call attention to another plan of confiscation that has grown out of these decrees and article 27, which are existing menaces to the oil producers, and I will skip over this matter of the direct dispute between the oil men and our Government on the one hand with the Mexican Government on the other. I simply touch on that matter because it is one that even though this other dispute may remain unsettled for a long period of time — ought to be settled now because of its obvious injustice and its lack of any benefit to the Mexican Government.

After the decree of February 18, 1918, the Mexican Government adopted the policy of refusing a permit to drill to any company which had not filed these documents required by the decree of February 18th. And inasmuch as 95 per cent of the oil producers engaged in Mexico had refused to do the thing which would be an admission of the lack of ownership of their own properties, they were refused the right to drill upon those properties, and are still so refused. In a later communication from one of the Mexican authorities, I think Mr. Santaella, he asserts that the only reason why the American oil producers had been refused the right to drill was because they refused to obey Mexican laws. That statement on his part is an intentional falsehood. The American companies, with the consent and approval and at the suggestion of our own State Department, refused to file these manifestoes, which would have been an acknowledgement of the confiscation of their own properties. The decree which they disobeyed is not a law of Mexico. It is merely an illegal decree issued by President Carranza, which his best legal advisers tell him is illegal, because it is beyond his power to issue any decree, under his extraordinary powers granted by Congress, except those that relate to matters connected with the department of finance, and this relates to matters connected with an entirely different department, that of Fomento.

In other words, the Mexican Government has attempted, by constitutional legislation, followed by decree, to obtain the surrender by the American petroleum producers of all of their rights in Mexico, and their acceptance in lieu thereof of some sort of a mining claim which would be more easily confiscated at some later date than those titles which they now have, because those which they now have are based upon a legal right and are held in such a way that they are entitled under international law to look to their own Government for the protection of such rights.

Failing to get them to surrender their properties willingly, they now refuse them the right to drill upon those lands. The refusal of the right to use a property, which you have the right to use, is certainly confiscation. That form of confiscation is being carried on today in Mexico, and, notwithstanding all their assurances that they do not intend to do anything to deprive Americans of their rights, there has been no attempting on the part of any Mexican official to explain why they have refused drilling rights to companies which they admit have the right to drill upon the land.

I do not of my own suggestion think of any other matter of which you might be willing to have me give some information, but I am ready to answer any questions that you see fit to submit to me.

Senator BRANDEGEE. I was going to ask you about this decree of April 2, which the stenographer took out.

Mr. DOHENY. The letter?

Senator BRANDEGEE. The letter by Mr. Fletcher.

Mr. DOHENY. Yes.

Senator BRANDEGEE. What ground did they take? I didn't have the opportunity to read it. Can you state substantially the position of our State Department?

Mr. DOHENY. Well, it took the ground that, under international law, the right of foreigners could not be set aside by mere legislation or the adoption of a new fundamental law, and that any act that led to that would be considered a sufficient ground for interposition, quoting exactly the words, I think, used by Secretary Bayard in a communication made to the Government of Peru during the presidency of Mr. Cleveland.

Senator BRANDEGEE. What was the reply of the Mexican Government to that representation of our own State Department? Is that in one of these books?

Mr. DOHENY. Yes, sir; I think it is.

Senator BRANDEGEE. Can that go in the record also?

Mr. DOHENY. I would like to submit a dossier we have made up, containing an immense amount of information collected by our attorneys on this subject. I am not familiar with the wording of these documents, nor with the purpose and intent of all of them, but if you desire I will have those portions marked with a pencil that I think you would be interested in.

Mr. WALKER. I made a mistake when I said the Government reply had been published. It has not been published. The United States Government asked for permission to publish it, and although the Mexican Government published a United States note without permission they have refused the United States Government the permission to publish this reply.

Mr. DOHENY. Nevertheless, we have included a copy of it with these documents.

Mr. WALKER. No. sir.

Mr. DOHENY. I will see that the committee gets a copy. I will file a copy of it, because we have a copy.

Senator BRANDEGEE. If you file this document you speak of —

Mr. DOHENY. The reply from the Mexican Government?

Senator BRANDEGEE. Yes; and the other thing you referred to — dossier. I don't know what you mean by it; I suppose you used a Spanish word; but this tabulation by your counsel to which you have referred — then we can order any portion of it that we think proper to be put in the record.

Mr. DOHENY. I will have it marked so as to call your attention to the portions I think are explanatory. In fact, the whole thing really is a record of the actions that have been taken by our own Government, the Mexican Government, and by our association in connection with this entire dispute.

Senator BRANDEGEE. What is the quality of the oil produced in your field, as compared with that in the Texas and California fields?

Mr. DOHENY. There are many different kinds of oil produced in the California and Texas fields, but in Mexico up to date we have only two distinct classes of oil, and both of them are the heavy type of oil. The oil which was first developed and which is produced in the Pamico district is of very heavy Baumé gravity, 10° to 12° Baumé, is viscous, as thick as cold honey, is a very satisfactory fuel oil, produces a very fine quality of asphaltum, does not yield a high per centage of gasoline, and is not refined to any great extent.

The oil that is produced in regions farther south, commencing about 5 miles south of Tampico, is a much lighter oil, averages about 20° Baumé, yields about 12½ per cent gasoline, contains a considerable percentage of kerosene if refined, and its ultimate commercial product will yield a substantial percentage of lubricant and 2 or 3 per cent of paraffin. It is usually refined for the purpose of producing two commercial products, mainly — that is, gasoline and fuel oil — although quite a substantial percentage of kerosene is also taken out in refining. This lighter oil which I refer to contains a much larger percentage of gasoline than any other oil of the same gravity produced in the world. The average percentage of gasoline in the oil produced in California and Texas is 5 to 7 per cent, and, as I stated before, this Mexican oil yields about 12½ per cent.

Senator BRANDEGEE. What is the most valuable ingredient of the oil as it comes out from the ground?

Mr. DOHENY. The gasoline. The lubricants are not so valuable.

Senator BRANDEGEE. Would it be possible in a general way to state the quality of the oil you produce in Mexico? Is it better or inferior to that of Texas?

Mr. DOHENY. Well, the oils we produce in Mexico are less valuable than the Texas oils. That does not mean they are inferior, but they produce a smaller percentage of the more valuable commercial product, such as gasoline, although they are much more valuable than some of the Texas oils. But the great production of the Ranger and other fields in northern Texas of light oils, carrying a higher percentage of gasoline, has raised the standard of the Texas oils from that of the very low standard that prevailed several years ago to among the best oils produced in the country.

Senator BRANDEGEE. I thought I remembered your stating yesterday, in regard to some oil that you got out in Mexico, that it took four and a half barrels of oil to equal in efficiency 1 ton of coal.

Mr. DOHENY. I said three and one-half.

Senator BRANDEGEE. I understood you to say a little while ago, referring to some oil used by the English, or some report made by them, that one barrel of oil was equal to 2 tons of coal.

Mr. DOHENY. One ton of oil is equal to 2 tons of coal.

The English speak of all fuel by the ton. As a matter of fact, during the war all the oils that were sold on that side were sold by the ton for export to the war zone. It is not a bad way to speak of oil where it is used for consumption in transportation, because the weight of the fuel has quite as much to do with its value, where it is carried a long distance, as the cost of it. This is not a direct answer to your question, but it contains some information as to why oil is more valuable as green fuel that as fuel under a stationary boiler, because the further oil is carried, as compared with coal, the cheaper it is. It takes 2 tons of coal to do the work of 1 ton of oil. That takes the place of a ton of freight which might be earning something, or if you look at it in another way, the same bunker space or the same tonnage capacity will carry a ship to its port of destination and back, where you would have to take coal at both ends of the voyage.

Senator BRANDEGEE. How many barrels of oil will it take to weigh a ton?

Mr. DOHENY. Approximately seven barrels. That depends on whether you use the United States ton of 2,000 pounds, the metric ton of 2,204 pounds, or the English ton of 2,240 pounds. The weight of oil is a little less than that of water — the weight of fuel oil.

I might suggest that, in order to put before the United States Government and the people of the United States an unprejudiced study of the entire Mexican situation, at the suggestion of a prominent New Yorker, four years ago I authorized him to organize for me a committee of 12 college presidents to take up the study of Mexico, in the interests of humanity and of Mexico and the United States, and to report to the President of the United States, and have the report published in book form. I never learned the names of those gentlemen, although I put up nearly $20,000 to meet the expenses which they were incurring.

I am mentioning this, not for the purpose of exalting myself as a giver of money for eleemosynary purposes, nor for the purpose of advertising myself as a man whose name ought to read "E.Z." instead of "E.D." but merely for the purpose of calling attention to the facts that there are people interested in Mexico who are also interested in an impartial and unprejudiced report of the conditions there by men qualified to make such a report, and which would be dignified by the character of the men themselves. And I was gratified to learn yesterday that among the gentlemen operating on that committee was Prof. Winton, who testified here.

Senator BRANDEGEE. Is the committee operating yet?

Mr. DOHENY. No. They dropped it, and I will explain why, because Prof. Winton did not seem to know. The committee was organized with Prof. Dabney, of the University of Ohio, I think, as chairman. I named one or two members of the committee myself, and one of the two I named could not act. I named Bishop Conaty, of Los Angeles, and also Dr. Norman Bridge, the treasurer of our companies. The other names I will secure for you and place in the record, because I am proud to have been associated, even though very indirectly, with these men.

Senator BRANDEGEE. You were about to state why they dropped it.

Mr. DOHENY. They had several meetings. I think Prof. Winton made a report to them last year on knowledge he already had about Mexico.

The CHAIRMAN. Yes, sir; he called our attention to that.

Senator BRANDEGEE. I will not bother you about that.

Mr. DOHENY. It was not stated before. Prof. Winton didn't

know. The work was carried on for several months, but it was being carried on while I was in Europe. I went over there after the war commenced and was there during the months of March and April, and while I was gone they had their meetings. When I came back I arranged with them to go through Mexico, and I attempted to arrange to get transportation facilities so they could go where they wished.

At that time there were two armed forces in Mexico opposing each other, it seemed, with nearly equal chances of success, and the Government of the United States had already made some overtures to them to lay down their arms and get together with representatives of South American countries and of the United States and arrive at some satisfactory settlement of the Mexican situation. The two leaders at that time were Francisco Villa and Venustiano Carranza. They were joint leaders of the constitutionalist forces against Huerta, and disagreed later on. At that time Villa held a portion of northern Mexico, and had advanced as far south as Mexico City and had placed the president that he favored in charge in Mexico City.

The Carranza forces were badly scattered. Gen. Obregon was somewhere in Hidalgo or Vera Cruz, and Gen. Carranza was at Vera Cruz, on the island of San Juan de Ulloa.

I attempted to get what is called in Mexico a safe conduct for these gentlemen through northern Mexico, and I was told by people in communication with Villa that that would be granted throughout his territory. I endeavored to get it, through a representative I had in Vera Cruz, from Gen. Carranza, but he would not grant it. Nevertheless, we intended to endeavor to make the trip, but about the time they were ready to go a battle took place between Gen. Obregon, who was returning to his home in southern Mexico, and the forces of Villa in the town of Silao, which resulted in the defeat of Villa, the scattering of his forces over northern Mexico, and the demoralization of transportation facilities to such an extent that the people who headed the organization made up their minds, with me, that it was not wise at that particular time to undertake a study of the situation, because it would have to be made under such unfavorable auspices. So it was dropped.

Later on, about two years ago, another gentleman who knew about the effort that I had made to have this carried out came to me and suggested that he was willing to take up the work and make a study of the Mexican situation. After giving it full consideration I told him I was willing to devote up to $100,000 for the purpose of making the study, as he unfolded the plan to me. I wrote him a letter of authority, a copy of which I will place in the record later on. I haven't it with me. I actually expended to date nearly $120,000, and the work is not yet completed.

But I have got with me a statement of the names of the men who were engaged in it, and I will file this list, so the stenographer need not take down the names, just for the purpose of showing you what the work was and that it was not propaganda work, not anti-Carranza work, nor intervention work.

(The list above referred to is as follows:)

DOHENY RESEARCH FOUNDATION – LIST OF PERSONS ENGAGED IN GATHERING MATERIAL, GIVING SOMEWHAT SPECIAL ATTENTION TO SUBJECT OPPOSITE TO HIS OR HER NAME.

Percy Martin, Stanford University, California . . . . .Labor
Theodore Macklin, Univeristy of Wisconsin . . . . Agriculture
Robert Cleland, Occidental College, California . . . . Mining
F. W. Powell, Columbia University, New York. . . . . .Transportation
W. W. Cumberland, Univeristy of Minnesota . . . . Manufacturing
Isaac J. Cox, Northwestern University . . . . .Education
Harry A. Bard, formerly commissioner of education, Peru. . . . . . . .Education
Arthur N. Young, Princeton University . . . . Public finance
W. F. McCaleb, Chicago University . . . . Banking
Chester Lloyd Jones, University of Wisconsin . . . . Commerce
Julius Klein, Harvard University . . . . Commerce
George Winfield Scott, formerly of Columbia University. . . . Foreign relations
W. L. Blair, journalist . . . . Government
H. I. Priestly, University of California . . . . Government
Albert Noel, journalist . . . . .Public health
James Robertson, Latin American Division, Department
    of Commerce . . . . .Public health
Wallace Thompson, journalist . . . . Social conditions
Miss Ida A. Tourtellot, Hampton Institute, Virginia . . . . Social conditions

These are the people who gathered the material, and gathered it in some way I know nothing about. I have had detached accounts occasionally that this, that, or the other man had gone into Mexico, with a passport or without a passport. Most of them were refused passports by Mr. Bonillas, the minister from Mexico, because it was the work of somebody they had determined to make an enemy of. The parties in power in Mexico had determined to make an enemy of me on account of my success, and I want that to go in the record. They have tried to prevent me from doing the things I would like to do to help out those people down there, and for whom I lay down to no man in desire to give assistance, both as a friend of humanity and a friend of the people who have always been friends of mine. There were 78,000 pages, more or less, of matter gathered by these men. This is a list of the people who were engaged in research and foundation work, and I don't suppose I have met 10 of the men engaged in it. I don't know what they have done. The work has not been completed. So, good or bad, it has not done much harm to Mexico and has not accomplished much in the way of bringing about intervention, if that was its purpose.

The CHAIRMAN. That was not its purpose in any sense.

Mr. DOHENY. Absolutely not. This is the list:

DOHENY RESEARCH FOUNDATION.

LIST OF PERSONS ENGAGED IN INTERPRETING MATERIAL, GIVING SPECIAL ATTENTION TO SUBJECTS OPPOSITE THEIR NAMES.

Elwood Meade, University of California. . . . . Irrigation
Frank Probert, University of California . . . . Mining
Victor S. Clark, editorial staff Atlantic Monthly and
    Living Age . . . . .Manufacturing and commerce
W. E. Dunn, University of Texas. . . . . Banking
W. T. Sedgwick, director School Public Health, main-
    tained jointly by Massachusetts School of Technology
    and Harvard Medical School . . . . .Public health

LIST OF PERSONS COMPOSING STAFF OF RESEARCH ASSISTANTS, TRANSLATORS, AND COMPUTERS IN VERY FINE DOUBTFUL POINTS.

Herbert Thompson	J. M. Butterfield
W. L. Blair	A. L. Tays
Percy Martin	Livingston Porter
W. W. McEuen	Franklin Schneider
H. H. Havermale	Albert Noel

Senator BRANDEGEE. I want to ask you a question about oil. How long is it possible to store oil?

Mr. DOHENY. Oil loses its value by evaporation from month to month, if it is stored, but it can be stored indefinitely with that constantly changing condition.

In regard to this "Doheny Research Foundation," I want to say that after having presented the letter, by the terms of which I authorized the work to go on, to the president of the University of California, that university kindly allowed them space in their building and many facilities of their institution for carrying on the work. I just received a letter, sent to me to London, from President Benjamin Ide Wheeler, of the University of California. This just came to me last night, and I would like to read it as showing the opinion which he has of the work of this research foundation, and which, of course, is information to me, because I never followed the progress of the work and did not know what they were doing.

(The letter referred to is here copied in full as follows:)

UNIVERSITY OF CALIFORNIA,
126 University Library, Berkeley, July 21, 1919.

MY DEAR MR. DOHENY: Now that we have created a full year of experience in the workings of the Mexican Commission founded and developed by you, I want to express to you my appreciation of the success which has attended the undertaking. It was evidently a venture. You were undertaking something toward which you could only grope. There was a lack of definite data regarding similar undertakings. I doubt if there had been any such a plan. You were willing, however, to go ahead and take the initiative. The university seconded your endeavors by giving you shelter. The value of the academic shelter is not to be underestimated. It means on the whole an assurance that inquiries conducted under the name of the university shall be disinterested and fair to all parties and points of view. Universities frequently make mistakes like other institutions, but they have the interesting quality of scientific, disinterestedness. At least that is so for most of the time and for most people.

Really the best assurance of disinterested inquiry rests with the character of the men employed by the commission. This commission has, in matter of fact, been made up of excellent men, upright, and honest, and able. It is evidently of great importance for the United States to get on well with Mexico. The only way for the two parties to get on together is for them each to understand the other — to know exactly where the difficulty lies and what the need is. The only way to get at that is through scientific enquiry on a scientific basis with a scientific goal. I reckon also with the consideration that we must bring this scientifically developed matter to public attention and public understanding. A considerable variety of publications will be necessary in order to bring the material factfully and effectively to the attention and the knowledge of the two communities. It will not only be necessary to publish scientific pamphlets and scientific books, but there must be tracts and pamphlets which appeal to the public interest — which get a hearing and stir the hearing into reasonable and sensible action. I think your Commission has made a good beginning. So far as I can now see it promises well for the future. Nothing can defeat its purposes unless it discloses itself as apparently devoted to some kind of propaganda or as having an "ax to grind." There are frequent inquiries made as to what the purposes of the commission are, and it would be undoubtedly easy to make a mistake. There is no safety except in absolute scientific disinterestedness. So far as I have been able to see nothing has been done that could impair the claims of the commission to scientific honesty. I believe it is our duty to go steadily ahead on the path we have been going and continue on earning a good name. I congratulate you on the work you have been able to do. It seems to me altogether worthwhile.

Very faithfully, yours,

BENJ. IDE WHEELER.

E. L. DOHENY, Esq.,
Care William Salomon & Co., London, England.

Mr. DOHENY. I would like to put this letter in for the benefit of those who may care to read this testimony.

The CHAIRMAN. It will be placed in the testimony following the list of names.

Mr. DOHENY. In other words, I would like to show the attitude of the oil people toward the people of Mexico, and to show we have not been unmindful of the needs of those people down there, as well as the rights of our own stockholders. When I first became acquainted in Mexico I became very well acquainted with a gentleman who was our second attorney, Mr. Joaquin de Casasus. We had to dispense with our first attorney, because he had to choose between the railroad company, whom he had for a long time represented, and our oil company, which had so recently become his client, because of the contract and threatened lawsuit which existed between them. So Mr. Casasus became our attorney and my very warm friend.

I ventured one day to say to him, in a moment of generosity, that I would like to have the opportunity of doing some good in the way of developing the best instincts of and of educating the people who were in our employ and who lived in our vicinity of the Huasteca region. I asked him if he would request his wife and ask Secretary Limantour if he would request his wife, to become the sponsors for an academy I would establish at Ebano, or Chijol, or some other suitable place to be selected by us jointly, for the education of the children of those who worked for us as well as those who might care to come from more distant localities. I offered to place at their disposal, for the purpose of carrying on this education, $50,000. I asked them to furnish us with the teachers and to be sponsors for the school, so we could not be accused of doing something contrary to the laws of Mexico. That was submitted to Mr. Limantour in my presence by Mr. Casasus. It was acknowledged, and I never heard another word about it.

Years later, when Mr. Madero came into power, I told Mr. Madero of my desire to do something to start an educational institution on our property, or near it, at some suitable point, to develop a technical and agricultural school. I told him of the developments we had made which justified now a larger institution than the one I had talked of to Mr. Casasus, and I suggested that one of the healthiest places on our property, a place called Chijol, would be suitable, and that I would get our company to grant a thousand or more acres of land, or hectares of land, if that amount were needed, and we would start an institution there for the training of Mexicans of any age who might desire to learn agriculture; that we would build machine shops and other places needed to do the work in the oil camps and educate the young men and give them technical training.

I offered to contribute for that purpose $500,000. I made the offer again later on through Mr. Calero, who had been the minister of foreign relations for Madero and who was at that time ambassador to the United States. Mr. Calero promised me to take it up with Mr. Madero and see if a law could not be framed that would permit of the organization of such an institution and to have for its control such trustees as might be selected to see that the money was properly used.

The death of Mr. Madero the next spring prevented that from being carried on.

I just mention those as incidents to show the feeling which our company has always had toward the people among whom we were doing business since nearly 20 years ago.

Senator BRANDEGEE. Was this to be a free academy?

Mr. DOHENY. A free academy; yes, sir.

The CHAIRMAN. You have, however, carried on the schools, the photographs of which you showed here this morning?

Mr. DOHENY. We have carried them on at our own expense with competent teachers and they are training a large number of pupils. They are not public schools, but they are open to the public; they are privately maintained, but open to the public.

Here are some more photographs showing how the people live down there. I would like to place these on file to show we take care of our employees (handing photographs to the chairman).

The CHAIRMAN. They are very instructive.

Mr. DOHENY. These show the homes of the peons.

The CHAIRMAN. What rent do you charge your employees for those houses?

Mr. DOHENY. I am afraid I could not answer that.

Mr. WALKER. Nothing, Mr. Doheny.

Mr. DOHENY. I am perfectly willing to answer that under oath, on account of the source of the information.

The CHAIRMAN. What is the source of their water supply?

Mr. DOHENY. We bring the water through a steel pipe line a distance of about 45 miles — or we did bring it that distance. Now we have developed some water about 4 or 5 miles away, good, clean well water, and they have baths and hydrants in their houses just exactly the same as the Americans have. Their source of supply of water is the same. Their ice is from the same place; their food is of the same quality, and their houses are inspected for sanitary purposes by our health officers.

The CHAIRMAN. What do they pay for water; do you know?

Mr. DOHENY. They pay nothing for water, nothing for light, nothing for fuel of any sort. I am quite sure that is true — I do not testify as to this under oath, but I am quite sure this is true as to every oil company operating in the Huasteca region — as to every American company, and the others, too, I think.

The CHAIRMAN. Mr. Doheny, you said you would see that the committee had a copy of the reply of Gen. Carranza to the note of Mr. Lansing. Would you care to give us in general words from your memory the purport of that reply, or do you prefer to wait until you can furnish us with a copy of the letter?

Mr. DOHENY. I think you would get it more nearly correct if Mr. Walker were to give it. Mr. Walker has been our representative here before the State Department in connection with all these matters, and I think his memory would be better as to the language of that letter.

Do you chance to remember it, Mr. Walker?

Mr. WALKER. I remember the purport of it.

Mr. DOHENY. Only the purport?

Mr. WALKER. Yes.

The CHAIRMAN. We will take that subject up later.

Mr. Doheny, you spoke of the increase in your taxes within a year, something about the percentage of increase being approximately 800. Is that simply a tax to the regular Government paid through governmental channels?

Mr. DOHENY. Yes, sir.

The CHAIRMAN. Did it include any other expense connected with your properties there?

Mr. DOHENY. No, sir. I think those other expenses are carried to "General expenses" if I remember rightly.

The CHAIRMAN. What are the other expenses? I do not mean in amount, but what is the occasion for them?

Mr. DOHENY. With the advent of the first revolutionary forces into the Huasteca region came the occupation of the oil territory by an opposing force to that which occupied the harbor of Tampico, and at the time that the Huerta forces, or Federals, were in charge of Tampico, the surrounding country was quickly occupied by what were called Constitutionalists, who were opposing Huerta, and were supposed to be following out the ideas of Madero and were determined to oppose the usurpation of Madero's power by one of his generals — Huerta.

The first demand upon us for the payment of taxes or contribuciones, or whatever they might be called, was from a general of the Constitutionalist Army who had organized a force in Vera Cruz, and who had come up from central Vera Cruz toward Tampico, and had located near Tuxpan. He sent word to Mr. Walker or Mr. Green, our superintendent, that he must pay $50,000 (pesos) under penalty of being prevented from shipping oil from our properties.

The CHAIRMAN. At that time were you paying taxes to the Huerta government on your oil shipments?

Mr. DOHENY. Up to that time we had been paying; but right there there are two subjects that really might be discussed at the same time. In reply to your last question, I will say that as soon as our Government turned its back on Huerta and refused to recognize him, we refused to pay him any more taxes. Up to that time we paid taxes to Huerta. This other man, being merely a revolutionist who was opposed to Huerta, and at that time not, so far as we knew, connected with any other particular revolutionist, we hesitated to pay anything to him.

The CHAIRMAN. He was in charge of the oil fields where your oil wells were?

Mr. DOHENY. He was located near the oil fields at that time.

The CHAIRMAN. He was not in Tampico itself?

Mr. DOHENY. No, sir; he was outside of Tampico, about 100 miles south. His name was Gen. Candido Aguilar.

The CHAIRMAN. Was he the same Candido Aguilar who was in the city of Washington recently?

Mr. DOHENY. Yes, sir; the same man. He was at that time a self-appointed general of forces he had collected in central Vera Cruz, and was what might be called at present a rebel or a revolutionist or a bandit, if you please. Those names are all interchangeable in the country at the present time.

Let me make a correction. I was mistaken in the amount that he demanded. It was $10,000.

The CHAIRMAN. If you have a memorandum there, you can, of course, refresh your memory from it.

Mr. DOHENY. That money was paid to him, or part of it, by Mr. Walker, who went to Tuxpam for that purpose, thereby risking his life in order to save our properties, and with the knowledge and consent and after consulting John Lind, the United States presidential representative in Mexico, through the American consul at Vera Cruz.

That was the first contribution which we ever made to other than the government in authority at Tampico.

The CHAIRMAN. That was to Candido Aguilar?

Mr. DOHENY. Yes, sir.

The next contribution which we made — and, by the way, this is connected with our refusal to pay taxes to Huerta — was to Gen. Carranfia, through Felicitas Villareal and Rafael Zubaran y Campany.

Mr. Walker was living in the City of Mexico at that time as our representative there, and the Huerta or Federal officials were in power in that city. They demanded of Mr. Walker that he pay the taxes which we had failed to pay upon oil exported, but on advices from me he refused. Finally his life was threatened. He was threatened with arrest, imprisonment, and execution by the treasurer of Mexico if he did not pay the tax. So I advised him by cable to make a draft for $100,000 in favor of the Huerta treasury and then get out of Mexico, which he did, coming down to Vera Cruz. I immediately stopped payment on the draft, on the theory that it was obtained under duress by a government which our Government refused to recognize, and we were not in honor or in any other way bound to pay it. Luckily for Mr. Walker, our troops had just taken Vera Cruz, so when he got to Vera Cruz he was at home.

But what I am going to state now is for the purpose of showing how we acted toward the Constitutionalist forces which at that time were headed by the present President of Mexico — Venustiano Carranza. I sought out his representative, Felicitas Villareal, who was the treasurer of the Constitutionalists, and Rafael Zubaran y Capmany. I told them of our refusal to pay taxes to Huerta and said that if they would give me their promise that if that draft came into their hands after they captured the City of Mexico they would return it to us and not present it for collection I would now pay them the amount of the draft in money, in New York, so that they could use it for the purpose of helping to finance their needs. I paid the cash and Dr. Bridge was with me in the Hotel Belmont in the city of New York. I also sent to see Señor Carranza, our attorney, or one of our attorneys, a man named Pedro Rendon, whose brother was the first man sacrificed by Huerta. I told him to assure Gen. Carranza of our friendship toward the cause of the Constitutionalists and of our refusal to pay taxes to Huerta and of our desire to act in accord with our own Government's attitude in connection with Mexico, and to tell him that if they needed fuel of any sort we would be glad to furnish them the fuel, keeping an account of it, and that we would refuse to pay taxes to Huerta, and that some time later when he came into authority we could adjust the matters and strike a balance as to the account against us for oil taxes and the amount which we might have charged against them for fuel oil delivered under our contract with the National Railways of Mexico.

This arrangement he agreed to and we carried it out to the extent of a credit to the Mexican Government of $685,000 and a charge against ourselves for taxes of $662,000. These figures are not exactly correct, but they are approximately correct.

About that time the situation had changed greatly. Huerta had resigned and left Mexico. Gen. Carranza and Villa had become estranged from each other. Carranza was living in Vera Cruz and Villa in some other part of Mexico.

When a representative from Mr. Carranza, the first chief of the Constitutionalist forces, arrived in Tampico with an account submitted by us to them of oils exported and a demand for the payment of the $662,000, of course, our representatives at Tampico were very much surprised, because they knew that the balance in our accounts with them were in their favor.

Nevertheless, he insisted upon our payment. Cablegrams were exchanged between our general superintendent in Mexico and myself. I instructed him not to pay. They threatened to detain our ships, but I continued to insist that he should not pay. Our ships were actually detained. An embargo was placed upon their movement. I telegraphed to Mr. Walker, who was spending New Year's Day with his family in the States on a vacation from Mexico, to immediately proceed to Galveston, where I would send to him a statement of our accounts against the Carranza Government with a copy of the draft which I had paid to Felicitas Villareal and Señor Zubaran y Capmany, and that he should go to Tampico and get such other evidences of our account against the Constitutionalists and of our indebtedness to them and proceed to Vera Cruz and get the account O.K.'d by Señor Carranza.

I had a little yacht at that time as to which, by the way, I will take the liberty, if you will allow me, of placing its history in this record. It was a yacht called *Wakival I*, which I purchased and sent down to Mexico to remain in the port of Tampico under a full head of steam so as to be a haven of refuge to any of our employees who might be compelled to seek shelter because of the strained relations between the United States and Mexico.

I kept that yacht there under a full head of steam, using it occasionally for traveling to Texas across the Gulf, until the time I speak of, when I cabled to have it sent for Mr. Walker's use to Galveston. He attempted to go into Tampico on the yacht in a heavy norther, and left it on the outer end of the south jetty, where what is left of its skeleton still remains. He escaped with his life, got a tugboat, and went down to Vera Cruz. He presented evidence which I had sent to him and which he collected in Tampico, to Mr. Carranza, and got the release of our tank steamers; but in the meantime, I must say, in justice to the State Department, that we had never up to that time asked for any aid or assistance or protection or interposition on the part of our Government, but I did then cable to our attorney, Mr. F. R. Kellogg, of Morristown, N. J., asking him to come to Washington and see Secretary Bryan about this matter.

A cable was sent to Mr. Carranza, signed by Mr. Bryan and by the late Sir Cecil Spring-Rice, who was British ambassador at that time to the United States.

As result of that cable the embargo was immediately lifted from our steamers, and as result of Mr. Walker's conversation with Señor Carranza an order was given to settle our account with the Government on the basis of our statement of the difference between us.

This is merely one of a hundred or more incidents which show the checkered career of a company doing business outside of the boundaries of its own country, and is given merely for the reason that it shows the attitude of our company toward the Constitutionalist forces when they were in need of help.

So far as we know, every American corporation doing business in Mexico extended sympathy or aid, or both — and we extended both — to Carranza from the time that President Wilson turned his back on Huerta. We were true to our own Government, and because of that were friendly and of aid to the Carranza Government.

The CHAIRMAN. Is the Carranza Government now in control of the oil fields near Tampico?

Mr. DOHENY. The Carranza Government, I believe, is in control of some of the oil fields. I read in the paper this morning that the Carranza forces had defeated the forces of Pelaez in the Tampico district, and I know that some of the forces are stationed on some of our properties farther south in what we call the Huasteca district. But outside of the immediate camps of the Carranzistas the country is held by a force under a local landowner whose name is Pelaez. He is one of the owners of properties leased to, some years ago, and which are still operated by the Mexican Eagle Co., which was then Lord Cowdray's company, and now is controlled by the "Royal Dutch."

This man Pelaez has an organized force of some numbers, and has held possession of a large portion of the country for the last two years. I think his force was organized at about the promulgation of the constitution in 1917 and in opposition to that constitution. He calls himself the only constitutionalist there is in Mexico, because he adheres to the constitution of 1857.

He was in a position to and did prevent us from shipping oil from our southern properties, from Casiano and Cerro Azul. He cut our pipe line three times between Casiano and Cerro Azul. His men threatened to kill our employees if they repaired it again. Not being desirous, however, of killing our employees, he decided on a plan of taking away a part of one of our pumps, which absolutely prevented the passage of the oil beyond that station. He held that until we agreed not to restore the pipe line nor to ship any oil until we paid him a tribute. I do not remember the exact date — Mr. Walker can probably give it — that I first received information that he demanded of us tribute for protection.

Senator BRANDEGEE. Protection against himself?

Mr. DOHENY. Against anybody.

I received the following radiogram from my steam yacht, my present yacht, *Casiano*. I may say as apology for owning a yacht, that I have owned a yacht, one or another, for seven years, and I have occupied one for just two months — so I am not guilty of being a yachtsman. I am just merely the owner of a yacht, because it was necessary to have one to bring Americans whose lives were threatened, out of Mexico, and we brought the little yacht there, at the time of the invasion of Vera Cruz, and at the time that Nafaratte declared war against the United States, and we brought out 192 on the yacht and an amount totaling 900 on our tank steamers, so that our presence in the harbor has been a source of safety or an immense amount of mental relief to a large number of Americans who took advantage of the offers we made to go to the States when these dangers threatened them. I really think their lives were saved, because I think their continued presence there would have caused a general massacre.

This last yacht that I have and which I am now using as a residence in the harbor of New York, has a wireless apparatus, as did the first one; and I had sent me on the 4th of February, 1916, the following radiogram:

Pelaez's forces again control Huasteca. He has sent us notice as follows: "I have assigned to Huasteca Petroleum Co. the sum of $30,000 every month, which should be paid without any excuse from January 1, 1916. In case the company should refuse to comply with this disposition we will proceed to stop all the work on the exportation of oil and also to advise the employees of the company to leave the different camps." First paragraph of notice states he has given protection to companies in his zone for past 16 months without their paying anything for its support. Therefore each company will have to pay hereafter, and we are taxed thirty thousand or fifteen hundred gold at present. Don't know what Aguila or Penn Mex are taxed. Latter camp looted on first stop. My fear is danger from other side if we pay, as Pelaez is now an outlaw, but Carranza unable or unwilling drive Pelaez out permanently. Also Pelaez now desperate and apt to take vengeance on Americans. Believe advisable shut down all developments for present until we are guaranteed protection from

Washington. Have told Flick and Green we will pay, if necessary. Will wire you full text communication from Galveston tomorrow, as believe matter should be taken up with Washington. Matter could be easily disposed of if present Government had not been recognized. Due Galveston early tomorrow. Would like return Sunday as payment due 10th.

That was sent by wireless from the yacht. It could not be sent from the telegraph office in Mexico; it had to be sent from the yacht by radiogram, because if it were put on the wires there it would immediately have come to the attention of the Carranza authorities and our people would have been imprisoned. This is from our general manager, Mr. Wylie:

Walker and I have discussed your message from yacht. Do not believe we can do other than pay Pelaez. Not in favor of abandoning camp and anxious to get new developments soon as possible. Sending your message to Doheny at Los Angeles and waiting reply.

Another, sent by Paddleford from Galveston. He says:

Arrived ashore 10:30 this morning. Am wiring Doheny full copy Pelaez communication. Fully agree with you and Walker that Palaez will have to be paid. My only anxiety is that Washington should know facts, so that in case of reprisal by other people we will have our Government back of us. Believe Pelaez will be driven out before March 1, and think Washington should insist that Carranza leave enough forces in the field to keep Pelaez out. Otherwise bringing in big well places us in precarious condition. Getting clearance for yacht to return tomorrow.

This was sent just before we brought in our big well which I told you about this morning, which yielded 250,000 barrels a day.

I call particular attention to this because, so far as our being the advocates and supporters of Pelaez, as charged in the newspapers and by Cabrera, in the Mexican congress, we were insisting that Carranza should keep force enough there so as to keep Pelaez out. And, of course, he could not do it, and has not done it up to date.

This is a communication giving further information on the question of the demand of Pelaez:

Following full text Pelaez communication: "The General this day wrote me as follows: 'To the representative of the Huasteca Petroleum Co. in Cerro Azul: Please go to Cerro Azul Camp today and notify the Huasteca Petroleum Co. that in view of the fact that for one year and four months the forces under my orders have given ample protection to the different companies that are located in the zone controlled by my forces without paying any contribution to their support, and that the said companies have been paying big sums to the cause of the Constitutionalist Government, I have thought it best, in order to save the poorer classes of people from suffering any damage that the said companies contribute every month to the support of said forces, I have assigned to the Huasteca Petroleum Co. the sum of 30,000 pesos every month, which should be paid without any excuse, from the 1st of January, 1916.

" 'Please notify the company that the amount that is already due should be paid on the 10th of this month, and in future payments should be made the last day of every month. In case the company should refuse to comply with this disposition we will precede to stop all the work on the exportation of oil and also to advise the employees of the company to leave the different camps.

" 'This for your information.

" 'Reform, liberty, justice, and law.

" 'Cerro Azul, *February 1, 1916.*

" 'The colonial chief of the column.

        " '(Signed)   D. MARTINEZ HERRERA.' "   PADDLEFORD

Those messages were always formal. They were not merely "Hands up"; they wrote them in the most formal way, as though they were decrees from a court.

I then wired Wylie to New York, as follows:

Just received yours from Paddleford. Please instruct him to pay the fifteen hundred monthly under duress until further notice or until no duress exists. We can not afford either to shut down or to oppose such demands. If Walker can call attention of minister quietly believe no harm would be done. Otherwise, not advisable under existing circumstances.

I decided what amount we would pay and did not leave it to him, and I decided on $1,500. Then this telegram to Paddleford by Walker:

Your telegram regarding Pelaez. Am going Washington tonight to show whole file to Lansing. Thoroughly appreciate your attitude and believe frank statement our position most beneficial to company from both viewpoints.

Mr. Walker received the following message from Wylie, our general manager:

Doheny wires you he expects leave Los Angeles Wednesday en route Tampico. Wants know if you will meet him Galveston. Says will wire date later.

Then this telegram from Wylie to Walker:

Doheny asks that you communicate with him the result of your various interviews regarding Paddleford's business. Paddleford delighted with your wire.

The telegram that I read before comes after that:

Doheny wires you he expects leave Los Angeles Wednesday en route Tampico. Wants know if you will meet him Galveston. Says will wire date later.

Now, that file contains evidence, such as it is, of the communications which passed between the officials of our company relative to the first demand made by the revolutionist or bandit that they called Gen. Pelaez. I instructed Mr. Walker to go to Washington, see our State Department, make a statement of the situation, go to Arredondo, and tell Mr. Arredondo what the situation was, and get the opinion of both as to what they thought we ought to do, but at the same time tell them that we expected to comply with this of our own election, because we were the best judges of what we ought to do to save our own property.

So I am telling this secondhand now. If you like, later on, you can put Mr. Walker on the stand to corroborate it or change it.

Mr. Walker reported to me that he went to the State Department and saw Mr. Lansing or Mr. Polk, stated the situation to them, and that he was going to put the matter up to Arredondo, and that they advised him that we should use our own best judgment; but they did not advise him that we were doing anything that should subject us to blame or criticism or criminal charge if we were to pay this money as demanded. Mr. Walker says he went to see Arredondo and told Arredondo what the facts were, and that Arredondo at first objected to the payment of it, and that Walker called his attention, as we had agreed he would, to the fact that we were paying to the Carranza Government at that time something like 60,000 pesos per month in taxes, and that that would be cut off by the action of Pelaez if we did not pay Pelaez the least amount he would be willing to take; and Arredondo agreed that it was a good thing for Carranza to have this money paid by us to Pelaez so as not to cut off the revenue he was getting. So that he was in the same boat with us. His revenue would be cut off if our revenue was cut off. And Mr. Walker and Arredondo agreed it was a good thing to do.

So Arredondo, the representative of Carranza, and through him Gen. Carranza, and through him his Government, was responsible, was a party to the payment of the first money to Palaez, the beginning of this tribute; and we have never made a payment since that has not been known; and the fact that we have been obliged to make payments since, in increasing sums, has been known to Carranza, who now charges us with supporting rebels by paying these amounts to protect his revenue and protect our oil property.

Senator BRANDEGEE. What do you mean by saying something about never having made a payment since?

Mr. DOHENY. I say we have never made a payment since that was not made with their knowledge.

The CHAIRMAN. Has our State Department been aware of the fact that you have been making payments to Pelaez?

Mr. DOHENY. Yes; not only aware of it, but so far as they could, without giving it in writing, they have approved of it.

Here is a communication which is better evidence of what I am stating than merely my verbal statement. This is a communication sent by Mr. Walker to the State Department November 5, 1917, addressed to the Hon. Frank L. Polk, counselor for the State Department:

MY DEAR MR. POLK: In view of the recent reported statement of Deputy Luis Cabrera in the Mexican Congress, to the effect that the Huasteca Petroleum

Co. has been voluntarily furnishing arms and munitions and paying tribute to rebel factions under mere pretense of fear or damage to properties and employees, we believe it essential to send you inclosed detailed memorandum denying the accusation and stating the actual experience of our company from the beginning of disorders in the oil fields, bearing on depredations and payments of forced tribute.

I believe that the files of the State Department contain record of every statement made in the adjoined memorandum.

I have the honor to remain, my dear Mr. Polk,

Your obedient servant,

H. WALKER,
For the Huasteca Petroleum Co.

The memorandum of facts presented by Mr. Walker to Mr. Polk with that letter is as follows:

MEMORANDUM OF FACTS PRESENTED BY THE HUASTECA PETROLEUM CO.

MATTER OF PAYMENT OF TRIBUTES TO MEXICAN FACTIONS EXERCISING DE FACTO CONTROL – FURNISHING OF ARMS AND MUNITIONS.

The Mexico City press reports that on October 17 Deputy Luis Cabrera, in a speech in the Chamber of Deputies, stated that the Huasteca Petroleum Co. (American) and a British petroleum company had been and are voluntarily lending support to armed rebellion in the oil fields, furnishing supplies and munitions. The facts are:

(1) During the past seven years of turbulence in Mexico all industries have been exposed to "forced loans," double taxation and seizure of supplies by armed bands in temporary control of the producing districts.

(2) American industrial concerns have been advised by American representatives, including Messrs. John Lind and John R. Silliman, to pay taxes to whatever party was in de facto armed control of the district in question.

(3) Certain American industries in Mexico like mines, smelters, factories and farms, when subjected to threat of violence for not complying with demands of armed forces for money or supplies, could abandon their properties with loss only of time and temporary production, and did so abandon them.

(4) Producing oil fields in Mexico can not be so abandoned. Wells can not be safely stopped. The oil must be continuously pumped away from the wells, or catastrophes of world-wide import result. It is therefore necessary for oil-producing companies in Mexico to continue pumping at all costs. This has made the oil fields a fruitful source of local levies.

(5) The experience of the Huasteca Petroleum Co. in this regard, of which record exists in the State Department, has been –

Under the de facto President Huerta:

(6) On May 15, 1913, Constitutionalist General Larraga, appearing in Ebano, San Luis Potosi, at the camp of the Mexican Petroleum Co., an allied concern, with a force of 200 troops. He arrested the superintendent, took such supplies as he needed, made a forced loan of $5,000, and went away with all the rifles in camp, which rifles the company had secured for "protection" at the request of Hon. Ernesto Madero, Minister of Finance, under President Madero.

(7) In October, 1913, the Huerta Government, through a packed and

spurious supreme court, imposed a fine of $400,000 United States currency on the company, and threatened stoppage of operations in case of nonpayment. The company, through its representatives in Mexico, having in mind the policy of financial blockade then followed by the American Government, referred the question of paying this fine to the Hon. John Lind, personal representative of the President of the United States. On Mr. Lind's request to resist payment of this imposed "fine," the Huasteca Petroleum Co. did resist, at the risk of the destruction of its business and at the jeopardy of the liberty of its officials in Mexico, and succeeded in delaying settlement, which was still pending when Huerta was forced to leave Mexico.

(8) In December, 1912, Constitutionalist Gen. Candido Aguilar appeared at the company's producing camp at Casiano, Vera Cruz, with a large armed force, demanding a loan of $10,000. He took supplies and all the rifles the company ever owned, which rifles also had been imported on request of Minister Ernesto Madero. At the same time another of his bands appeared at the Potrero camp of the Eagle Oil Co. and demanded the same sum.

The Eagle Oil Co. (British owned) refused to make the payment. Aguilar's men stopped the company's pumps, causing the oil and gas to break out around the well and under the Buenavista River. The escaping oil and gas have since been ignited by lightning and burned for three months. The well is forever in a dangerous condition by reason of the stopping of the pumps in December, 1913.

The Huasteca Petroleum Co., desirous of cooperating with the American Government in its Mexican policy, referred the Aguilar request to Mr. Lind, then in Tampico, through the American consul. Mr. Lind advised the company to pay the "loan," which it did promptly. Its pumps were not then and never after stopped.

I want to interject this in the middle of this memorandum: That at that time it was a well-known fact that the British assisted in the sale of a large amount of Huerta bonds and they were distinctly favorable to the Huerta Government at that time. Our Government had shown its animosity to Huerta and its desire to support his opponents. So that our action was in line with our own Government and that of the British was in line with the supposed sympathies of the British Government.

(Continuing the reading of the memorandum referred to:)

(9) The Larraga and Aguilar visits deprived the companies of their last arms, and subsequently they have been defenseless and at the mercy of whatever armed forces occupy the oil districts.

I want to add that we have never since been allowed to have any arms there, and foolish as it may seem for Americans that can fight, as proven lately, we have gone into that country without arms and allowed ourselves to be abused in every way that makes a red-blooded man feeling like wishing to die.

(Reading further:)

(10) The only arms and cartridges ever owned or imported by the Huasteca or Mexican Petroleum Cos. were delivered to the above-named constitutionalist generals.

DURING THE VILLA REVOLT.

(11) Gen. Aguilar left the oil fields and moved to Tuxpam in May, 1914. Local residents of the district organized under the leadership of Manuel Pelaez in opposition to the Carranza faction. They were classed as Villistas, though they had no sympathy with Villa. During the Villa revolt, August, 1914 — November, 1915, they levied on all the companies for supplies and one for "Monelava" paper money. As the American Government favored neither side in the contest, the company handled each demand as it came up with troubling the State Department for instructions, but notified the American consulate of everything it did.

So that even before the United States had taken sides between Villa and Carranza we were obliged to pay tribute first to one man and then to the other, and we never knew what their allegiance was until they declared themselves, and then we did not know whether they were telling the truth or not.

Senator BRANDEGEE. Do you mean Villa and Carranza?

Mr. DOHENY. Yes. Villa and Carranza both, and often parties that vowed allegiance to neither one.

(12) When the Eagle Oil Co. failed to deliver "Monelava" money demanded by Pelaez in the spring of 1913 his forces stopped their pumps, renewing the damage done by Aguilar's troops in 1913. The paper money was delivered and pumping resumed.

(13) The stoppage of the "Aguila" Co.'s pumps, in execution of his threat by Pelaez, proves that his menaces are serious, and answers the charge attributed to Mr. Cabrera that the companies paying tribute to Pelaez are only pretending payment under duress.

AFTER THE DE FACTO RECOGNITION OF FIRST CHIEF CARRANZA.

(14) By recognition of the Carranza branch of the revolution of 1913 the American Government gave the oil companies a basis for their conduct toward the factions. Carranza was recognized as in de facto control. Pelaez, in fact, occupied the oil region. In view of the American Government's evident desire to consolidate the Government under Gen. Carranza, the officials of the company agreed to accompany, and did accompany, Gen. Vera and Col. Teran, of the Carranza forces in Tamaulipas, to meet Pelaez in the jungle for the purpose of urging his surrender to the recognized faction. During the parley Pelaez learned that the Carranzista general, Galindo, had arrived in Tuxpan with forces and was threatening his rear. The parley ended, and Pelaez has subsequently been suspicious of conferences.

(15) The Huasteca Petroleum Co. has, notwithstanding, whenever asked to bring Pelaez together with constitutionalist commissioners to talk surrender, cooperated to that end. As an example, in September, 1917, its officials were able to put Deputy Eugenio Mendez, of the Carranza Congress, in touch with Pelaez's chief of operations for a parley.

This was within one month of the time when Deputy Cabrera is reported as charging the companies with voluntarily supporting the Pelaez rebellion.

(16) In the first days of February, 1916, Pelaez made a demand for a

regular payment by the producing oil companies, for protection, of what amounted to $1,200 per month, under threat of stopping oil pumps, just as he had stopped the "Aguila" pumps 10 months previously, and sending the American workers out of the country. The demand was communicated to the president of the Huasteca Petroleum Co. on February 8, 1916, by radiogram sent from his yacht, which put out from Tampico for the purpose, this being the only possible means of submitting the demand in time for its approval to prevent destruction.

The officials of the company in Mexico had, and have, strict orders to make no agreement to pay money to armed factions without approval of the president of the company. The president of the company would not approve the payment, in view of the recognition of the Carranza faction, without consulting the American State Department, in spite of the destructive effect of refusal to pay.

Notwithstanding that, I am now accused of having been a supporter of the rebels, although I ran the risk of having our property destroyed by delaying until we could put the matter before the proper authorities here.

(Reading:)

(17) The representatives of the Huasteca Petroleum Co., on February 6, 1916, laid the question before the American State Department and the Mexican ambassador designate at Washington. Both authorities advised the company to make the payment to avoid destruction.

This is a declaration in a letter to the State Department, telling our State Department that they authorized us to make this payment. We have since received no letter from the State Department calling attention to this sentence and saying that it was not warranted by any action on their part.

(Reading further:)

The same advice was given at the same time to the Penn.-Mex. Oil Co. The Aguila Oil Co. was, we are informed, advised by the British Government to pay the tribute.

The reason only three companies were mentioned here was because only three companies were moving oil and the only ones that could be forced into payment by the stoppage of pipe lines, etc.

(Reading further:)

All oil-producing companies in the district controlled by Pelaez have since paid the monthly tribute demanded by him. His forces occupy their camps and eat at the restaurants furnished for employees. The companies must keep food and other supplies on hand. These the Pelaez forces take as they need them, just as the Larraga and Aguilar forces did in 1913, and as the Treviño (Carranzista) forces did at Ebano from November, 1914, to May, 1915. This form of contribution to the need or caprice of controlling forces in Mexico can not be prevented except by abandonment of properties which, in the case of oil-producing properties, can not be considered.

(18) No successful military expedition has as yet been sent against Pelaez's movement. His forces have absorbed much of the arms and cartridges and

many of the men sent against them. In December, 1916, the movement was credited with having armed 2,900 men with captured rifles and munitions.

(19) In December, 1916, the superintendent of the Huasteca Petroleum Co. made a special trip to the United States to report to the president of the company that Pelaez, having learned that the de facto government's tax receipts from the oil produced in his district had greatly increased, had demanded an increased monthly payment. The State Department was again consulted, and letters were exchanged in the matter, of date December 22, 1916, and January 5, 1917, in which the decision arrived at was set forth. Conditions as to payment of monthly tribute have not subsequently changed.

(20) It is within the knowledge of the counselor of the State Department that in the month of February, 1917, pressure was brought to bear upon the Huasteca Petroleum Co. from important sources to make a shipment or shipments of rifles and cartridges to the Pelaez forces, and that the Huasteca Petroleum Co. would have nothing to do with such procedure without the request and consent of the State Department and opposed the proposal for reasons then explained, principal among which was the evil effect of strengthening any Mexican rebel faction with military supplies.

It did not then, it did not before, it has not subsequently ever delivered arms or munitions of any sort to forces in rebellion against the Carranza Government.

I want to say here that while we have never declared our sympathies in Mexico, there is one thing that we always have declared, and that is that it is dangerous to let arms go into any Mexican's hands at a time when there is likely to be a feeling stirred up against Americans, and we have always opposed sending any arms to any faction in Mexico, so far as our opinion has been asked, and we will always do that so long as an unstable Government exists there.

(21) It is the belief of the officials of the Huasteca Petroleum Co. that no other oil-producing concern has furnished arms or munitions from the United States to rebels against the Carranza Government. Such delivery is impossible, first, on account of the American embargo, and, second, on account of the careful search by customs guards of all ships arriving at Tuxpan and Tampico, the only possible ports for such traffic.

It is not to be believed that Mr. Cabrera made the false and damaging statements attributed to him by the Mexican press. If he did in fact make the statements reported he has been grossly misinformed as to the attitude and acts of the Huasteca Petroleum Co. He is reported to have said:

(1) That the company gives arms to rebels.

This is answered by the facts set forth herein in (6), (8), (9), (10), and (20).

(2) That the company gives supplies to the rebels voluntarily, as that its claim of duress is a pretense.

This is answered by the notorious results of refusal to pay tribute to Aguilar and to Pelaez, set forth in (8) and (12).

(3) That the company has given supplies to the Pelaez rebels.

This is true only as set forth herein. The result of refusal of supplies to Pelaez and his troops, while they are predominant in the producing district at this time, when the United States and their allies need petroleum and its products more urgently than ever, would be a more far-reaching calamity than before we were at war.

The Huasteca Petroleum Co., and we believe other American companies, has from the beginning of the disorder in Mexico attempted in every way to cooperate with the policy toward Mexico assumed by the American Government and at the same time to continuously produce and supply the petroleum products so vital for the United States in peace and war. Special conditions of disorder and disputed authority have forced the company to pay tribute in various forms to more than one faction at a time. The work could not be suspended. From the time Gen. Aguilar occupied Casiano, its producing fields and its terminal have been controlled by opposing armed factions. It has had to satisfy the exigencies of both, maintaining a neutrality as perfect as possible, and it has never in any way favored either side except when acts of favoritism were patently desired by the American Government.

Respectfully submitted.

H. WALKER,

For the Huasteca Petroleum Co.

I suppose it is all right to put this in the record, is it not, Mr. Walker?

Mr. WALKER. I presume so, but this is a private communication to the State Department. Has this committee the power to subpoena such documents? This is brought here in response to your subpoena.

The CHAIRMAN. I think we are entitled to it. At any rate, we have got it and we will keep it.

Senator BRANDEGEE. Is this Candido Aguilar the son-in-law of Carranza?

Mr. DOHENY. He is the son-in-law of Carranza; yes.

Senator BRANDEGEE. Is there any doubt about that?

Mr. DOHENY. He is reputed to be and I think he is, although there is always some doubt about most everything.

Senator BRANDEGEE. I did not know whether he was recognized by his father-in-law.

Mr. DOHENY. I think he is.

The CHAIRMAN. He was reported to be on a mission for Carranza about two weeks ago.

Mr. DOHENY. When the property Ebano was occupied for four or five months by contending forces we had one white man, an American, killed on the property, but probably it was because he was with Mexicans and was running away from the attacking force. I think the killing was merely an incident of the attack at that time. This man's name was Ely, an American citizen from Iowa, who had children living in Mexico and some children in the United States.

The CHAIRMAN. We are not going into the details of killings and robberies and so forth in Mexico with Mr. Doheny, because we have various witnesses who will testify to those things who were on the ground and will be able to testify from personal knowledge. I do not know, at this time at least, that there is anything else that the committee desires to interrogate you about, Mr. Doheny. Your testimony has certainly been very clear, and enlightening, and very interesting, and, to state my personal opinion, it should be appreciated by the people of the United States, to whom it will go sooner or later. We thank you.

Mr. DOHENY. I expect to be in New York for several weeks to come, and if it is deemed necessary to have me here again for the purpose of clearing any point or adding to the information in any way or correct any misstatements I will be glad to come over at any time at the request of the committee.

The CHAIRMAN. I thank you.

Senator BRANDEGEE. You may have answered what I am about to ask, as I have not been here during all of your testimony, but have you been in the room while the witnesses who testified before you were on the stand?

Mr. DOHENY. Yes, sir.

Senator BRANDEGEE. Did you hear the testimony of the witness, more particularly, I think, of Dr. Inman, who testified about the improved conditions of Mexico now over what they were a few years ago?

Mr. DOHENY. Yes, sir.

Senator BRANDEGEE. Have you given any testimony as to the general conditions in Mexico?

Mr. DOHENY. I think no general testimony; no, sir.

Senator BRANDEGEE. Have you been in any portions of Mexico, except where your oil fields are located?

Mr. DOHENY. At various times I have been at very many places besides those. I commenced to go into Mexico, I think, as I stated in my introductory statement, in 1878.

Senator BRANDEGEE. I mean more recently — in the last three or four years — have you traveled about Mexico?

Mr. DOHENY. In the last three or four years, no; except in the vicinity of our oil fields.

Senator BRANDEGEE. The object of my question was to get your judgment as to whether, and, if so, at what rate, general conditions are improving in Mexico since Gen. Carranza took possession or became President. How rapidly is the country increasing in prosperity or how rapidly are peaceful conditions being resumed and law and order being established?

Mr. DOHENY. I think that is partially answered by testimony I gave this morning, to this effect: That three years ago I went to Mexico and two years ago I went to Mexico, and on both occasions I took with me large parties and went down over our property for a distance of 90 miles south of Tampico and went over our property for a distance of 35 miles. I had a number of ladies with me in the party at both times. There did seem to be some fear in the United States that they were going into dangerous places, but when I arrived down there and talked with our own people I judged the situation to be as it turned out to be — safe for them to go where they wished to go.

Senator BRANDEGEE. Where was that?

Mr. DOHENY. That was two years ago.

Senator BRANDEGEE. Not when, but where, did you say it was?

Mr. DOHENY. We wished to go all over our oil fields, and I went there, and I took my wife with me, and several gentlemen with their wives. We found it safe. Very recently I was asked about the possibility of making a trip at this time, or rather I asked about it, and I was told by no means to do it. A Mexican gentleman arrived in New York a few days ago, whose name I will not mention for obvious reasons, but who is a very warm friend of President Carranza, or of President Carranza's government, and I asked him for the purpose of information whether or not a certain party who wished to go to Mexico could go safely by rail. The fact of the matter is that a California company had wired to me to know if I could send down on one of our tank steamers one of their representatives. We are not allowed to carry passengers on our tank steamers, and there is some little trouble in getting the department to give us permission to do it, and at the same time we feel that we will be responsible in some way or other for what they may do when they arrive there.

I wanted to be in a position to tell them that they could send him by rail, and I asked about it, and his answer was, not by way of Monterey and Victoria, but he said, "if you want to send him by Monterey, Saltillo, San Luis Potosi, and around in that way, it will be safe all right, but to go down through the State of Tamaulipas, it is not safe to go. The State of Tamaulipas joins the Rio Grande and the Gulf of Mexico, and the City of Tampico is in that State, and capital is Victoria, and Osuna, the man appointed governor by President Carranza, is governor of the State, and in his State the railroads are reported to be unsafe to travel on at the present time.

Senator BRANDEGEE. Are you now having to pay tribute to anybody for protection at the present time?

Mr. DOHENY. We are paying tribute to Pelaez.

Senator BRANDEGEE. Now, Mr. Doheny?

Mr. DOHENY. Now.

Senator BRANDEGEE. Every month?

Mr. DOHENY. Every month.

Senator BRANDEGEE. At what rate, now?

Mr. DOHENY. I do not know the rate.

The CHAIRMAN. Do you know the total payment to all of the companies?

Mr. DOHENY. The total payment to all of the companies is less than $30,000.

Senator BRANDEGEE. In your judgement, is it within the power of Carranza to disperse these bands which you have to pay tribute to?

Mr. DOHENY. My judgement would be that it is not within his power, or else he would have done it, because it is the one big blot on his claim of dominating Mexico, and the most valuable spot in Mexico, the most valuable spot in all the world is this — under his claim of jurisdiction — but it does not prevent these people from levying tribute.

The CHAIRMAN. I will ask you another question or two, Mr. Doheny. Have you had your attention called recently to a statement or affidavit which must be filed before the Mexican consul in New York City, and other Mexican consular officers, by anyone desiring a passport from that Government in order to go to Tampico?

Mr. DOHENY. Yes, sir; that is a new requirement. Our employees going to Mexico to the oil fields near Tampico have been required to sign the following affidavit. This fact was brought to my attention by the officers of my company this week. The affidavit reads as follows:

The undersigned, under oath, deposes and says that he has been warned that the Tampico oil region is a dangerous district on account of the activities of bandits operating in said region. That deponent, by reason of his business as employee is on his way to that region, and travels at his own risk. That in case some accident might happen to him, hereby he formally renounces the right that he or his heirs might have, to present a claim to the Mexican Government, either directly or through any other channel.

Senator BRANDEGEE. It is a rather significant statement, "his heirs," do you not think?

Mr. DOHENY. It certainly does not encourage a man to seek a job in the oil fields.

The CHAIRMAN. Are you a member of the organization for the protection of American rights in Mexico, as testified to here?

Mr. DOHENY. Yes, sir.

The CHAIRMAN. Some of the witnesses who testified in your hearing seem to have the idea, or desire to convey the idea that that association, with yourself at the head of it, is organized for the purpose of bringing about a war between this country and Mexico. Do you have any such purpose?

Mr. DOHENY. I would like to correct a misstatement in your statement just now, if you will allow me.

The CHAIRMAN. Certainly.

Mr. DOHENY. I am not at the head of it.

The CHAIRMAN. You are a member of it?

Mr. DOHENY. I am a member of it, and I am glad that the opportunity is allowed me to say something about the organization, because I had it in mind to ask permission to do so, but it slipped my mind, among many other things. The fact of the matter is this, that I am chairman of an organization known as the Oil Producers' Association, and we were presenting a united front against what we believe to be the unjust claims of the Mexican Government, and with such effect that other people having properties in Mexico desired to join with us, and they came to my office and suggested the organization of a larger association to be made up of groups, of which we are only one. There are seven groups in the association for the protection of American rights in Mexico, and the exact names of the groups Mr. Boynton can give you, as he is the managing director of the association, employed under a salary to do the work.

The first chairman elected was Mr. Con Kelley, of the Anaconda Copper Co., and I believe I was elected vice chairman at that time. I went to Europe immediately afterwards, as did Mr. Kelley, and who presided or what was done during my absence I do not know, as I have not had the time to read the minutes, but I do know that arrangements were made to do effective work, for the truth, the whole truth, and nothing but the truth, to have that put in the papers about Mexico. Of course, there is a good deal of trouble in getting the whole truth. However, I have not seen anything that has been published that has been anything but the truth, so far as it could be determined.

The purpose of this organization is indicated by its name only. It has no other purpose. I will say further that there has never been a word said in any meeting that I have attended which would indicate that the members of it are in favor of intervention, or any member of it. I will state further that as a matter of fact one of the gentlemen whose name is on the committee of the League of Free Nations, was one of the charter members of the association, and was the principal speaker at a meeting which I attended, and that is Mr. Thomas W. Lamont, of J. Pierpont Morgan & Co. Another party that association are of themselves a sufficient guaranty that they favored Mexico, and who is a representative of the committee of the National Association for the Protection of American Lives in Mexico, is a vice president of the Guaranty Trust Co., which is our treasury. The names of the gentlemen who represent the different groups in that association are of themselves a sufficient guaranty that they are not propagandists in favor of intervention in Mexico, and never will be connected with anything that is not creditable in that or any other line of effort. They are well-known men who would not be connected with anything that was not perfectly right and proper, and the name of the association indicates that it is only for their rights, and, I hope, a very propitiously right movement at this time.

Senator BRANDEGEE. Mr. Lamont is owner of the New York Evening Post, is he not?

Mr. DOHENY. Yes.

Senator BRANDEGEE. And the New York Evening Post does not indicate that he or that paper is in favor of intervention?

Mr. DOHENY. No; we regard the New York Evening Post as leaning over the other way a little bit.

The CHAIRMAN. Mr. Doheny, have you had any experience with other propagandas at any time, if I may use the word without meaning to reflect upon any gentlemen, or with other propangandists who have sought to create the impression that to educate the American people as to the purported views with reference to Mexico, along the line of some of the recent views we have had here; that is, to the effect that Americans were sending out distorted statements of conditions there with some ulterior purposes in mind — I mean, have you come in contact with those efforts for several years past, or at any period during the last six or seven years?

Mr. DOHENY. Yes; but not in any very direct contact.

The CHAIRMAN. Do you know Dr. David Starr Jordan?

Mr. DOHENY. Yes; I have heard of him, and have met him.

The CHAIRMAN. Do you also know Rev. Henry Allen Tupper?

Mr. DOHENY. By name, very well.

The CHAIRMAN. Did you hear of the efforts of either of these gentlemen along this line that I have indicated?

Mr. DOHENY. Well, I am quite familiar with the incidents that happened at El Paso, which were reported in the newspapers, and which, among other things, reported David Starr Jordan as having been so desirous of having the sympathy of the United States continued with the Carranza government that he made the charge that Villa was instigated to make his raid into Columbus by American interests, and was furnished money by them, and that they were particeps criminis to the raid. I was very sorry to read the next day that he got out of El Paso without the thing happening which had been threatened.

The CHAIRMAN. Do you happen to know of your own knowledge whether any of the gentlemen whose names have been mentioned here by any of the witnesses, or by myself, have received any funds from Carranza or those associated with him?

Mr. DOHENY. Well, I hoped that that might not be brought up, Mr. Chairman, but I had evidence that one of them received money.

The CHAIRMAN. You were requested by the committee to bring with you such evidence that you had on that.

Mr. DOHENY. Yes, sir.

The CHAIRMAN. Have you brought it?

Mr. DOHENY. Yes, sir.

The CHAIRMAN. Will you produce it?

Mr. DOHENY. I have sent a photograph of it to the State Department at the time it came into my possession, several years ago.

The CHAIRMAN. What is that?

Mr. DOHENY. It is a draft. No. 8, made out in favor of the Mexican treasurer general by the Huasteca Petroleum Co. in payment of the sum of $3,466.86, to discharge the bar dues for the months of May and June, 1915. It is signed by our representative in Mexico and paid in New York.

The CHAIRMAN. Were there any indorsements? That draft was paid in New York?

Mr. DOHENY. Yes, sir. It is voucher 1061, contains the cancellation of the stamp signed by our representative in Mexico, and was indorsed by the treasurer general of Mexico, paid to the order of Dr. Henry Allen Tupper, for value received, Vera Cruz, July 31, 1915, and it was receipted — payment was receipted in New York, August 19, 1915, signed, Henry Allen Tupper.

The CHAIRMAN. Was that gold money — that is, United States gold money, currency?

Mr. DOHENY. That was United States currency; yes, sir.

Senator BRANDEGEE. What was the value received?

Mr. DOHENY. We were never told.

The CHAIRMAN. Do you know whether Dr. Tupper was in El

Paso with Dr. Jordan at the time of these occurrences?

Mr. DOHENY. The papers reported that he was; yes, sir.

The CHAIRMAN. Will you leave this draft with the committee, or do you prefer to have it returned?

Mr. DOHENY. I would be perfectly willing to furnish it, either the original draft or a photographic copy of the draft. Have always felt as though we ought to retain the original draft, because it may be very significant, and it might be possible that we will be called upon to prove its existence, in which case a photograph might not be satisfactory.

The CHAIRMAN. A photographic copy will be satisfactory to the committee.

I will state, Mr. Doheny, that the purpose of the committee, or at least of myself, in requesting you to bring this paper with you, as a witness, was that there were various Americans who were very active — so they stated themselves, and as was stated to the committee members — in securing recognition of Carranza by this Government, and among those gentlemen were Mr. Tupper, and the names of others are well known to myself, at any rate, and there may be some further evidence brought out along that same line; and knowing that uncontrovertible evidence, at least, existed that some of our philanthropists had received accommodation of some character from the Carranza government at about the time of his recognition, I desired to have it in evidence now.

Mr. DOHENY. We sent a photographic copy of this draft to the State Department at the time we received that from the bank, so that the State Department has been informed of its existence.

The CHAIRMAN. As the Foreign Relations Committee have an important hearing tomorrow, have requested a full attendance, at least, for the morning session of all its members. Of course, Senator Brandegee and myself are members of the committeee, and we being compelled to attend the meeting of the committee tomorrow, will not have a session of this hearing, but we will endeavor to have a session tomorrow afternoon, and invite certain other witnesses, if it is possible for us to do so, as we have their addresses here and can reach them by telephone.

Mr. DOHENY. I would like to say this, Mr. Chairman. At the time that we brought in that great well in Mexico, that has been described in the testimony here, we had on the ground a photographer whom we had been employing for a couple of years to take pictures of various portions of the camp, and he was there the day it was drilled in, and he has taken moving pictures, showing Tampico Harbor and the vicinity of the canal where most of the murders took place, and showing the character of the country, and this wonderful well, the most wonderful in the world, and the picture is just as clear as though you were at the well, except the smelling of the oil, and I showed it to the Geographical Society about three years ago, and if this committee should arrive at the conclusion that it would be valuable in any way to have that shown here at some place in Washington, I have the films in New York. I showed them in London, and I would be very glad to bring them over and show them to the Foreign Relations Committee of the House and Senate, or any others who might desire to see them. It may be that it would be desirable to have them show the character of the country, and the work being done by the Americans in this land, which seems to be a storm center.

The CHAIRMAN. I am sure that it would be very interesting, and I will take up the matter before the full committee.

Mr. DOHENY. I would be very glad to bring it over next week or the week after.

Senator BRANDEGEE. That well that you described, does that well keep up?

Mr. DOHENY. I will say that we laid two pipe lines before we drilled the well, and the well furnishes all the oil that we can carry in the two pipe lines. It does that besides the —

Senator BRANDEGEE. There is restraint there also?

Mr. DOHENY. Yes, sir.

Senator BRANDEGEE. Did you not say that it was 250,000 barrels capacity?

Mr. DOHENY. Two hundred and sixty-one thousand barrels, and 10 per cent overflow, wasted, in 24 hours, and is now 45,000 or 50,000 barrels, with 900 pounds back pressure.

Senator BRANDEGEE. How many years has that been flowing?

Mr. DOHENY. It will be three years next February.

The CHAIRMAN. I desire to make the further statement in connection with those remarks I made a few moments ago, as to the purpose of securing this last testimony: I do not want it to be understood, as chairman of this committee or personally, in intimating that there is anything wrong in any American securing pay for his services, if they did secure such remuneration, in attempting in any way to secure the recognition of Mr. Carranza; but in view of the fact that various charges have been made as to selfish interests along the border and in this country being desirous of bringing trouble with Mexico, and bringing raids on the other side of the country, some of the gentlemen who made such statements are posing as friends of the Mexican people, I think this further testimony to show that they may have had their expenses paid and received remuneration for such friendship — I think that it is the duty of the committee to show it, and if we can get the evidence we will show it.

Mr. Secretary, has there been any return on the subpoena, or have we heard anything from Mr. de Bekker?

The SECRETARY. No, Mr. Chairman; the address given us at the Bush Terminal investigation shows that no such person is known at the Bush Terminal, and there has been an attempt to locate him at 130 West Forty-second Street, the address given by Mr. McDonald, and the Sergeant at Arms notified me at noon that he had no returns from there.

(Thereupon, at 5:20 o'clock p.m., the hearing was adjourned, subject to the call of the chairman.)

THE WEALTH OF MEXICO IN 1911

AND

AMERICAN LOSSES DURING THE MEXICAN REVOLUTION

Summary Report of Senate Hearings
by
Senator Albert B. Fall

The Wealth of Mexico

Class.	American.	English.	French.	Mexican.	All other.
Railway stocks	$235,464,000	$81,237,800		$125,440,000	$75,000
Railway bonds	408,926,000	87,680,000	$17,000,000	12,275,000	38,535,380
Bank stocks	7,850,000	5,000,000	31,000,000	31,950,000	3,250,000
Bank deposits	22,700,000			161,963,042	18,560,000
Mines	223,000,000	43,600,000	5,000,000	7,500,000	7,830,000
Smelters	26,500,000			7,200,000	3,000,000
National bonds	52,000,000	67,000,000	60,000,000	21,000,000	
Timberlands	8,100,000	10,300,000		5,600,000	750,000
Ranches	3,150,000	2,700,000		14,000,000	
Farms	960,000	760,000		47,000,000	1,250,000
Live stock	9,000,000			47,450,000	3,800,000
Houses and personal	4,500,000	680,000		127,020,000	2,760,000
Cotton mills		450,000	19,000,000	6,000,000	4,750,000
Soap factories	1,200,000			2,780,000	3,600,000
Tobacco factories			3,238,000	4,712,000	895,000
Breweries	600,000		178,000	2,822,000	1,250,000
Factories	9,600,000	2,780,000		3,270,200	3,000,000
Public utilities	760,000	8,000,000		5,155,000	275,000
Stores:					
Wholesale	2,700,000	110,000	7,000,000	2,800,000	14,270,000
Retail	1,780,000	30,000	680,000	71,235,000	2,175,000
Oil business	15,000,000	10,000,000		650,000	
Rubber industry	15,000,000			4,500,000	2,500,000
Professional	3,600,000	850,000		1,560,000	1,100,000
Insurance	4,000,000			2,000,000	3,500,000
Theaters	20,000			1,575,000	500,000
Hotels	260,000			1,730,000	710,000
Institutions	1,200,000	125,000	350,000	74,000,000	200,000
Total	1,057,770,000	321,302,800	143,446,000	792,187,242	118,535,380

NOTE.—From the testimony taken and other evidence in the possession of the committee, the committee reports that the total amount of American investments in Mexico in 1911 were more nearly $1,500,000,000 than the total set forth in the column above, $1,057,770,000.

TOTAL WEALTH AND APPROXIMATE PROPORTIONS, AMERICAN, BRITISH, MEXICAN.

The total wealth of Mexico as it appears in this table was $2,434,241,422, of which Americans owned $1,057,770,000; English, $321,302,800; and the Mexicans, $792,187,242. The figures given in the table as to British ownership should, from the best information in my possession, be increased from $321,000,000 to at least $800,000,000. The figures for American investment in mines should be increased very largely.

Mexican, largely in lands, town lots, etc. — Of the Mexican ownership over one-half was in lands, town lots, bank deposits, and bank stocks.

American investments are in tax-paying, labor-employing operations. — American investments in individual agriculture holdings are hereinafter set forth. The balance of the American investments was in railroads, mines, factories, oil, rubber, and property of this class, i.e., producing and labor-employing, tax-paying business — with the exception of about $50,000,000 in national bonds.

The Americans owned 78 per cent of the mines, 72 per cent of the smelters, 58 per cent of the oil, 68 per cent of the rubber business.

Railroads — Americans and English capital — Eighty-eight per cent are railroads. — The total railroad mileage was about 16,000 miles, in which American and English capital was invested (to extent about 88 per cent) and which their capitalists had constructed to that extent.

The Letcher table shows only an investment of about $3,150,000 in ranches and about $13,000,000 in timberlands, farms, houses and lots, and personal property.

This statement is entirely incorrect as specific testimony before this committee shows that more than 3,000 American families of an average of five persons each owned their own homes either in colonies or in separate locations, all of whom were engaged in agriculture and that the actual average loss to such families has been approximately $10,000 each, or a total in this one item of $30,000,000, not taking into consideration the value of the land nor of the houses and other improvements which could not or have not been destroyed.

In this connection we are not considering the very large amounts invested in cattle ranches devoted purely to stock raising, nor in estimating this loss have we included the loss upon rubber, coffee, sugar, and other like large plantations.

ADDITIONAL LOSSES IN RAILROADS, ETC.

The testimony will show that in addition to the $30,000,000 lost by these smaller agriculturists who have been driven out of Mexico and a comparatively few of whom have been able to return, the loss to the national railroads of Mexico have been, at a conservative estimate, $80,000,000 through destruction not only of rolling stock but through the destruction of the actual corpus of the property itself by the burning of the bridges, destruction of railroad stations, sidings, etc., the tearing up of steel and burning it, so that when straightened for temporary use it is unsafe for traffic.

The total mileage of the railroads in Mexico in 1910-11 was approximately 24,600 kilometers, of which a little less than 14,000 kilometers, is included in the national roads, as to the loss upon which direct testimony was given, showing as just stated, damage to the amount of $80,000,000. Other testimony shows that the remaining 10,000 kilometers not known as the national roads have suffered at least an equal amount of damage per kilometer; that is to say, approximately $60,000,000 to such roads, or a total of railroad loss alone in the amount of $140,000,000; that is to say, that it would require at least $140,000,000 now to place the twenty-four thousand plus kilometers of railways in Mexico in the condition in which they were found in 1910-11.

DAMAGES TO OIL AND MINING COMPANIES ONLY ESTIMATED.

In so far as the testimony adduced before the committee is concerned, we have little or none and have sought none concerning the actual loss to oil companies through confiscation of their properties; through damage to their business; through destruction of their wells and consequent loss of oil, nor upon any other account whatsoever; except that the testimony shows the cash loss to pay rolls and by virtue of robberies of actual cash to these companies within the last few years, has amounted to more than $233,833.

The mining companies, in so far as the committee knows, have made no claims for damages through the State Department and few of their representatives have come before the committee except as upon page 1429, part 9, testified to.

Through other evidence the committee has knowledge not only of the closing down of producing mines due to revolutionary acts and inability to get supplies, etc., but of the further fact that smelters, reduction works, improvements upon and around mines, mining machinery of all classes, etc., have been destroyed all over the Republic.

The closing down of an operating mine means not only loss of time and interest upon the investment, but aside from any actual destruction by vandalism means the filling of shafts with water, the caving in of underground works, decay of mine timbers, etc.

The committee are privately informed by one of the officials of a great American company engaged in mining and other development of like character in Mexico, that its losses have amounted to approximately $25,000,000 during the last 10 years.

Another mining company in which more than 8,000 Americans are interested, has, we are informed, paid out approximately $1,500,000 in blackmail or bribes to prevent destruction of millions of dollars worth of property invested in improvements, etc., in connection with its work.

DAMAGES OTHER PROPERTY.

Power lines have been cut; power plants destroyed; irrigation works dynamited; canals cut; factories burned; railroad and mining contractors' and subcontractors' supplies, tools, stock, and equipment, etc., destroyed; banks, trust companies, investment companies, money exchanges, etc., looted of cash and put out of business; brokers, commission men, general agents, dentists, wholesale and retail merchants have lost their investments and as well their books of trade, implements of their profession, their stocks of merchandise, etc.

Those who have attempted to continue business by going back to their locations when temporary peace appeared to justify their return, have been held up and compelled to pay blackmail to every new bandit and tribute to every odd one in their community.

The committee, however, have been particularly interested in and have largely confined their investigation to the losses of the individual American, which losses, in proportion to those of the large corporations or large capitalists, have been as 100 to 1.

The larger corporations, as shown by the evidence in the case, have been able, through the employment of Mexican officials, to secure even the use of an army for the protection of their properties, while the individuals or colonists located in an outlying district have been compelled to lose a life's savings and to witness the murder or outrage of their friends or their families.

Oil companies have been obliged to pay to Candido Aguilar, son-in-law of Carranza, first, ransom or blackmail or exactions for the protection of their properties, and when he was driven off have, through payments to Pelaez amounting to $30,000 per month, been able to secure his protection against other bands as well as against Carranza.

American railroad conductors; firemen; locomotive engineers; brakemen and other railroad employees, in one instance alone to the number of 500, have been run out of Mexico never to return, with the total loss of all they might have invested in their homes in Guadalajara or elsewhere.

CORPORATIONS PAYING FOR PROTECTION TO PROPERTY NOT ALWAYS ABLE TO SECURE SAME FOR THEIR EMPLOYEES.

Individuals in the employ of corporations have been robbed, mistreated, and murdered because protection extended to the corporation property proper was by the bandits not always extended to the individual in the employ of the corporation; and this notwithstanding the established fact that our corporations have done everything in their power to protect their employees, and to ransom them when seized by bandits.

MEXICAN PROPAGANDA.

Carranza propagandists in this country have filled the papers with attacks upon "predatory interests" who were seeking intervention in Mexico for selfish purposes.

Churches have resounded with denunciation from the pulpits of the same "predatory interests" who —

Desired to have not only the treasure of the United States poured out, but the blood of its sons spilled for the protection and accretion of their ill-gotten "dirty dollars" in the Republic of Mexico.

THIS COMMITTEE PRESENTS CASE OF INDIVIDUAL AMERICAN.

Where has the voice been lifted in behalf of the common, every day, homemaking, honest, industrious American with his family, teaching the Mexican modern methods of agriculture and handicraft, who has, while tied to a tree, seen his daughter raped and his wife disemboweled in his presence?

The country and the Congress of the United States having heard from those American interests who have been able to secure a hearing through the press and having heard from those good friends of Carranza who have been conscientiously or unconscientiously, sincerely or hypocritically, directing his propaganda and assisting in the expenditure of his funds set aside for propaganda purposes, this committee determined to present, as it is endeavoring to present, the case of the individual American who has received no protection from his Government and only through this medium can make his loss and his sufferings known to the public.

The summary of losses under this heading may be found by reference to page 89 of this report. The total thereof, as found in the evidence, is $50,481,133.

NATURE AND AMOUNT OF PRESENT HOLDINGS AND PROPERTIES IN MEXICO OF CITIZENS OF THE UNITED STATES.

The nature and amount of the present holdings of American citizens in Mexico can only be ascertained by reference to the facts hereinbefore submitted and by deducting the losses herein set forth, except in that, under the Mexican mining law, taxes upon mining property are payable every three months and same must be paid by the owner or his attorney in fact, in person, either in the City of Mexico or in the headquarters of the district in which his mine is situated.

Failing payment of such taxes within three months after same are due, title to the property is forfeited and anyone else whosoever can relocate same and take it over, together with any improvements of whatever kind or character attached to any portion of the property, including, of course, all development work, etc.

The law as to real estate in the different States provides also for the forfeiture of property for nonpayment of taxes.

The person who, or corporation which, has been able to secure an attorney, could change him whenever the Government changed, or secure a new attorney with every change of Government and thus have representation before the tax office, and being financially able to make the payments have been able to prevent legal forfeiture.

The individual prospector and small mine owner, living himself probably upon his mine in an inaccessible district in Mexico, if he lived to reach the coast or border, has been compelled to leave Mexico and lose his life's savings and work invested in his property, not having the money with which to employ an attorney on the ground; and not able to pay over and over, again and again, the amount of taxes claimed to be due as the tax collector came in or faded out of office every few days, has lost forever the title to his property.

Of course, it may be possible that if the American lives long enough to see some responsible government established in Mexico and to see an administration here in power which will endeavor to assist in enforcing his legal claims, some of these forfeitures may be set aside.

Of course, if the real estate owner enjoys the same good fortune, he may, before the weight of years has bowed his head too low — or possibly some heir to his misfortunes may regain right to the possession of what was once an orange grove or a beautiful wheat field — not recognizable now because the orange trees have been chopped and burned, and its location, as well as that of the wheat field, grown up in cactus, cat claw, and mesquite.

Source: *Investigation of Mexican Affairs,*
op. cit., pp. 3322-3326.

STATISTICAL TABLES

(1910 – 1929)

TABLE 1.   Mexican Foreign Trade (1910) D-390

TABLE 2.   Mexican Exports (1910 - 1911) D-392

TABLE 3.   American Investments in Mexico
            (Estimate - 1911) D-393

TABLE 4.   Most Profitable U.S. Public Companies
            Operating in Mexico (1900 - 1911) D-394

TABLE 5.   Losses Claimed by Americans in Mexico
            (1910 - 1920) D-395

TABLE 6.   U.S. Oil Companies & Entrepreneurs with
            Operations in Mexico Prior to May 1, 1917 . . . D-396

TABLE 7.   Effect of 1917 Constitution on Oil
            Companies D-397

TABLE 8.   World Petroleum Production and Mexican
            Output (1927) D-398

TABLE 9.   American Investments in Mexico by Industry
            (Estimates - 1929) D-399

TABLE 1

MEXICAN FOREIGN TRADE (1910)

The foreign trade of Mexico during the calendar year 1910 amounted to $245,885,803, United States currency. The imports were valued at $107,061,955 and the exports $138,823,848. The share of the United States in the import and export trade was $61,029,681 and $105,357,236, respectively.

The following table shows the total value of the imports into and exports from Mexico, by countries, during 1910:

COUNTRIES	IMPORTS	EXPORTS
United States	$61,029,681	$105,357,236
Austria-Hungary	1,010,659	. . . . . .
Belgium	1,876,090	3,496,265
Canada	1,228,578	740,876
Central America	56,228	785,144
France	9,424,083	5,485,561
Germany	11,982,678	3,619,767
Great Britain	11,509,098	17,096,100
Italy	1,037,422	. . . . . .
Spain	2,890,529	1,112,630
South America	1,472,250	21,036
West Indies	113,035	996,330
All other countries	3,431,624	112,903
Total	107,061,955	138,823,848

The principal articles of import into and export from Mexico during 1910 were as follows:

ARTICLES	VALUE	ARTICLES	VALUE
IMPORTS		EXPORTS	
Animal products	$8,613,392	Mineral products:	
Vegetable products	23,488,828	Gold	$24,484,372
Mineral products	28,501,623	Silver	38,700,017
Textiles and		Other	18,662,526
manufactures	11,608,822	Vegetable	
Chemical and pharma-		products	43,919,578
ceutical products	6,226,057	Animal products	10,140,766
Liquors, spirituous and		Manufactures	1,875,226
fermented	3,416,000	All other articles	1,041,363
Paper, and		Total	138,823,848
manufactures of	2,696,710		
Machinery and apparatus	12,211,856		
Vehicles	3,925,927		
Arms and explosives	1,549,128		
All other articles	4,823,612		
Total	107,061,955		

The exports to the United States in 1910, according to invoices certified at the several American consulates and agencies in Mexico, were valued at $105,194,293. The total exports from each district were as follows:

DISTRICTS	VALUE	DISTRICTS	VALUE
Acapulco........	$98,245	Mazatlan........	$3,744,398
Aguascalientes	11,574,512	Mexico.........	13,466,737
Chihuahua.......	6,972,556	Monterey........	10,531,048
Ciudad Juarez.....	1,879,378	Nogales.........	11,656,788
Ciudad Porfirio		Nuevo Laredo.....	120,740
Diaz..........	500,353	Progreso	13,456,281
Durango	13,898,443	Salina Cruz.......	325,127
Ensenada........	161,645	Saltillo	3,085,201
Frontera	862,877	San Luis Potosi....	4,895,383
Guadalajara	506,468	Tampico	829,725
Hermosillo.......	2,026,646	Tapachula	245,045
La Paz..........	264,712	Vera Cruz	4,484,684
Manzanillo.......	17,260		
Matamoros.......	90,041	Total.........	105,194,293

Source: *Commercial Relations of the United States, 1910.*
Washington, D.C., GPO, 1911. p. 42.

TABLE 2

MEXICAN EXPORTS (1910 - 1911)

The following table shows the articles of export from Mexico and their values during 1910 and 1911:

ARTICLES	1910	1911
Mineral products:		
Gold..........................	$24,484,372	$28,911,905
Silver	38,700,017	42,418,566
Other	18,662,526	21,095,334
Vegetable products	43,919,578	41,180,724
Animal products...................	10,140,766	2,121,624
Manufactures....................	1,875,226	2,219,576
All other articles..................	1,041,363	1,044,839
Total....................	138,823,848	145,992,568

The values of the declared exports through American consulates and agencies in Mexico to the United States for 1911 follow:

ARTICLES	VALUE	ARTICLES	VALUE
Arsenious acid	$33,098	Jalap root	$47,201
Animals, alive........	2,667,580	Lumber and	
Antiques and curios....	2,454	woods	389,048
Beans	122,642	Leather........	16,000
Beeswax	4,429	Minerals:	
Bones and horns	25,577	Copper	22,821,283
Broom root	63,178	Gold.........	19,569,160
Chicle	523,080	Graphite	71,411
Chile..............	199,413	Lead.........	6,302,801
Coffee.............	2,835,937	Onyx	80,156
Cottonseed products ...	18,988	Quicksilver	41,992
Cotton waste	14,740	Silver........	9,176,196
Fibers:		Zinc.........	114,359
Hemp...........	1,447	Unclassified....	6,175,683
Ixtle.............	483,490	Oils:	
Lechugilla	4,901	Crude petroleum.	483,015
Palm.............	122,012	Essential oils ...	17,589
Sisal.............	10,971,960	Pearls	9,881
Zapupe...........	9,151	Peas, chick......	283,818
Fertilizers:		Pecans.........	229,649
Blood and bone	60,876	Rubber	8,739,220
Guano	15,761	Sarsaparilla root ..	14,561
Fruits and vegetables,		Shellfish	65,382
fresh.............	231,643	Sugar	23,498
Glycerin	55,594	Tobacco	34,997
Hair, animal........	66,056	Vanilla beans	118,219
Hats, palm leaf	324,006	All other articles ..	605,467
Hides and skins.......	4,976,933		
Honey.............	15,651	Total ...	99,417,479
Household goods......	136,296		

Source: *Commercial Relations of the United States, 1911.*
Washington, D.C., GPO, 1912. p. 72.

TABLE 3

AMERICAN INVESTMENTS IN MEXICO
(Estimate - 1911)

Type of investment	Amount in millions of dollars	Per cent of total
Railroads	644.3	61.7
Mining	249.5	23.9
Government bonds	52.0	5.0
Banks	30.6	2.9
Oil	15.0	1.4
Rubber	15.0	1.4
Real estate	12.2	1.2
Manufacturing	11.4	1.1
Miscellaneous	14.6	1.4
Total	1,044.6	100.0

Editor's Note: This estimate would be very low, reflecting primarily only those large companies reporting back to stockholders. It also almost completely ignores the value of the new oil discoveries and oil fields, then held in secret by most oil companies and entrepreneurs. Source of this table: *America's Stake in International Investments,* by Cleona Lewis, Washington, D.C., 1928. Reportedly prepared originally by William H. Seamon, an American mining engineer with long experience in Mexico. See Marvin D. Bernstein's *The Mexican Mining Industry, 1890-1950.* p. 313.

TABLE 4

MOST PROFITABLE U.S. PUBLIC COMPANIES
OPERATING IN MEXICO (1900-1911)

Company	Capital	Dividends (in per cent)	Years covered
Mexican Telegraph Co.	$3,589,400	355	1882-1910
Moctezuma Copper Co.	2,600,000	153	1902-1910
Greene Consolidated Copper Co.	8,640,000	71	1901-1907
International Lumber and Development Co.	6,000,000	59	1905-1910
Mines Co. of America	6,934,075	54	1903-1910
Mexican Telephone and Telegraph Co.	1,000,000	45	1906-1910
Guanajuato Power and Electric Co.	5,000,000	37.5	1902-1910
United States and Mexican Trust Co.	1,000,000	36.75	1906-1910
Mexican Northern Railway	3,000,000	33.5	1895-1906
Guanajuato Development Co.	4,000,000	30	1906-1910
Mexican Petroleum Co.	36,000,000	27	1907-1910
Intercontinental Rubber Co.	37,050,000*	21	1907-1910
German-American Coffee Co.	3,270,250	10	1905

Editor's Note: Contains data only on those companies which were required to report to their stockholders. Does not include privately held companies and those controlled by one entrepreneur or family, such as those of Doheny, Hearst, the Guggenheim family & others. The data on this table taken from Marvin D. Bernstein's *The Mexican Mining Industry, 1890-1950*. p. 314. Dr. Bernstein compiled his statistics from *The Mexican Year Book*, 1912; *Moody's Manual*, 1912; and *Poor's Manual*, 1912, 1907. The asterisk (*) indicates authorized capital. Other figures indicate capital actually issued.

TABLE 5

LOSSES CLAIMED BY AMERICANS IN MEXICO
FIRST 10 YEARS OF REVOLUTION
(1910 - 1920)

Small Rancher, Farmer & Non-Corporate Claims

	FAMILIES	LOSSES
Colonists and families outside of colonies, engaged in agricultural persuits, including some plantation companies	3,400	$38,119,774
Miscellaneous individuals engaged in business on small scale	. . . .	4,273,084
Miscellaneous companies engaged in business on small scale	. . . .	8,088,275
Total	. . . .	50,481,133

Damage to oil companies, other than loss of pay rolls, not included in this list.
Damage to mining companies, other than dynamiting of one plant, not included in this list.
Damage to railroads not included in this list.

Total Claims Filed by 1920

Summary of losses — American.

Deaths.	$14,675,000
Personal injuries	2,846,301
Property, individual.	50,481,133
Railroad, American (estimated)	112,000,000
Mining (estimated).	125,000,000
Oil; stock ranches; coffee, sugar, and other plantations; factories; banks; city residences; power plants; irrigation systems, etc.	200,000,000
Total	505,002,434

Editor's Note: Over 85 per cent of the claims filed against the Mexican Government were made by the large-scale business interests operating in Mexico: oil, mining & railroads. By 1920 most of the oil and mining, and those railroads not taken over by the government, were in the hands of large corporations or trusts.

Source: *Investigation of Mexican Affairs.* Vol. II, pp. 3398-99.
(66th Congress, 2nd Session, Senate Doc. 285) Washington, D.C., 1920.

TABLE 6

U.S. OIL COMPANIES & ENTREPRENEURS
WITH OPERATIONS IN MEXICO PRIOR
TO MAY 1, 1917

American International Fuel &
  Petroleum Co.
Anderson, M. C., et al
Atlantic Lobos Oil Co.
Axtell, Dr. B. C., estate of
Balch, Ernest
Beckman, A. W.
Cortez-Aguila Petroleum Co.
Cortez Oil Corporation
Dalton, W. H.
Doub, D. L.
East Coast Oil Co.
Exendine, Jasper
Hall, G. L.
Hall, J. L.
Harris, G. S.
Hawkins, L. O.
Huasteca Petroleum Co.
Hodgins, P. J.
Johnson Land & Fiber Co.
Kearney, Ed. T.
Kettering, Mrs. Lena
Lot Seventeen Oil Co.
Mexican Coal & Coke Co.
Mexican Crude Rubber Co.

Mexican Gulf Oil Co.
Mexican Petroleum Co. of California
Mexican Plantation Co.
Mexican Sinclair Petroleum
  Corporation
Mexico Land Securities Co.
New England Fuel Oil Co.
Oil Fields of Mexico
Panuco Boston Oil Co.
Penn Mex Fuel Co.
Postelle, J. M.
Rathbone, Charles
Rhoades, J. Beach
Sutherland, W. H.
Tamiahua Petroleum Co.
Tamesi Petroleum & Asphalt Co.
Tampico Oil & Refining Co.
Texas Petrolene & Asphalt Co.
Tillman, A. N.
Tuxpam Petroleum Co.
Weill, Melville K.
Wilson, Burton W., and associates
Wright, M. P.
Yates, Mrs. Carrie

Editor's Note: The above list is indicative of the problems related to identifying ownership of specific companies. Huasteca Petroleum Company and the Mexican Petroleum Company of California were Doheny companies; The Oil Fields of Mexico Company was founded by Percey Furber; and Penn Mex Fuel Company, by Mike Benedum.

TABLE 7

EFFECT OF 1917 CONSTITUTION ON
U.S. OIL COMPANIES

U.S. Companies Which Applied for Confirmatory Concessions under the Constitution of 1917:

Penn Mex Fuel Co.
Texas Petrolene & Asphalt Co.
East Coast Oil Co.
New England Fuel Oil Co.

U.S. Companies & Individuals Holding Titles in the Name of Mexican Companies but Refusing to Accept the New Provisions of the Constitution:

Atlantic Refining Co.   Subsidiaries, La Atlantica Compania Mexicana Productora y Refinadora de Petroleo, S. A., D. W. Johnson & Cia., Successores.
Atlantic Gulf Oil Corporation.   Subsidiary, Cia. Petrolera del Agwi.
Humble Oil & Refining Co.   Subsidiary, Cia. Petrolera Tamaulipas, S. A.
Island Oil & Transport Corporation.   Subsidiary, Cia. Petrolera Capuchinas, S. A.
Standard Oil Co. of California.   Subsidiary, Richmond Petroleum Co. of Mexico, S. A.
Standard Oil Co. of New Jersey.   Subsidiary, Cia. Transcontinental de Petroleo, S. A.
Leopold Newborg.
W. L. Hernstadt.
Malcolm C. Anderson.   Mexican company, Cia. Petrolera Los Chijoles, S. A.

Source: *Oil Concessions in Mexico.* Senate Document 210. 66th Congress, 2nd Session. pp. 3-4. Washington, D.C., GPO, 1927.

TABLE 8

WORLD PETROLEUM PRODUCTION & MEXICAN OUTPUT
(1927)

WORLD PETROLEUM PRODUCTION OF LARGE COMPANIES, 1927
(Daily output in barrels)

		Working Capital
Dutch-Shell	344,200	$217,000,000
Standard (N. J.)	214,700	598,000,000
Gulf	212,500	110,000,000
Standard (Calif.)	150,000	95,000,000
Standard (Ind.)	118,000	167,000,000
Standard (N. Y.)	100,000	220,000,000
Texas Corp.	107,500	127,000,000
Anglo-Persian	102,600	34,500,000
Totals	1,349,500	$1,568,500,000

MEXICAN OUTPUT PERCENTAGES FOR LARGE U.S. OIL COMPANIES
(Daily output in barrels)

STANDARD (IND.)		STANDARD (N. J.)	
United States	25,000	United States	114,800
Mexico	23,000	Mexico	8,500
Venezuela	70,000	Canada	800
		Colombia	55,000
Total	118,000	Peru	25,000
		Argentina	800
		Roumania	5,000
GULF		Poland	1,300
United States	145,500	Neth. East Indies	3,500
Mexico	7,000		
Venezuela	60,000	Total	214,700
Total	212,500	TEXAS CORP.	
		United States	106,500
		Mexico	1,000
		Total	107,500

Source: *O'Shaughnessy's South American Oil Reports,* March 1928.

TABLE 9

AMERICAN INVESTMENTS IN MEXICO BY INDUSTRY
(ESTIMATES – 1929)

Type of Investments	Amount in U.S. dollars (In millions)
Bonds	$160,000,000
Railways	300,000,000
Mining industry	400,000,000
Petroleum industry	400,000,000
Manufacturing	60,000,000
Commercial operations	50,000,000
Public utilities	37,000,000
Banks	3,500,000
Land holdings	138,000,000
Total U.S. Investment	$1,550,500,000

Source: Thomas F. Lee: *Latin American Problems*, N.Y., 1928. p. 146.

EDITORIAL NOTE:

PETROLEUM: Divided between more than ninety companies, including most of the largest U.S. oil companies.

MINING: Absorbed largest part of U.S. capital. Most important was the Guggenheim-controlled American Smelting and Refining Company, with smelters in all the leading mining districts of Mexico, and with essentially a monopolistic control over copper and silver mining. After the Guggenheim interests, remainder divided between 300 U.S.-controlled mining interests and companies.

MEXICAN TELEPHONE & TELEGRAPH COMPANY: Subsidiary of International Telephone and Telegraph (ITT). A second major U.S.-controlled utility, the American & Foreign Power Company, Inc. owned many municipal Mexican power and light companies, but reported earnings from its Mexican properties in 1928 of only one and a half million U.S. dollars.

LAND HOLDINGS: With many small U.S. ranchers and settlers. Larger units included the famous Hearst ranch, considerably undervalued at two million U.S., the Three Oaks ranch of E. K. Warren & Son, the Cudahy (meat packing interests) ranch, the Morris & Co. ranch, the Palomas Land & Cattle Company ranch, the Coralitos Land & Cattle Company, and the Grove ranch. Many of these were companion ranches to ranches owned in Texas, New Mexico and

Arizona. To the south, land holdings by Americans included the Cuatotolapan Sugar Company, the Mexican-American Fruit Company, the Cuyamel Fruit Company, and the Janatha Plantation Company. Most of the mahogany harvested in southern Mexico was carried on by U.S. companies, and the American Chicle Company controlled most of the chicle harvested for chewing gum in the states of Campeche and Yucatan.

U.S. INVESTMENTS: In an earlier table we note that U.S. investments in 1911 amounted to a little over one billion dollars. During the next eighteen years of instability and revolution the estimates increased fifty percent, to one and a half billion U.S. dollars. If these estimates are correct, one might conclude that the revolution had little if any effect upon U.S. investments in Mexico. One should be most cautious in taking this view, however. We must consider this increase in light of inflationary rises during these years. Additionally, the value of the petroleum industry (shown here at 400 million) increased substantially when compared to the 1911 figure of fifteen million. Possibly this reflects a more realistic appraisal of the true value of U.S. owned oil fields rather than any significant increase in investment by U.S. companies.

Sources

CHAPTER ONE

Edward L. Doheny's version of his life and contributions appear in the document section of this book. Another detailed, if self-serving, version was given during his testimony in the Teapot Dome Trial, which was reported on extensively by both *The New York Times* and *Washington Star*. Dr. Fritz L. Hoffman was the only scholar to gain access to the extensive Doheny collection of reports and interviews at Occidental College before their disappearance. His article, "Edward L. Doheny and the Beginnings of Petroleum Development in Mexico," appeared in *Mid-America*, Vol. xxiv (New Series, 13) in 1941. That article provides an excellent if uncritical history of the oil entrepreneur's early years. Mexican sources on Doheny have never been fully researched. There is much in the records of the Dpto. de Hacienda and Dpto. de Fomento on both Doheny and his oil companies in the Golden Lane. The Mexican press carried reports and articles on Doheny, particularly between 1910 and 1925. The Spanish-language *Diario del Hogar* and *El Imparcial*, both published in Mexico City, were invaluable. The English-language *Mexican Herald*, also published in Mexico, contained articles on the Mexican oil industry, as well as on all entrepreneurs in Mexico. The official publication, *Boletin del Petroleo*, contains a wealth of statistics and data on production after it began publication in 1915. *Mexico's Oil. A Compilation of Official Documents* (Mexico City, 1940), published by the government of Mexico in defense of its oil expropriations, is a rich source of documentary materials on all early oil operations in Mexico, including that of Edward L. Doheny. There are many errors, particularly in its history of the early period before 1910, yet it still serves as an excellent point of departure. Gabriel Antonio Menéndez's *Doheny El Cruel. Episodios de la sangrienta lucha por el petróleo mexicano* (Mexico City, 1958), is the only full-length study of Doheny in any language. Menéndez is a historian whose primary interest is in labor unions, and he emphasizes Doheny's wealth and "exploitation," both of Mexico and its people. Doheny's brilliant geologist, Ezequiel Ordóñoz, wrote two published pieces, "El petróleo en México," *Revista Mexicana de interieria y arquitectura*, March 15, 1932, and a report published in the sourcebook, *Mexico's Oil*. Neither, unfortunately, gives any personal picture of Doheny. Clarence W. Barron's *Mexican Problem* (Boston, 1917), is primarily a public relations piece on behalf of Doheny and his companies, and presents data provided by Doheny himself. *They Told Barron* (N.Y., 1930), contains several talks with Doheny, revealing that Doheny had fired the scholar, Dr. E.J. Dillon, from his payroll for not writing articles favorable to him and his views relating to the 1917 Carranza constitution. *Mexican Petroleum* (N.Y., 1922), published by the Pan American Petroleum & Transport Company, contains a detailed 300-page pro-Doheny history of his Mexican oil companies and their operations. Paul H. Giddens' *Standard Oil Company—Indiana* (N.Y., 1955) contains information on Standard Oil's early relations with Doheny, though there is apparently much in Standard's archives on Edward L. Doheny which remains to be researched. On the darker side, *Huasteca Petroleum Company vs. El Sr. William H. Mealy, Vice President de la Compañia Mexicana de Combustible, S.A.* (Mexico, n.d.), published in Spanish, demonstrates some of the ruthless actions undertaken by Doheny and his companies against small entrepreneurs. Doheny's misuse of government officials, and his prevarications, are detailed extensively in John Ise's *The United States Oil Policy* (New Haven, 1928), as well as in J. Leonard Bates' *The Origins of the Teapot Dome* (Urbana, 1963). Of particular value was Burl Noggle's *Teapot Dome: Oil and Politics in the 1920s* (N.Y., 1962), from which I have taken several quotes. I have also quoted from Sam T. Mallison's *The Great Wildcatter* (Charleston, 1953), regarding Doheny's relations with Mike Benedum, and from Percy Furber's *I Took Chances* (Leicester, England, 1954). Both these entrepreneurs had dealings with Doheny. See also *Moody's Manual of Investments* for the period, as well as *The New York Times* and *Wall Street Journal*, from 1910 to

1925. I regret I did not examine the records of the New York Stock Exchange, which conducted several investigations of the rapid rise and fall of Doheny's Mexican Petroleum Company. Doheny's relationship with Cecil B. DeMille is taken from *The Autobiography of Cecil B. DeMille* (Englewood Cliffs, N.J., 1959). Data on his relationship with Sir Weetman Pearson may be found in his biography, *Member for Mexico* (London, 1966), written by Desmond Young. See also Peter Calvert, *The Mexican Revolution, 1910-1914. The Diplomacy of Anglo-American Conflict* (Cambridge, 1968). Calvert made extensive use of the Pearson papers, now located at Whitehall Securities Ltd., in London. For Albert Fall's relationship with Doheny, see *The Memoirs of Albert B. Fall* (El Paso, 1966), edited by David H. Stratton. Stratton's introduction and notes are particularly valuable, suggesting that Doheny paid for the writing of Fall's memoirs as a public relations tool during the Teapot Dome scandal. Fall's personal files and records are scattered through four university libraries, though all seem to have been purged of Doheny correspondence. I would also recommend Mark T. Gilderhus' "Senator Albert B. Fall and 'The Plot against Mexico,'" in the *New Mexico Historical Review,* vol. xlviii, no. 4, 1973, which is valuable for the research, but not for the conclusions which understate Fall's close and long-term association with Edward Doheny. A personal memoir by a close associate may be found in Caspar Whitney's *Charles Adelbert Canfield* (N.Y., 1930), privately printed in an edition of 200 copies. This book may be hard to find. Canfield was Doheny's partner in California and Mexico, and there is much here favorable to Doheny and his companies. For a book of a family nature, I recommend Lucille V. Miller's "Edward and Estelle Doheny," in *The Ventura County Historical Society Quarterly*, vol. vi, no. 1, November, 1960. Ms. Miller was personal secretary to Estelle Doheny from 1931 to 1938, and a later curator of the Doheny collection of rare books. An antiquarian book dealer who had sold Estelle Doheny many of her rare books issued *The Dohenys of Los Angeles* (Los Angeles, 1975), an item of *curiosia* rather than substance. I am weakest on my sources concerning the life and activities of Clarence W. Barron. Biographical data is included in the previously-mentioned book *They Told Barron*, as well as in the *New York Times* and *Boston Transcript* obituaries of October 4, 1928. All efforts to obtain evidence on Barron's records, files, and correspondence from the Dow, Jones Company proved unproductive. Perhaps the inferences drawn from circumstantial evidence will stimulate someone there to research the archives in an effort at refutation. Lawyers tell me that circumstantial evidence is more solid legally than eye-witness accounts, so I rest my case on that evidence alone. One or two quotes on Doheny come from oral interviews with the sons of Tampico wildcatters, old enough to remember Tampico well during the oil boom days. I am particularly grateful to Mordelo Vincent, Jr., whose keen memory belies his eighty-four years.

CHAPTER TWO

The principal printed source on Mordelo Vincent, *A Man Remembers* (N.Y., 1970), was written by his son, Mordelo L. Vincent, Jr. This is an honest, hard-hitting autobiography of oil wildcatting in Tampico, and along the Golden Lane between 1910 and 1927. Mordelo Jr. pushed tools on his father's rigs, and his is one of the few eyewitness accounts we have today of life in Tampico during those years. The book is roughly written and badly organized, but well worth reading. Published by Vantage, it was only casually distributed and will be hard to find. Another brief source on Mordelo Vincent can be found in the previously cited *Mexico's Oil*. Interestingly, this Mexican government publication suggests that Vincent, born in Mexico, ran one of the few oil operations in the Golden Lane that the government viewed as Mexican in origin rather than foreign. Data on the operations of Addison H. Gibson, William H. Zahniser, and Franklin C. Mooney, and his AGWI companies, is revealed in annual *Mooney's Manuals*, as well as in *The New York Times* and *Wall Street Journal*. The Gibson Foundation still operates in Pittsburgh, but its officials know nothing of the whereabouts of his papers. Neither does his oil company in Texas, which survives as of this writing, and contributes its profits to the Gibson Foundation. Franklin C. Mooney's grandson still lives in Long Island, New York, but the location of Mooney's files and correspondence is unknown. I wish to thank Mordelo Vincent Jr., of Lake Charles, Louisiana, who suffered patiently with me through seven lengthy oral interviews, and to Claude Buckley Jr., of San Antonio, Texas, and Edmund Buckley Jr., of Houston, Texas, who provided additional insight. I wish to thank as well, Georgie Burden of McAllen, Texas. Georgie's grandparents immigrated to Mexico with Mordelo Vincent's father after the Civil War. She is a cousin of Mordelo Vincent Jr., and her lively comments proved helpful.

CHAPTER THREE

The Mexican government records referred to in Chapter One contain much on the business operations of Henry Clay Pierce. I also gathered much of my material on Pierce's early career and relationship with Standard Oil from Allan Nevins' *John D. Rockefeller. The Heroic Age of American Enterprise* (N.Y., 1940), Ralph W. and Muriel E. Hidy's *History of the Standard Oil Company, New Jersey. Pioneering in Big Business, 1882-1911* (N.Y., 1955), and George S. Gibb and Evelyn H. Knowlton's *History of the Standard Oil Company, New Jersey. The Resurgent Years, 1911-1927* (N.Y., 1956). All three of these excellent studies contain good material on the character and abilities of Pierce, and on his relationship with Rockefeller and Standard Oil. Also of benefit was the material on Pierce found in the Pearson archives, and reported by both Desmond Young and Peter Calvert, previously cited in Chapter One. An enterprising scholar should find more there on Pierce. The technical and public press contained numerous articles on Henry Clay Pierce, one of the best being "Death of Henry Clay Pierce," which was published in *Mexican Commerce and Industry*, vol. ix, no. 7, July 1927. This journal has been helpful in providing me with information on a number of American entrepreneurs in Mexico during these years. Data on Sir Weetman Pearson's operations in Mexico is derived from the books of Desmond Young, Peter Calvert, and Lon Tinkle's *Mr. De. A Biography of Everette Lee DeGolyer* (Boston, 1970). DeGolyer, a brilliant millionaire oil geologist, brought in some of Pearson's largest wells in Mexico. The DeGolyer Foundation in Dallas, Texas, contains DeGolyer correspondence and records. One should also consult the *Boletin del Petroleo* for the period after 1916. Percy N. Furber's *I Took Chances. From Windjammers to Jets* (Leicester, England, 1954), is an overlooked autobiography based on the author's daily diaries. It provides the basis for the Furber section in this book, and for quotes in other chapters attributed to Furber. Also helpful was "History of the Fubero Oil Fields," *Transactions of the American Institute of Mining Engineers*, vol. lii, 1915. *Mexico's Oil*, the government history, all but ignores Furber, and no one remembers that he was the first man recorded to have drilled oil in Mexico in 1894. The *Mexican Yearbook for 1922-24* (Los Angeles, 1924), edited by Robert G. Cleland, contains a valuable statistical and narrative chapter on the Mexican oil industry, including lists of all oil companies in Mexico and citing particular concessions. The 1921 edition of the same yearbook, while less valuable, does contain an early history of oil in Mexico, stating that Captain George Glidden formed a Boston-Mexican Oil Company in 1881 and brought in a successful well. He died, according to this writing, in New Orleans, and his widow sold his Mexican properties. I did not include this brief mention in the narrative, as I could find it verified in no other source. If true, Glidden may have been the first to drill an oil well in Mexico, and he may be the Boston sea captain the Mexicans claim committed suicide when his venture failed. The principal published source on Mike Benedum may be found in Sam T. Mallison's *The Great Wildcatter* (Charleston, 1953). Both Benedum and his partner, Joseph C. Trees, were interviewed extensively as part of the Oral History Project at Columbia University, sponsored by Allan Nevins. Benedum contributed over 60,000 words to his own oral autobiography.

CHAPTER FOUR

Oral interviews constitute the principal sources on the Buckley brothers. Claude Buckley Jr. of San Antonio, Texas, and Edmund Buckley Jr. of Houston, Texas, were particularly helpful. Mrs. Malcolm Milburn of Austin, Texas; Reid Buckley of Camden, South Carolina; and former New York Senator James Buckley of Washington, D.C., were also consulted. Reid Buckley was kind enough to provide some written material on his father. A tape of oral interviews he had made in earlier years, containing interviews with early oil entrepreneurs, had been misplaced, and therefore was not available for my research. I also wish to thank the Benjamin Belt family, of Texas and California, who provided some written materials, as well as one Buckley family member who asked that her name not be cited. I also wish to thank Alberto Diaz, no relation to Porfirio that I know of, for providing me with data on William Buckley's relationship with General Peláez, particularly the documentation on Buckley's proposal to assassinate Carranza. Priscilla L. and William Buckley Jr.'s *W.F.B.—An Appreciation* (N.Y., 1959), is a privately printed family collection of narratives on William Buckley Sr. The writings on Buckley's Mexican experiences are sympathetic and laudatory, as might be expected. Charles Lam Markmann's *The Buckleys. A Family Examined* (N.Y., 1973) is the best, if also the most sympathetic, biography of the northern branch of the Buckley family. It all but ignores the two Buckley brothers who remained in Texas. Ferdinand Lundberg's *The Rich and Super-Rich* (N.Y., 1968), contains a brief, caustic review of the northern branch of the family, and is of only incidental interest.

One of the few portraits of the revolutionary Manuel Peláez may be found in Carl W. Ackerman's *Mexico's Dilemma* (N.Y., 1918). Ackerman visited the Golden Lane for the *Saturday Evening Post*, and talked with Peláez officers. Also of value are Jack London's articles in *Collier's* in 1914, two of which recount his experiences in Tampico and along the Golden Lane, while reporting on the American occupation forces there. London's writings on Mexico are recommended more for their flavor than conclusions. Jack London espoused American interests and his views resemble those of the imperialistic advocates who initiated the Spanish-American war. Sources on Standard Oil's operations in Mexico, and on the larger oil companies, come from both American and Mexican materials. The American sources on Standard are primarily those referred to earlier in the source section on Henry Clay Pierce. In addition, I would recommend documents filed in the U.S. District Court, Eastern District of New York: *Merimos Viesca y Compania, Inc. Plaintiff against Pan American Petroleum & Transport Company, et al.* (N.Y., 1930-1934-1936). The thick three volumes in this suit contain a wealth of material on Standard's oil operations in Mexico, as well as both Doheny's and Standard's use of "White Guards" to police its properties. For an earlier view of the nature and profits of Standard's operations in Mexico, including its relationship with Henry Clay Pierce, I recommend *Report of the Commissioner of Corporations on the Petroleum Industry. Part I. Position of the Standard Oil Company in the Petroleum Industry.* 2 volumes. (Washington, D.C., 1907). This voluminous document led to the breakup of the Standard Oil Trust a few years later. For the Mexican side, I consulted *Mexico's Oil*, Carlos Diaz Dufoo's *La cuestion del petroleo* (Mexico, 1921), Jorge Espiñosa de los Reyes' *Relaciones economicas entre Mexico y Estados Unidos, 1870-1910* (Mexico, 1951), Jesús Silva Herzog's *Petroleo Mexicano. Historia de una problema* (Mexico, 1941), and the most recent Mexican exposition, Lorenzo Meyer's *Mexico and the United States in the Oil Controversy, 1917-1942* (Austin, Texas, 1977), translated by Muriel Vasconcellos. One of the more recent pro-Mexican scholarly studies was written by Merrill Rippy, *Oil and the Mexican Revolution* (Leiden, Netherlands, 1972). Rippy has written a scholarly study based on thorough research, concluding the book has covered "The story of Mexico's struggle to free herself from foreign domination in her oil industry," since there presumably could have been no revolution "without freedom from foreign interference." For those seeking opinions contrary to those proposed in this book, I would recommend all of the foregoing sources. For the data on Strauder Nelson, I am indebted to Claude Buckley, Jr., of San Antonio, Texas; Madeline and Schriner Nelson, also of San Antonio; and particularly to Mr. and Mrs. Rugeley Ferguson, of Halotis, Texas. The Fergusons not only gave gladly of their time, answering my many questions, but also provided me with important documents and correspondence written by Strauder Nelson in earlier years.

CHAPTER FIVE

The two sources I relied on most extensively are David M. Pletcher's *Rails, Mines, and Progress* (Ithaca, N.Y., 1958), and Grant Shepherd's *The Silver Magnet* (N.Y., 1938). Pletcher's study of seven American entrepreneurs in Mexico, most of whom failed, is an historical classic, and should be required reading for anyone with an interest in the subject. Grant Shepherd's autobiography contains a rich body of material of his father, and is an important source on fifty years of life in Mexican silver mining. There is a wealth of material to be found on Alexander Shepherd in the morgue of the *Washington Star*, as well as in the mining journals of the day. I am also indebted to Carl Blake, of Chicago, Illinois, whose father worked at the Batopilas Mine for a number of years before and after 1900. Carl Blake was kind enough to provide me with family papers as well as report on several visits he made to the property in more recent years.

CHAPTER SIX

The Mulatos Mine swindle was widely reported in the leading American mining journals of the day. One of the most interesting accounts appears in John Baragwanath's autobiographical *Pay-Streak* (Garden City, 1936). Baragwanath actually worked as a mining engineer for both the American Smelting and Refining Company as well as the Hayward interests in San Francisco. Although he knew the story of the Canizeros fraud intimately, he chose for some reason to relate it in his book as a tale told him by a friend who worked with Alvinza Hayward. The legal case relating to the Aguayo brothers and Canizeros was detailed in the *San Francisco Examiner* and *Weekly Examiner*. John Hays Hammond's role in this story is told in *The Autobiography of John Hays Hammond* (N.Y., 1935). Robert S. Towne has been reported on extensively in

American mining journals. He is also frequently mentioned in books by Marvin Bernstein and Isaac Marcosson, listed in the sources on Chapter Seven. Towne's own Mexican enterprises are revealed in tax reports filed by him and his estate with the government of Mexico, and may be found in the archives in Mexico City. The investments of James W. Gerard in Mexican mining are detailed in his autobiography, *My First Eighty-Three Years in America* (Garden City, 1951). Gerard's obituaries in *The New York Times, Washington Star,* and *Washington Post and Times Herald,* were also consulted.

CHAPTER SEVEN

All studies of American mining entrepreneurs in Mexico should begin with Marvin D. Bernstein's *The Mexican Mining Industry, 1890-1950* (Albany, N.Y., 1965). This first-rate scholarly work provides many sources on Americans in Mexican mining which will not be detailed here. Suffice it to say that I have used these sources, and Bernstein has guided much of my research, suggesting fruitful areas for further inquiry. Harvey O'Connor's *The Guggenheims* (N.Y., 1937), and Isaac F. Marcosson's *Metal Magic. The Story of the American Smelting & Refining Company* (N.Y., 1949), made use of personal interviews and previously confidential archival sources. Both have provided data for this book. *The Mexican Mining Journal,* and a host of American mining journals, carried articles on the Guggenheims in Mexico. Another good source is the records in the Dpto. de Minas, in Mexico City. John Hays Hammond's experiences with the Guggenheims and American Smelting's operations in Mexico are detailed in his autobiography. Hammond's book, and articles in *The Mexican Mining Journal,* tell the story of the ill-fated Pedro Alvarado, and his mine at Parral. The Madero family economic story is told by Marcosson, as well as in a number of Mexican biographies of Madero. Data on American Smelting's acquisition of the Rosita coal mines is detailed in *Moody's Manual.* Reports on that acquisition are available in the records of the Mexican Dpto. de Minas. Pancho Villa's words were taken from Grant Shepherd's autobiography.

CHAPTER EIGHT

Fred Wilbur Powell's *The Railroads of Mexico* (Boston, 1921), contains a good general history of American railroad concessions, and an extensive bibliography of sources. Data on Arthur E.

Stilwell comes from a chapter on Stilwell in Pletcher's book, mentioned in sources on Chapter Five, as well as from a full-length scholarly biography, *Arthur E. Stilwell, Promoter with a Hunch* (Nashville, Tennessee, 1971), authored by Keith L. Bryant, Jr. *Poor's Railroad Manual* and *Moody's Investments* provide annual reports on major American railroad operations in Mexico. Information on Collis P. Huntington is taken from H. H. Bancroft's *Chronicles of the Builders of the Commonwealth*, vol. v (N.Y., 1891), and his extensive obituary in the *American Monthly Review of Reviews* for September 1900. Harriman's role in the Southern Pacific Mexican venture is discussed briefly in George Kenan's *E.H. Harriman* (Boston, 1932). A number of American railroading magazines contain articles on "SP de Mex" operations. The *American Railway Age* was particularly useful. N.C. Wilson and F.J. Taylor's *Southern Pacific* (N.Y., 1952), contains a chapter on its Mexican operations, including details on the efforts of J.A. Small. Additional articles on Small appeared in *Railway Age*. The records on Edward N. Brown, with an English-language biography of Brown, may be studied in the archives of the Mexican National Railroad. See also his obituary in the *New York Times* and *Washington Post*. Edgar Turlington's *Mexico and Her Foreign Creditors* (N.Y., 1930), and *The Public Finances of Mexico* (N.Y., 1921), by Walter F. McCaleb, provide a hint of the role of American investment bankers in Mexico. Financing sections in *Moody's*, and notes of stock and bond financing and the firms handling these money-raising efforts appear in Mexican financial archives. Notes of who arranged stock and bond financing, and which firms acted as brokers, appear occasionally in *Moody's*, and regularly in financing sections of the *Wall Street Journal*. Data on James Speyer was gathered from Lyman H. Weeks' *Prominent Families of New York* (N.Y., 1897); "The Banking House of Speyer & Company," *The Independent*, April 2, 1903; and in another issue of that same periodical for December 26, 1912. Other references to Speyer may be found in *World's Work*, October 1905; the *Magazine of Wall Street*, February 7, 1920, and in the *Fortune Magazine* issue for August 1931. For Otto Kahn, see "Otto the Magnificent," in *Outlook*, July 4, 1928, and David Lawrence's "American Business and Business Men," *Saturday Evening Post*, March 15, 1930. A social history of Speyer and Kahn appears in Stephen Birmingham's *"Our Crowd." The Great Jewish Families of New York* (N.Y., 1967).

CHAPTER NINE

Data on Frederick S. Pearson was obtained from over a score of articles on Pearson in *Electrical Engineer, Electrical World,* and *Public Utilities Reports.* See also *Moody's Manual* relating to public utilities. Pearson's obituary appeared in *The New York Times* and *Boston Globe,* following the sinking of the *Lusitania.* Ernesto Galarza's *La Industria Eléctrica en México* (Mexico City, 1941), contains information on the companies of Pearson and on the Braniff brothers. It is the best scholarly study on Americans and others in the Mexican utility business. Other sources on the Braniff brothers are limited to Mexican consular reports. There were brief notes on both brothers as well in the English-language *Mexican Herald.* Materials for American and Foreign Power and ITT were derived from *Moody's Manual for Utilities.* There exists no history of American and Foreign Power, but Robert Sobel's *I. T. T.* (N.Y., 1982) contains interesting sections on Colonel Behn and his brother Hernand. Data on the Behn strategy for Third World nations and its Mexican venture is included as well. Consular reports from U.S. offices throughout northern Mexico contain much information on American ranches and farming enterprises there. There is a lot of data on both the Warren and Hearst enterprises in the U.S. National archives records. For Warren, see also an obituary in the Evanston, Illinois *Press* and *Chicago Tribune* for January 17, 1919. On William Randolph Hearst, I consulted O. Carlson and Ernest Sutherland Bates' *Hearst, Lord of San Simeon* (N.Y., 1936), Ferdinand Lundberg's *Imperial Hearst* (N.Y., 1936), and W.A. Swanberg's *Citizen Hearst* (N.Y., 1961). A good general scholarly work referred to was George M. McBride's *The Land Systems of Mexico* (N.Y., 1923). There is a wealth of material on Porfirio Diaz and his era. The most recent Mexican biographies are Bernardo Reyes' *El General Porfirio Diaz* (Mexico, 1960), and Jorge Fernando Iturribarria's *Porfirio Diaz ante la Historia* (Mexico, 1967). The multi-volume work, *Historia Moderna de Mexico. El Porfiriato,* edited by Daniel Cosio Villegas (Mexico, 1963-1967), contains a wealth of studies contributed by Mexican scholars on the Diaz era. Two thick volumes deal with economics during the period. An article critical of the *cientificos* was written by E. Alexander Powell in *The American Magazine* (May-October, 1910). Most helpful was José Yves Limantour's own autobiography, *Apuntes sobre mi vida publica, 1892-1911* (Mexico, 1965). Unfortunately, Limantour mentions nothing of his personal life, and little about his friendship with American entrepreneurs. I have also relied on the accounts of many Americans who knew both Diaz and his *cientificos*, such as that written by Percy Furber. I have also used Edward I. Bell's *The Political Shame of Mexico* (N.Y., 1924). Bell was editor of two newspapers in Mexico City for many years, and his accounts are the product of first-hand knowledge. Both Bell and Furber supplied the information for the final section on Gustavo Madero.

Several titles were referred to extensively in the research for this book, but have not been mentioned specifically in any one chapter. I would mention particularly José Domingo Lavin's *Inversiones Extranjeras* (Mexico, 1954), and James M. Callahan's *American Foreign Policy in Mexican Relations* (N.Y., 1967). The former presents an overall Mexican study of foreign investment, while the latter contains an excellent sixty-page chapter on the American economic invasion of Mexico under Diaz.

DOCUMENTARY SOURCES

Document I   Andrew D. Barlow, "United States Enterprises in Mexico." *Commercial Relations of the United States with Foreign Countries.* vol. I. pp. 403-533. Washington, D.C., 1905   (Barlow was U.S. Consul General in Mexico City.)

Document II   Based on a report on Mexico prepared for the Department of Commerce by U.S. Consul General Arnold Shanklin, *Commercial Relations of the United States with Foreign Nations*, 1909. pp. 509-570. Washington, D.C., 1910.

Document III   Robert W. Dunn, *American Foreign Investments.* pp. 89-107. World Peace Foundation, N.Y., 1926.

Document IV   Max Winkler, *Investments of United States Capital in Latin America.* pp. 222-253. Pan American Union. Washington, D.C., 1928.

Document V   *Investigation of Mexican Affairs.* U.S. Senate, Committee on Foreign Relations. Washington, D.C., 1920. 2 volumes.

* * * * *

Index

Ackerman, Carl W., 44, 407
Aguayo, Leocadio, 77-84
Aguayo, Manuel, 77-84
El Aguila Oil Co., 8, 36, 44
Aguilar, General Candido, D357, D366-367, D370
AGWI. See Atlantic, Gulf and West Indies Steamship Lines.
All America Cables, Inc., D147
Alvarado, Pedro, 101-102, 409
American & Foreign Power Co., 130-131, D173-174, D399, 411
American Chicle Co., D149
American Smelting & Refining Co., 88, 100-107, D10, D43, D143, D164-165, D166-172, D176
Amparo Mining Co., 89
Atcheson, Topeka and Santa Fe Railroad, 2, 112, D275
Atlantic, Gulf and West Indies Steamship Lines, 20-24
Atlantic Gulf Oil Corp., 20-23, D154-155

Bagge, Nils Olaf, D263-272
Baker, John, 47
Banco Minero de Chihuahua, 71, 73, 140
banking (see also investment banking), D6, D12-13, D69, D149
Baragwanath, John, 408
Barbiou, Narcisso, 22
Barron, Clarence W., 13-15, 402, 403
Basave, Carlos, 117
Bates, Ernest Sutherland, 411
Bates, J. Leonard, 402
Batopilas mine, 59-74, D40, D145, D166
Behn, Hernand, 131, 411
Behn, Sosthenes, 131, 411
Bell, Edward I., 412
Belt, Benjamin B., 41, 406
Benedum, Michael L., 33-36, 402, 406
Bernstein, Marvin, 409
Beyer, Charles E., 41
Blaine, James G., 83
Blake, Carl, 408

Blake, W.R., 154
Boise Cascade Corp., 130
Braniff, Oscar, 129-130, 132, D66, 411
Braniff, Thomas, 129-130, 132, D66, 411
Briden, Dick, 80
Broden, Dominick, 84
Brown, D.C., 87
Brown, Edward N., 116-119, D195-222, 410
Brown, Capt. Harry, 33-34
Bryan, William Jennings, 45, D212-213, D215-216
Bryant, Keith L., 410
Buckley, Claude Jr., 404, 406, 408
Buckley, Claude H., 41-47
Buckley, Edmund Jr., 404, 406
Buckley, Edmund L., 41-48
Buckley, James, 46, 406
Buckley, Reid, 46, 406
Buckley, William Jr., 46, 406
Buckley, William F., 41-47, D241-250
Bulnes, Francisco, 155, D248
Burden, Georgie, 404
Burden, Jack, 41
Burke, Tommy, 47

Cabrera, Luis, 117
Calvert, Peter, 403, 405
Camacho, Luis, 32
Canfield, Charles A., 2-3, D275, D285, 403
Canizeros, Luis, 75-85
Canizeros, Santiago, 76
Carlson, O., 411
Carranza Constitution, 1917, 47-48, D335-345
Carranza, Venustiano, 45, 131, 154, D244, D259-260, D358-360, D367-368, D371-372
Casasús, Joaquin D., 6-7, 117, 130, 137-140, D248, D277, D354
El Charro Oil Co., 49
Chase National Bank, 126
Central Mexican Railway, 143

414

cientificos, 6, 130, 137-143, 155, D238, D246-249, D258-259, 412
Cities Service Oil Co., 22, D140, D163
Clayton, General Powell, 4, D279
Cleland, Robert G., D351, 405
Continental Mexican Petroleum Co., 49
Corral, Ramón, D247, D258
Corralitos Land Co., D22, D149, D176
Cortez Petroleum Co., 49
Cosio Villegas, Daniel, 411
Crawford, George, 36
Crawford, Henry E., 89-90
Creel, Enrique C., 67, 71-72, 117, 130, 137-140, 154-155
Creel, George, 10-11
Creel, Juan, 72
Crocker, Charles, 109
Cumberland, W.W., D351

Daley, Marcus, 89
Daniels, Josephus, 12
Davis, Britton, D22
DeGolyer, Everette Lee, 405
de la Barra, Francisco, 31
de la Barra, Ignacio L., 117
de la Barra, Luis, 31
DeMille, Cecil B., 12, 403
Devine, Hamilton, 49
Di Giorgio Fruit Co., D149
Diaz, Alberto, 406
Diaz, Carmilita, 136-137
Diaz, Felix, 44, D238
Diaz, Porfirio, 6-7, 28, 31, 67-68, 71, 83, 85, 90-91, 99-100, 111, 113, 135-137, 154, D236, D246-247, D258-260, D287, D290-292, 411, 412
Dillon, Dr. E.J., 402
Doheny, Edward L., 1-16, 17, 27 33-37, 44, D149-150, D273-380, 401-404, 407
Doheny, Estelle, 10, 14-15, 403
Doheny Research Foundation, 10, D350-353
Dondé, Rafael, 83
Dufoo, Carlos Diaz, 407
Dunn, Robert W., 412
Durango Cattle Co., D23

Eagen, General John, 83
Edelen, A.W., 105
Electric Bond & Share Co., 130
Erath Gas & Distillate field, 55
Espiñosa de los Reyes, Jorge, 407

Fall, Albert B., 9, 12-13, 45, D235-240, D381-388, 403
Fargo, William G., 63
Ferguson, Rugeley, 408
Field, Marshall, 97-98
First National Bank of N.Y., D145
Fisk, James, 109
Flanagan, James W., 49-50
Ford Motor Co., D148
Foy, John H., D9
Frisbie, General John B., 113, 132-133, D23
Fuentes, Luis, 145
Furber, Percy N., 26, 30-33, 136-138, 142, 402, 405, 412

Galarza, Ernesto, 411
Garrison, William Lloyd, 10
Gerard, James W., 88-91, 154, 409
Geronimo, 134
Gibb, George S., 405
Gibson, Addison H., 19-23, 404
Giddens, Paul H., 402
Gilderhus, Mark T., 403
Gillette, Dan, 80, 82
Glidden, Captain George, 406
Goldman, Sachs & Co., 126
Gonzalez, Abraham, 155
Green & Co., 49
Gregory, John, 10
Guanacevi Mining Co., 134
Guanajuato Power & Electric Co., 130, D147
Guaranty Trust, 126
Guggenheim Exploration Co., 101-102, D43
Guggenheim family, 88, 122, 125, D142
Guggenheim, Benjamin, 97
Guggenheim, Daniel, 97, 101
Guggenheim, Isaac, 97
Guggenheim, Meyer, 93-102
Guggenheim, Murray, 97
Guggenheim, Simon, 95
Guggenheim, Simon Jr., 97

Guggenheim, Solomon, 97
Guggenheim, William, 97
Guggenheim's Sons, M., 97-98, D40
Gulf Oil Co., 20, 35, 48, D163

Hammond, John Hays, 83-84, 101-102, 129-130, 408, 409
Hanzen, Harry, 20
Harriman, E.H., 102, 123, 410
Hayward, Alvinza, 80-85, 408
Hayward, Hobart, and Lane, 80-85
Hearst, George, 134
Hearst, Phoebe A., 134-135, D22
Hearst, William R., 134-135, D22, D176, 411
Heckscher, August, 31-32
Hidy, Muriel E., 405
Hill, Charles, 97-98
Hoffman, Dr. Fritz L., 401
Holden Smelting & Refining Co., 98
Huasteca Petroleum Co., 5, D138, D156-157, D159-160, D297-299, D301-379
Hudson, C.R., 117
Huerta, Adolfo de la, 38, 43-44, D244-246, D357-358
Huntington, Collis P., 71, 109, 113-114, 122, 410

International Petroleum Co., 49
ITT (International Telephone & Telegraph Co.), 130-132, D173, D399, 411
Interoceanic Railway, 119
investment banking, D136, D149-150, D152-153, D221-222, D393
Ise, John, 402
Iturribarria, Jorge Fernando, 411

Janin, Alexis, 80
Jones & Co., 49
Jones, Chester Lloyd, D351
Jones, E.R., 105
Juan Felipe Oil Co., 49
Juarez, Benito, 149

Kahn, Otto Herman, 125-126, 410
Kansas City, Mexico & Orient Railroad, 111-112, 140, D55, D85, D146
Kansas City Smelting & Refining

Co., 86-88
Kenan, George, 410
Kenna, E.D., 3, D275-276
Kerens, R.C., 3
Kidder, Peabody & Co., 122, 126, D149
Klein, Julius, D351
Knowlton, Evelyn H., 405
Kuhn, Loeb & Co., 125-126, 143, D146, D149

Lamont, Thomas W., D375
land (inc. agriculture & ranching) 132-135, D4-5, D21-30, D69, D77-82, D86-87, D96, D98-99, D105-106, D109, D119, D121, D123-126, D128-129, D148-149, D176-177, D393, D395
Lane Franklin K., 10, D181-193
Lavin, Jose Domingo, 412
Lehman Brothers, 126
Letcher, Marion, 112
Limantour, José Yves, 4-5, 31, 109, 113, 117, 119-120, 123, 130, 140-143, 145, D244, D247-248, D284-285, 411
Limantour, Julio, 31, 130, 142-143
Loaiza, Wenceslao, 80, 82, 84
London, Jack, 407
London Exploration Co., 80
Lundberg, Ferdinand, 46, 406, 411

McAdoo, William G., 12
McBride, George M., 411
McCaleb, W.F., D351, 410
McCook General A.M., 83
Macedo, Miguel, D248
Macklin, Theodore, D351
Madero, Ernesto, 104-105
Madero, Evaristo, 104
Madero, Francisco I., 29, 104, 136 143, 147-148, 155, D244-245, D260-262
Madero, Gustavo, 29, 104, 143-145, D261, 412
Madero family, 102-105, 409
Maginnis, A.P., D288-289
Mallison, Sam T., 402, 406
manufacturing, D5-6, D36-39, D70, D82-83, D105-106, D107, D147, D393

850262817

Marcosson, Isaac, 97-98, 409
Markmann, Charles Lam, 406
Martin, Percy, D351
Martinez del Rio, Pablo, 3, 6-7, D276-280, D285
Masons, York Rite, 31
Mayo Indians, 68
Mellon, Andrew, 14, 35, 49
Menéndez, Gabriel Antonio, 402
Metropolitan Life Insurance Co., D146
Mexican Central Railroad, 3-4, 27, 112-113, D3, D56, D197, D275, D280-281
Mexican Chamber of Commerce, 91
Mexican Eagle Oil Co. See: El Aguila Oil Co.
Mexican International Railway, 112-113, 116, 122, 125
Mexican Minerals Railway, 87
Mexican National Railroad, 113, 116-118, D3, D198-199, D201-208
Mexican Northern Power Co., D86-87
Mexican Northern Railway, 87, 112, D56
Mexican "Pete." See: Mexican Petroleum Co.
Mexican Petroleum Co., 5-16, 34-35, 38, D27, D138, D154, D290, D293, 294, D297-299, D301-379
Mexican Society, 90
Mexican Telephone Co., (Later, Mexican Telephone & Telegraph Co.), 131, D6, D19, D147, D173
Mexican Telegraph Co. (See: Mexican Telephone Co.)
Meyer, August, 87
Meyer, Lorenzo, 407
Milburn, Mrs. Malcolm, 406
Miller, Lucille V., 403
Minas Cinco, 89-90
mining, 59-108, D3-4, D10-12, D39-52, D70, D76-77, D92, D94, D97, D110, D113, D121, D129-130, D142-145, D164-172, D223-234, D263-272, D390-395, D399
Molino, Oligario, D258
Monterey Iron & Steel Co., D38
Montgomery, Charles, 80-82
Mooney, Franklin C., 23-24, 404

mordida, definition of, 6
Morgan, J.P., 122-123, 126, D140, D149
Morrow, Dwight R., 51
Mulatos Mine, 75-85

National City Bank of New York, 126, D149, D174
National Railroad of Mexico, 112, 116-117, D118, D196-197, D201
Nelson, Cecil, 54
Nelson, Madeline, 408
Nelson, Schriner, 408
Nelson, Strauder G., 53-57, 408
Nevins, Allan, 405, 406
Nevins, W.G., 3
Newhouse, Edgar L., 99-100, 145
Noggle, Burl, 402
Nuñez, Roberto, D248

O'Boyle, M.W., D9
Obregón, Alvaro, 45, 50-52
O'Conner, Harvey, 98, 409
Ohio-Mexican Oil Co., 49
oil, 1-58, D66, D74-75, D76-77, D126, D137-142, D154-164, D241-250, D273-380, D393-394, D396-399
Oil Fields of Mexico Co., 31-33
Ordóñoz, Ezequiel, 4-5, D284-285, 402
Orozco, Pascual, 106-107, 114, D264, D268
Palmilla Mine, 101-102
Palomas Land & Cattle Co., D149, D176
Pan American Petroleum & Transport Co., 5, D159
Pani, Alberto J., 117-118
Pantapec Oil Co., 46
Pearson, Frederick S., 127-129, 411
Pearson, Sir Weetman, 8, 17, 27-29, 32, 44, 49, 120, 137, 403, 405
Peláez, Manuel, 36, 44-45, D300-363, D373, 406, 407
Pemex, 55-56
Penn-Mex Fuel Co., 35-36, 49, D158, D161-162
Phelps Dodge Co., 100, D142-143, D170

Pierce, Henry Clay, 3-5, 8, 26-30, 49, 117, 143, D283-284, 405, 407
Pierce Oil Co., 30, D141
Pimentel, Emilio, D248
Piñeda, Rosendo, D248
Pletcher, David M., 155, 408, 410
Porfirio Diaz Tunnel, 67
Porter, General Horace, 63
Potosi & Rio Verde Railway, 87
Potosi Electric Light Co., D20
Poundstone, R., 80
Powell, E. Alexander, 411
Powell, F.W., D351, 409
Puebla Tramway, Light & Power Co., 129
Pullman, George M., 59, 63, 97

Ramos, José, 45
railroads, 109-120, D2-3, D55-57, D70, D76-77, D82, D85-86, D89, D92, D95-96, D100-101, D102-103, D123, D129, D145-147, D195-222, D393, D394, D395
Reed, Douglas, 43
Remington, Frederick, 134
Reyes, Bernardo, 411
Reyes, Rafael, 142
Rhodes, Cecil, 3, D313-314
Rio Chonchos Agricultural & Electric Power Co., 130
Rippy, Merrill, 407
Robertson, J.A., D24
Robertson, James, D351
Robinson, A.A., 2-3, 27, D275, D280-282
Robinson, J.R., 63
Rockefeller, John D., 26-29, 98
Rogers, Henry H., 34-35
Romero, Matias, 109, 137, 142, 147-148, 154
Rosita Coal Mines, 104-105, 409
Royal Dutch Shell, 49
Rubio, Romero, 83

Schiff, Mortimer L., 126
Shanklin, Arnold, 412
Shepherd, Alexander R., 59-74, 140, 408

Shepherd, Grant, 64-67, 70, 73, 107, 408, 409
Shepherd, Jack, 59, 63
Sherman, General William Tecumseh, 59
Sidewell, J.S., 41
Sierra, Justo, D248
Silva Herzog, Jesús, 407
Sinclair, Harry, 14, 49
Sinclair Oil Co., 36, 48, D139, D157, D162-163
Slattery, Michael J., D223-234
Small, J.A., 113-114, 410
Sobel, Robert, 411
Solomon & Co., D149
Sonora Railway, 113
Southern Pacific of Mexico ("SP de Mex), 113-116, D145-146
Southern Pacific Railroad, 112, 123, D102-103
Spencer Trask & Co., D176
Speyer & Co., 113, 119, 121-126, 143, D146, D149, D221
Speyer, Ellen Leslie Lowery, 123
Speyer, James J., 122-123, 410
Standard Oil Company, 4, 26-30, 32, 34-35, D287
Standard Oil Co., Indiana, 48-49
Standard Oil Co., New Jersey, 36, 40 48-52, D138-139, D154, D162
Standard Oil Trust, 49, 407
Starr, Eddie, 18-19
Stevens, Lyndon H., 72
Stilwell, Arthur E., 111-112, D55, 410
Stratton, David H., 403
Sullivan, James, 109
Swanberg, W.A., 411

Tamiahua Petroleum Co., 49
Tancasneque Oil Co., 49
Taylor, F.J., 410
Teagle, Walter C., 49, 151
Teapot Dome, 9
Tehuantepec Railroad Co., 120
Tepatate Oil Co., 19-24
Terrazas, Luis, 72, D237
Terrazas family, 67, 155

Texas Co., 20, 48-49, D140, D159, D162

Thalmann, Ernst, 117, D146

Thompson, Edward H., 133, D30

Thompson, Wallace, D351

Tinkle, Lon, 405

Toluca Electric Power & Light Co., D20

Torres, Luis, 83

Towne, Robert S., 86-88, D143, 408-409

Transcontinental Petroleum Co., 43, 50-52

Traven, B., 85

Treat, Milo, 36

Trees, Joseph, 33-36, 406

Tupper, Dr. Henry Allen, D376-377

Turlington, Edgar, 410

Tuxpam Petroleum Co., 5, 49

Ulises Petroleum Co., 49

Union Oil Co., 43

utilities, 127-133, D6-7, D19-20, D69, D85-86, D147, D173-175, D176

Villa, Pancho, 107, 114, D264, D269

Vincent, Mordelo Jr., 20-24, 43, 404

Vincent, Mordelo Sr., 17-24, 404

Warner-Quinlan Co., 22-23, D162

Warren, Edward Kirk, 133-134, D176, 411

Waters-Pierce Oil Co., 3-4, 17, 27, 40, D37

Weeks, Lyman H., 410

Whitney, Caspar, 403

Whitney, William C., 101

Williams, Harry, 33-34

Willis, Marshal "Irish," 64-65

Wilson, Henry Lane, 148, D251-262

Wilson, John H., D23

Wilson, John M., 41

Wilson, N.C., 410

Winkler, Max, 412

Wolf, Addie, 125

Wylie, Herbert G., D295-297

Yaqui Indians, 68, 70

Young, Charles Sumner, 31

Young, Desmond, 27, 403, 405

Zahniser, William H., 19-23, 404